THE PSYCHOLOGY OF BEHAVIOUR

THE PSYCHOLOGY OF BEHAVIOUR IN ORGANIZATIONS

Second Edition

Elizabeth Chell

Alcan Professor of Management, School of Business Management
University of Newcastle upon Tyne

First edition 1987
Reprinted 1989, 1990 (twice), 1991
Second edition 1993

Published by
THE MACMILLAN PRESS LTD
Houndmills, Basingstoke, Hampshire RG21 2XS
and London
Companies and representatives
throughout the world

ISBN 0–333–57000–6 hardcover
ISBN 0–333–57001–4 paperback

A catalogue record for this book is available
from the British Library.

Printed in Hong Kong

Contents

Tables

Figures

Preface to the Second Edition

The rationale of the original text still stands. Despite the movement in higher education to mass education, mass audiences and the implications for teaching methodology, I believe, perhaps even more fervently, in the need for a 'middle way' which avoids the superficial treatment of the subject. This book is intended to provide such a 'middle way'. It avoids the textbook approach – breadth of coverage but wanting in depth – and is selective, treating particular topics in a detailed manner. It is recognized that students on management courses cannot be expected to read all the original texts and papers upon which particular theoretical developments are based. Indeed, it is questionable whether it is appropriate that they should do so. After all, the managerial contexts in which past research has been carried out have changed and, while there are some seminal works which should be read, we must consider the longer-term applicability of some theories and the accompanying research findings. The study of leadership is a very good case in point. As a history of ideas in management and organizational behaviour/psychology, it makes a fascinating study. But few theories in leadership have stood the test of time. Even some of the most well known, for example Fiedler's contingency theory, have been subjected to heavy criticism.

The danger of not reading past theoretical contributions to the subject is, I can hear someone saying, the tendency to 'reinvent the wheel'. This is another reason why books like *The Psychology of Behaviour in Organizations* (and there are many examples covering complementary aspects of organizational behaviour) are important. They give students a sense of the richness of the subject – both its systematic and imaginative treatment.

This book should appeal to a wide and diverse audience. It is, of course, primarily directed at students of organizational behaviour but will be of interest to students of applied social psychology and of organizational psychology. It will also be of interest to postgraduate students pursuing an MBA degree and, not inappropriately, post-experience students taking short courses in various aspects of executive management. In this and other ways it is hoped that the book will reach a wider audience of practising managers, for it is only through interaction and dialogue with the practitioner that a subject such as this can produce ideas which are relevant and which lend themselves to the development of better management practice.

PLAN OF THE BOOK

The book covers subjects which represent three levels of analysis of behaviour in organizations. As organizations are staffed with people, it is at this level of analysis that the book begins.

Chapter 1 examines the nature of personality and shows how important it is to think of personality not as something which is wholly determined from within but which is affected by the context within which the person operates. The theoretical basis of this account – interactionism – is outlined and examples of applications at the place of work – for example, psychological climate and stress – are described. The approach to understanding personality is reconsidered through an examination of Hampson's social construction theory. Another theoretical approach is that of attribution theory. This process considers the way individuals attribute causes to events; it is important when we consider what might count as evidence for a particular attribution. The implications of these analyses for understanding behaviour in organizations are clearly spelt out.

Chapter 2 tackles the issues of personality development. The issue is one of whether personality changes throughout the life course, or whether perceived differences are merely superficial responses to new situations which leave the basic personality unchanged. Different approaches to dealing with this matter are outlined and their implications for management discussed. Additional material considers how transitional events impact upon the individual, his/her psychological well-being and coping strategies.

Chapter 3 presents the real challenge to management in terms of their understanding what motivates, and how to motivate, subordinates. The coverage of this chapter incorporates need, reinforcement, equity and expectancy theories. A discussion of management style as a motivator is also included.

Organizational life is rarely about individuals acting independently; often tasks are too complex for one person to tackle and accomplish single-handedly. Efforts need to be coordinated and goals integrated. Thus the second level of the discussion directs attention to the role and function of groups and teams within organizations.

Chapter 4 outlines the nature and function of groups, and in particular examines the effect of normative structure and conformity on decision-making behaviour.

Chapter 5 suggests that of fundamental importance to the organization are its management teams, work groups and specialist groups. The question pursued is how to make such groups operate effectively – indeed, how might one build an effective team in the first place? Several approaches to answering these questions are covered in detail.

Chapter 6 concerns leadership theory. In 1986, when I wrote the first edition of *The Psychology of Behaviour in Organizations*, leadership research appeared to be in the doldrums. Since that time there has been much rethinking of the role that personality plays in explaining leadership behaviour. This has been demonstrated in the revived interest in the charismatic personality, and in 'transactional and transformational' models of leadership. The chapter concludes with a conceptual model of the skill of leadership.

The third area of discussion focuses upon the organization as such.

Chapter 7 examines what organizations are and the effect of organizational structure on behaviour. The Weberian model of the bureaucratic organization is described in some detail with a critique based on Clegg's analysis. There is a discussion of power and commitment in organizations, and, in addition, socio-technical and contingency models of organizations are described. A critical examination of the role of the organizational psychologist as interventionist is also included.

Organizational environments continue to be characterized as turbulent, imposing a need for responsiveness, flexibility and, in short, change. Chapter 8 therefore looks at pressure for change. In particular the question of the continued relevance of organizational development is examined. The techniques and approach of organizational development are outlined and a plan for the evaluation of change programmes put forward.

Chapter 9 discusses the issue of controlling and managing organizations. It covers scientific management and Taylorism, worker participation in management, quality control circles and total quality management. The issue is the extent to which employees have a say in how they are managed, and the psychological and structural factors which affect the balance between worker and managerial control.

Finally, I would like to add that I am delighted that this book has gone into a second edition. I hope that the book will continue to be of use to students and teachers of organizational behaviour in the years to come.

University of Newcastle upon Tyne   ELIZABETH CHELL

Acknowledgements

Producing the revisions has been quite a protracted process and I should acknowledge most sincerely my debt of gratitude to Belinda Holdsworth and her predecessor Frances Arnold at the publishers for the encouragement they have given me and for the patience they have displayed. Carrying out these revisions has coincided with the process of leaving one institution and taking up a quite challenging post in another. This has made life extremely interesting and it has made the preparation of the manuscript even more protracted!

It is 'normal' in a personal statement of acknowledgement such as this to thank one's family and friends for their support. In my own case I have to say that since the first edition of this book, my family has dwindled and I have lost some five members of it, those particularly close to me being my father and my grandmother. This has meant that I have been called upon to be supportive and to draw upon my own inner reserves. While this has, on occasions, been a strain, I have throughout enjoyed the support of a few dear friends – friends whom I have come to appreciate more and more.

E. C.

The author and publishers gratefully acknowledge permission from the following to reproduce copyright material:

Figure 1.1, 'Sources of Stress' from J. Marshall and C. L. Cooper, *Executives under Pressure*, © 1979 Judi Marshall.

Figure 1.2, 'The Person–Situation–Act model' from *International Small Business Journal*, 3, 3, p. 50, © 1985, Woodcock Publications.

Figure 2.1, 'Erikson's Eight Stages of Personality Development' from E. H. Erikson, *Childhood and Society* 2nd edn, © 1963 Norton.

Figure 2.2, 'Levinson's Model of the Life Course' from N. Smelser and E. H. Erikson (eds), *Themes of Work and Love in Adulthood*, p. 283, © 1980, Harvard University Press.

Figure 2.3, 'The Six Interacting Systems of Personality and their Integration' from A. Powell and J. R. Royce, 'Paths to Being, Life Style and Individuality', in *Psychological Reports*, 42 (1978) © Joseph Royce.

Figure 2.4, 'Self-esteem Changes during Transitions' from J. D. Adams, J. Hayes and B. Hopson, *Transition: Understanding and Managing Personal Change*, p. 13, © 1976 John Adams, John Hayes and Barrie Hopson.

Figure 2.5, 'The Transition Cycle' after N. Nicholson, 'The Transition Cycle: Causes, Outcomes, Processes and Forms', from S. Fisher and C. L. Cooper (eds), *On the Move: The Psychology of Change and Transition*, p. 87, © 1990 The Society for the Psychological Study of Social Issues, reprinted by permission of John Wiley & Sons Ltd.

Figure 3.1, 'The Porter–Lawler Model of the Process of Motivation' adapted from L. W. Porter and E. E. Lawler III, *Managerial Attitudes and Performance*, © 1968, Irwin-Dorsey.

Figure 6.1, 'The Managerial Grid' from R. R. Blake and J. S. Mouton, *The Managerial Grid: Key Orientations for Achieving Production through People*, © 1964, Gulf.

Figure 8.1, 'The OD Cube: A Typology of Intervention' adapted from an idea devised by R. A. Schmuck and M. B. Miles, *Organization Development in Schools*, 1971, University Associates.

Figure 8.2, 'A Cyclical Model of Interpersonal Conflict' from p. 72 of R. E. Walton, *Interpersonal Peacemaking*, © 1969, Addison-Wesley.

Table 2.1, 'Summary Comparison of the Transformations of Personality during Various Phases of the Life Span' from J. R. Royce and A. Powell, *Theory of Personality and Individual Differences: Factors, Systems and Processes*, p. 250, © 1983, Prentice-Hall, Inc., Englewood Cliffs, New Jersey.

Table 3.1, 'A Comparison of the Basic Need Theories proposed by Maslow, Alderfer, McClelland and Herzberg' from E. H. Schein, *Organizational Psychology*, 3rd edn, p. 30, © 1980, Prentice-Hall.

Table 4.2, 'An Evaluation of Six Different Decision-making Techniques' adapted from K. Murnighan, 'Group Decision-making: What Strategies

Acknowledgements

Should You Use?', *Management Review*, February 1981, p. 61, © 1981 American Management Association, New York.

Table 5.2, 'Two Prevailing Organizational Paradigms' from R. Thomsett, *People and Project Management*, p. 37, © 1980. Reprinted by permission of Prentice-Hall Inc., Englewood Cliffs, New Jersey.

Table 5.3, 'The Characteristics of Belbin's Eight Team Roles' from R. M. Belbin, *Management Teams*, p. 78, © 1981, Heinemann Educational Books.

Table 6.1, 'Fiedler's Contingency Model of Leadership Effectiveness', adapted from F. Fiedler, *A Theory of Leadership Effectiveness*, p. 37, © 1967, Fred E. Fiedler.

Table 7.3, 'A Comparison between Three Major Structural Arrangements in Organizations', adapted from F. Blackler and S. Shimmin, *Applying Psychology in Organizations*, © 1984, Methuen.

Table 8.1, 'General Characteristics of High- and Low-Innovating Companies', from R. M. Kanter, *The Change Masters*, © 1984, Unwin.

Table 8.2, 'Eight Sources of Organizational Change Problems', from M. Woodcock and D. Francis, *Organizational Development through Teambuilding*, pp. 6–7, © Gower.

Table 9.1, 'Technology- versus End-User-Centred Approaches to Organization Work Design', adapted from F. Blackler, 'Information Technology and Competitiveness: Signposts from Organizational Psychology', paper presented to the Occupational Section of the British Psychological Society Conference, Nottingham, January 1986.

Material abstracted and adapted from D. M. McGregor, *The Human Side of Enterprise*, © 1960, McGraw-Hill (tables 3.2 and 5.1).

Material abstracted and adapted from T. Burns and G. M. Stalker, *The Management of Innovation*, © 1961, Tavistock Publications (table 4.1).

1 What Types of People?

THE NATURE OF PERSONALITY

The concept of personality has undergone considerable revisions over the past decade. The idea that personality is something which is internal to the individual and manifests itself outwardly through their behaviour has been questioned (Hampson, 1982, 1988; Harré, 1979; Mischel, 1968). However, this traditional, trait concept of personality lingers on, particularly in the mind of the lay person and of the traditional personality theorist (Hampson, 1984). We must ask therefore what the lay person and the personality theorist are trying to describe when using the concept of personality. At work and socially, it would seem that people apply trait attributions in an attempt to understand why people are behaving in the way they are doing. This *cognitive* process gives a sense of order to what might otherwise appear to be senseless, uncoordinated behaviours. 'Traits' may therefore be thought of as classification systems, used by individuals to understand other people's *and their own* behaviour.

In this chapter, we will ask and attempt to answer the questions, 'What is the intellectual basis for rejecting or at least modifying the trait view of personality, and what are the implications of such changes for understanding behaviour in organizations?' A partial answer is given by examining the nature and influence of situations on people's behaviour. The application of such an analysis can be viewed in terms of the way the work situation is perceived, how perceptions of the job affect work attitudes, and how both personal characteristics and situational factors can make for stress reactions. A second part of the answer lies in an understanding of how people label situations and consequently what *meaning* these situations have for them. Social norms and rules shape the person's interpretation of the situation and thus suggest the *role* that should be enacted in order to manage that situation effectively. The third aspect of the answer is found in our understanding of what people are doing when they perceive and describe other people's actions. Essentially they are trying to discover the *causes* of other people's behaviour: why they behaved in the way that they did. In this way, it is said, we attribute responsibility and blame for actions *and* we come to know ourselves. One well-researched application, that of attributing success and failure, is examined. In this and other ways it will be made clear that how personality is shaped has considerable implications for work-related behaviours. Indeed, it will be clear that in answer to the question, 'What types of people?' the answer is that it is people who can respond appropriately to the exigencies of the situation – job, task demands, role, etc. – who will be perceived to be the most effective. The abilities to find a niche, to cope or to adapt to a set of circumstances are likely to be the criteria for success in today's rapidly changing organizational life. But it is to an explication of the various approaches to understanding personality that we turn first.

DISILLUSIONMENT WITH THE TRAIT CONCEPT OF PERSONALITY

The trait theorist espouses the following definition of personality: that personality refers to 'more or less *stable, internal* factors that make one person's behaviour *consistent* from one time to another and *different* from the behaviour other people would manifest in comparable situations' (Hampson, 1982, p. 1, my emphasis). 'Traits' may therefore be said to represent 'predispositions to behave in certain ways in a variety of different situations'. Put in a slightly different way, the term 'trait' may be said to refer to 'stylistic *consistencies* in interpersonal behaviour' (Hogan *et al.*, 1977, p. 256, my emphasis). Thus, while there may be day-to-day fluctuations in people's behaviour, there is nevertheless a stable core which is identifiable. Given this, and the further assumption that people are consistent in the ways they express these purported underlying traits, then it should be possible to predict their future behaviour.

It was the idea of consistency that led Mischel to launch an attack on trait psychology (Mischel, 1968). Where Mischel's attack was most successful was in undermining the belief that people express the same trait across different situations or even the same trait in the same situation. Thus, for example, a person who is characterized as 'honest' may not exhibit honesty in all conceivable or actual situations. Indeed, given the same set of circumstances on more than one occasion, a person *may* react differently.

Just how consistent are people? Bem and Allen (1974) threw further light on the issue by suggesting that different people may exhibit consistency on some traits and considerable variability on others. It should therefore be possible to predict some of the people some of the time, but not all of the people all of the time! However, the controversy continues with Mischel questioning this suggestion of 'partial' behavioural consistency (Mischel, 1984). Furthermore, he suggested that what people *mean* when they apply the concept of consistency to themselves is not that they consistently exhibit those behaviours which are appropriately applicable to the expression of the trait across different situations (Mischel, 1984). Rather, they assess their consistency in terms of the expression of those behaviours which *for them* are the most relevant or typical of that trait. Another feature of this process is that *temporal stability* is often confused with cross-situational consistency (Mischel and Peake, 1982). That, is the number of times a particular behaviour is exhibited is confused with the manifestation of behaviours typical of the trait across a wide range of situations. In this way, people come to believe in their personal consistency of reliably exhibiting a trait.

Real consistency seems to be associated with physiological or maladaptive behaviours. Thus, when a person cannot handle a situation, i.e. has not the skills or competencies to do so, he or she often resorts to the expression of a rigid behaviour pattern which may be inappropriate or insensitive to the requirements of situations.

Under such conditions, relatively cross-situationally consistent 'characterisitic' behaviour patterns that are less context-sensitive become more likely. This increased consistency of problematic, disadvantageous behaviour should be seen when competency requirements for appropriate functioning exceed the individual's available competence. Such rigidity may be expected especially in highly stressful situations. (Mischel, 1984, p. 359)

Although Mischel has been one of the most trenchant critics of trait theory, he is not alone (see Chell, 1985b). Indeed, Harré (1979) usefully summarizes the main criticisms of trait theory as outlined below:

● Classical trait theory (as typified by Eysenck and Cattell) assumes that the manifestation of trait behaviour is independent of situations and persons with whom the individual is interacting. This assumption would appear to be questionable, given that the manifestation of a trait behaviour is usually in response to specifiable situational conditions.

● Collections of traits form clusters (e.g. intelligent, neurotic, introverted), and such clusters suggest further attributions, for example, dark, thin, bites his nails. This suggests that there is a connection between the attributions made in trait psychology and the content of cultural stereotypes. There were two aspects of this issue: (a) just as 'birds' 'beaks' and 'feathers' tend to co-occur in the 'object' world, so do certain trait descriptors (cf. Joe, 1971); (b) raters cannot be entirely objective in that they too implicitly assume trait co-occurrence. Mischel (1968) has elaborated this point further by suggesting that the attribution of traits made by raters said more about the raters than it did about the ratees. That is to say, the raters were using their own categories to describe the behaviour they were assessing. This was based on their implicit personality theories of trait co-occurrences. Whether the implicit theories described the personalities of the ratees was thus open to question.

● When people account for their own behaviour they point to some feature of the situation; when they account for other people's behaviour, they tend to make reference to traits. This is especially true where the behaviour might be thought to be reprehensible in some way. This suggests that trait *ascriptions* are part of a moral commentary upon oneself and others; in general they lead to the disapproval of others and credit for oneself.

● There are various empirical difficulties with trait theory: For example, it has been suggested that (a) trait attributions are more a product of language, i.e. they are devices for speaking about other people, than they are exhibited in objective features of action. (b) Trait descriptions are gathered by means of questionnaires; they are reports of what people would do in imagined situations. However, when people's actual behaviour is observed across a wide variety of situations, through a reasonably extended time span, then traits 'disappear'. (c) Many important dispositions – extraversion, neuroticism, etc. – are not attributed on the basis of observed manifestations of the behaviour in question but rather as a result of analysis of psychometric data. As Harré puts it: 'they dissolve in the acid of careful investigation'.

● Kenrick and Funder (1988) also acknowledge the problem of over-reliance on a single psychometric measure of personality. They conclude that, ideally, multiple observations across a variety of situations, conducted by more than one person are required in order to begin to measure the consistent nature of any one individual's personality.

● On the question of consistency, this seems to be confined to physiologically based behaviour (for example, patterns of eye contact, addiction to tobacco) and to pathological personalities. In the latter case, pathologically or mentally disturbed patients tend to be rigidly consistent in their behaviour. *Real* consistency is regarded as being a sign of maladaption.

● There are, in addition, some conceptual difficulties with regard to traits: that is, what are traits? Traits have been described as categorizing concepts which vary in breadth (Hampson *et al.*, 1986, 1987). Traits or dispositional concepts such as extraversion are so broad that a very wide range of very different kinds of human activity exemplify it. In contrast, narrow traits such as 'talkative' refer to a more limited range of behavioural instances (ibid.). One issue is: Can traits be used for prediction purposes using psychometric methods? Should psychologists be developing alternative methods (for example, based on interactionist theory) and/or idiographic techniques?

- Trait measures can be used only to predict broad behavioural tendencies; they cannot predict how a person will respond in a specific situation (Epstein and O'Brien, 1985). Much depends on what it is you are trying to achieve. If you wish to give an *explanation* of a person's behaviour then the trait measure is not the appropriate tool. It is important, however, as a basis for an explanation to examine systematically what people do and the conditions under which they do it over a lengthy period of time and a variety of situations.

- Traits construed as dispositional concepts to respond in certain ways in specific situations are linked contingently to those settings in a variety of different ways, for example, behaviourally, interpretatively, cognitively and emotionally. Why assume one underlying structure to account for such different contingent relations? For example, consider the following statements: s/he is shy; s/he is alert; s/he is a logical thinker; s/he is sad. Do the descriptors have to refer to an underlying trait, or could we account for some if not all of those behaviours by a knowledge of the context in which the behaviour was exhibited? For instance, you would expect a person to be sad when attending a funeral; you might expect them to be alert if they were motivated to do well in their studies, etc.

- Trait concepts may be linked conceptually to responses or contingently and perhaps learned. For instance, to comply is to respond to requests and to be obedient is to carry out orders: both suggest conceptual connections. On the other hand, there are several responses other than blushing which may count as a response to a socially embarassing situation.

- There is a problem of knowledge: how do you know a person 'has' such and such a trait? (Usually you observe their response to particular situations and make an inference.) If, however, you widen the concept of trait to include needs, abilities and attitudes, these are dispositions which are not manifested nearly so frequently or so obviously. They may be no more than action *tendencies* given the person's belief state at the time; why assume they refer to some internal 'thing'?

- Hampson (1984) goes further and suggests that traits do not reside *within* individuals, but, as it were, *between* individuals in order to give recognition to the social filter of interpretations and categorization of behaviours into trait terms.

● In addition, a point made by Jones and Nisbett (1972), we tend to see people in a limited range of situations and attribute the trait on the basis of that limited information. Furthermore, our first impressions – the so-called 'primacy effect' – of a person count more because on subsequent occasions we filter out information which is not consistent with those impressions. Our assessments of others *may* therefore be biased and partial.

● In order to avoid inconsistencies in the manifestation of the trait, the trait theorist could partition the situation element. So, for example, X is dominant in S1, X is servile in S2. The problem with this analysis is that it would open the floodgates and merely proliferate trait concepts.

● Further, there is the philosophical point that the personality theory subscribed to indicates underlying assumptions about human nature. Trait theory is an 'automaton' theory; the individual's actions are merely manifestations of his or her traits. There are alternative conceptions which do not assume an underlying stimulus–response model. Such a conceptualization is the ethogenic theory of Rom Harré (see later section).

Trait theory has thus suffered a rough ride during and since the 1970s. Although such criticisms were incisive and brought trait psychology to crisis point, the 'attack' prompted a thorough examination of both the conceptual basis of the theory and the methodology associated with it. In the next section a brief historical overview is presented of alternative theories to traditional trait theory. This is used to enable a consideration of how situations influence, and may be used to help explain, work-related behaviours.

THE INFLUENCE OF SITUATIONS IN DETERMINING BEHAVIOUR: INTERACTIONISM

Mischel (1968) in his attack on trait theory suggested that behaviour could be explained as being a function entirely of the situation people found themselves in. This position was known as 'situationism'. It was found to be untenable; indeed, Bowers (1973) argued cogently against it. Mischel therefore shifted his ground somewhat and argued for a reconceptualization of personality from the position of a cognitive social learning theorist, that is, he assumed that behaviour was a learned response, and that past experience had a part to play in how people interpreted stimulus situations and reacted to them (Mischel, 1973, 1981). Instead of thinking of people as a composite of traits, he suggested a set of five cognitive social learning person variables. These were their *competencies* – i.e. a person's abilities and skills; *constructs* – their conceptual framework which governs how they think about the things that happen around them; *expectancies* – which means that people have learned expectations about other people's and their own behaviour in certain situations; *values* – people have preferences, they evaluate objects, events, situations and people in positive and negative ways; *self-regulatory plans and strategies* – people are purposeful and goal-oriented, in order to achieve their aims they formulate plans which shape their activities and orientation to particular situations.

There were other developments in interactionism. For example, Argyle and Little (1972) and Argyle (1976) gathered empirical evidence to substantiate the claim that behaviour is a function of both person and situation variables. Indeed, they went further and suggested that the main determinant of behaviour was the interaction between these two sets of variables. The main problems would appear to be (a) how to conceptualize persons; (b) how to conceptualize situations; and (c) how to conceptualize interaction.

Persons have been variously conceptualized in terms of single traits; demographic and other descriptive variables (Newton and Keenan, 1983); and/or variables akin to Mischel's social learning variables (Harré, 1979). It was recognized early on that there was a need to classify situations and to recognize what are their pertinent features as they affect behaviour (Frederiksen, 1972). Indeed, more recent developments have focused primarily on this particular issue (Magnusson, 1981). As regards the concept of interaction, there are two possible formulations: interaction between person and situation variables can be thought of in terms of *physical* or *psychological* interaction. In the case of *physical* interaction, the underlying model assumes a stimulus–response or mechanistic level of interaction. Person and situation variables (the independent variables in the model) give rise to (cause) the behavioural response (the dependent variable). The interaction thus has unidirectional causality (Bowers, 1973; Ekehammer, 1974; Endler and Magnusson, 1976; Pervin, 1968). *Psychological* interaction, on the other hand, assumes an *organismic* model of human nature. How a person perceives and cognizes the situation is paramount. In this interpretation of person, situation interaction, it is the *meaning* which person holds for the situation which 'causes' him or her to behave in a particular way, and as such it is the cognitive constructs of the person and the symbolic meaning signalled by the situation which 'shape' behaviour.

Epstein and O'Brien (1985), in their historical review of the 'person–situation' debate, state most emphatically that

Mischel performed an important service in drawing attention to the widespread, inappropriate use of trait theory. For example, it had become a common practice to infer traits from single items of behaviour and from single signs in projective tests, and to use trait measures to predict single items of behaviour. (Ibid., p. 515).

These authors point out further that most of the criticisms which Mischel (1968) and others had levelled against trait theory have been countered (see Kenrick and Funder, 1988, for a more recent defence of trait theory) except, they suggest, for one: this was the inability of psychologists using self-ratings and the results of objective tests to achieve correlations beyond 0.30. The problem psychologists had overlooked was that single items of behaviour have limited reliability and generality. It is important, they suggest, to aggregate items over both situations and occasions in order to measure traits that are both broad and stable. Traits measured in this way allow for the prediction of *broad dispositions*, but they do *not* enable the prediction of single behavioural acts. Put graphically, they state,

An extrovert can be expected to be extroverted most of the time, but it would be foolish to wager that someone will greet you with a slap on the back and play a practical joke on you when you meet him or her at 2.00 p.m. tomorrow. (Epstein and O'Brien, 1985, pp. 516–7)

While defences such as these have, to some extent, restored trait theory, they have neither stifled interactionism nor put an end to what Pervin (1990) terms the 'internal–external' issue which has underlain the person–situation controversy. Pervin comments that 'although we are all pretty much interactionists at this point, there remains considerable disagreement about *what* in the person interacts *how* with *what* in the situation' (Ibid. p. 14).

THE APPLICATION OF INTERACTIONISM TO AN UNDERSTANDING OF WORK-RELATED BEHAVIOUR

In what ways may this person (P) × situation (S) interactionism be applied to work situations? It is too facile to simply say that the work situation is defined by the task. Apart from the omission of a number of key environmental variables (see next section), it begs the question of what the task is and what the incumbent has made of the job. Stewart's work on the nature of managerial jobs distinguishes between core activities which must be performed and are common to all jobs of a given category and peripheral activities which may or may not be performed (Stewart, 1982). Here the incumbent has discretion and autonomy to shape the job to meet his or her needs and to manage the situation to the level of his or her competence or incompetence. Hacker (1981), in his attempt to analyse work situations, distinguished between the following: (a) the actual and perceived features of the situation; (b) the situation as manifested – the *real* situation; (c) the degree of autonomy of the worker; (d) the extent to which the worker redefines the situation; (e) the nature and sequencing of task requirements and the process of job regulation; (f) individual differences in reactions to situations, particularly where higher-order activities such as planning and goal setting are concerned as these can transform *real* situations; (g) the lack of correspondence between the worker's perception of her reaction to the situation and her actual reaction; (h) the results produced, including feelings of job satisfaction, well-being and experience, and how these outcomes are perceived.

Defining and analysing situations is clearly a complex activity, involving problems of conceptualization and measurement. Part of this complexity resides in the fact that it is insufficient to measure workers' objective situations, rather it is essential to understand their subjective work environment. This particular problem is even more apparent in the research carried out on *psychological climate*.

1 Psychological Climate

James and Sells (1981) use the concept of *psychological climate* (PC) to indicate how the individual's perceptions of the situation give it psychological significance and meaning. In their analysis, a person's beliefs about the situation affect PC. Aspects of the situation which exert most influence are linked, perhaps not surprisingly, to the individual's direct and closest experiences of the work environment. Key environmental variables were thought to be: (a) role characteristics, such as role ambiguity and conflict; (b) job characteristics, such as job autonomy and job challenge; (c) leader behaviours, including goal emphasis and work facilitation; (d) workgroup and social environment characteristics, including cooperation and friendliness; (e) organizational and subsystem attributes which directly affect the individual's experience, for example, fairness of the reward system.

In a study by James and Jones (1979) such environmental variables were used in combination with a set of person variables (e.g., achievement motivation, self-esteem, job challenge and involvement, compliance, etc.) to determine what factors influenced job satisfaction. They found that job

(PC) perceptions and job attitudes (satisfaction) were reciprocal causes of each other. They also found that individuals who were more involved with their jobs were more likely to be satisfied with their jobs, but that this was in part a function of education; more highly educated individuals were less satisfied. One problem from a management perspective was that job satisfaction is not necessarily related to job performance. It would therefore be of considerable interest for this type of research to be extended so that it examined the implications of PC for productivity and effectiveness on the job.

2 Stress at Work

The nature and causes of stress at work is an area which has been extensively researched over the past decade or so (Cooper and Payne, 1980; French, Rogers and Cobb, 1974; Ivancevich *et al.*, 1982; Marshall and Cooper, 1979; Sarason and Sarason, 1981). It would appear that stress is caused as a result of the interaction between the demands of the situation, and the individual's ability to meet those demands, that is, where there is a lack of 'fit' then stress results (Ivancevich and Matteson, 1984). Current research would appear to concur that one aspect of individual differences in reaction to situations is how the situation is perceived: thus the environment produces 'potential' stressors and it is the judgement made by the individual that his or her environment is threatening in some way that produces felt stress. The underlying model of person–environment interaction is thus one of *psychological* interaction.

Marshall and Cooper (1979) have attempted to determine what are the sources of managerial job stress. As regards environmental sources of job stress, they have suggested the following factors should be considered: the job, including working conditions, and work load; aspects of the role, including role ambiguity, role conflict, and role responsibility; relationships with the boss, superiors, subordinates and colleagues; career development, such as job security, promotion, and mid-life crisis; organizational structure and climate as it affects personal autonomy, freedom to influence decisions, participation, and quality of working life. In addition, there are extra organizational sources of stress which include: family, life crises, marriage, dual career patterns, and job mobility. As regards the characteristics of the individual, these include their personality, such as neurotic tendencies, emotional instability, rigidity, etc., and behaviour patterns, as exemplified by coronary prone behaviour pattern Type A. The elements of this model are summarized in more detail in Figure 1.1 below.

11

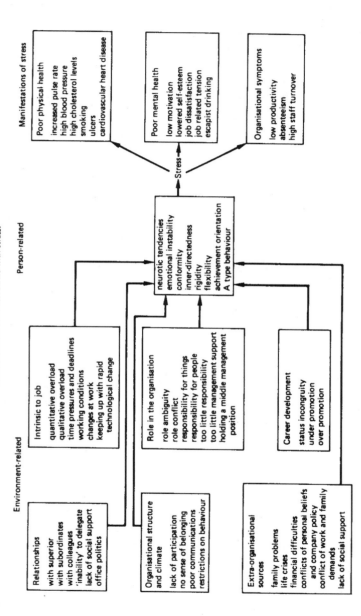

FIGURE 1.1 *Sources of stress*

SOURCE J. Marshall and C. L. Cooper (1979) *Executives under Pressure* (London: Macmillan).

In general, Marshall and Cooper found that the person-related variables, anxiety-prone and ambitious, and three job–environment-related variables – work overload, lack of autonomy and concern about career development – frequently explained different individuals' stresses on a company-wide basis. They emphasized, however, that stress reactions were extremely individualistic. In their words, 'stress is the outcome of the interaction of a particular individual with a particular environment at a particular point in time' (Marshall and Cooper, 1979, p. 74). However, they found it useful to subdivide their sample of managers according to the criteria of level and function. This revealed that different factors were salient in causing stress reactions within different departments and different levels of management.

The work of Ivancevich and Matteson (1984) concerns the nature of the interaction between person and environmental variables where the independent variables of interest are stress-related behaviour patterns. These behaviour patterns – Type A and B – were first observed by Friedman and Rosenman. The characteristics of these behaviour patterns are now well known. They include, for Type A, extreme competitiveness, single-mindedness, ambition and aggression. Such individuals are often preoccupied with meeting deadlines. They appear to be engaged in a chronic struggle to attain an ever-increasing number of goals over shorter and shorter time spans. They are impatient and are sometimes given to explosiveness of speech. They are motivated to assert control over their environment, indeed, this would appear to be a very basic need, to avoid feelings of helplessness and lack of control (Seligman, 1975). While such behaviour patterns have clear implications for the individual's effectiveness at work – particularly as a colleague – there are far more serious implications in terms of the individual's susceptibility to coronary heart disease (CHD). Type B individuals are quite the opposite of Type As. They are relaxed and set themselves more realistic goals. They are moderate achievers whose work performance can vary from a moderate pace to plodding. Such individuals may need environmental stimulation and motivation to increase their performance rate (Chesney *et al.*, 1981b; Snow and Glass, 1981).

The model of Type A–B environment interaction developed by Ivancevich and Matteson (1984) relates conceptually to the James and Sells (1981), James and Jones (1979) research described above. That is, the interaction is conceived in terms of the individuals' 'cognitive representations of relatively proximal work-related events, expressed in terms that have *meaning* and are important to the individual' (Ivancevich and Matteson, 1984, p. 498). The work environment for these researchers consists of three categories of variable: (a) *substance* – people, events, processes, norms, etc.; (b) *qualities* – for example, the degree of control which may be exerted, pace of work flow, job challenge, etc.; (c) relations – that is, facets of the work environment are related to each other to form an integrated system. In addition, in considering how the individual interacts within the work environment, it is important to consider the individual's past experience. That is, individuals, in interpreting their work environment, use not only perception, but also learning, memory and recall.

Is it possible to characterize the work environments which may be optimal for Type A–B individuals? Ivancevich and Matteson (1984) have suggested that the optimal Type A work environment is controllable, fast-paced and extremely challenging. However, if work demands are too excessive, and work goals unattainable, this will result in frenetic behaviour on the part of both Type A and Type B individuals, with an elevated pattern of cardiovascular activity (Snow and Glass, 1981). The optimal work environment for Type Bs is routine, moderately paced and moderately challenging. Such people work most effectively and have lower blood pressure in work environments that encourage dependence on others and on established routines (Chesney *et al.*, 1981b). In this way, the degree of congruence between person and environment can be assessed.

THE ROLES PEOPLE PLAY: AN ANALYSIS OF THE SITUATION–ACT MODEL

Person–situation interactionism has largely interpreted 'interaction' as being *psychological* interaction. This type of analysis has been taken a stage further by ethogenists, such as Rom Harré, by emphasizing the *meaning* which the situation holds for person. The person must act within situations; situations are rule-governed and how a person behaves is often prescribed by these socially acquired rules. The person thus adopts a suitable role in order to perform effectively within the situation. The social situation is defined by the label given to it by the culture, for example, doing the shopping. Each situation has rules which make certain acts relevant and meaningful in that situation, so that the range of behaviours that could potentially occur is limited by the nature of the situation: people do certain things in some situations and refrain from doing them in others (see Figure 1.2).

The situation dictates what role the person (or actor) shall play. Thus, the characteristics of the individual which are important are those related to the situation, for example, knowledge of the situation, intended out-

14

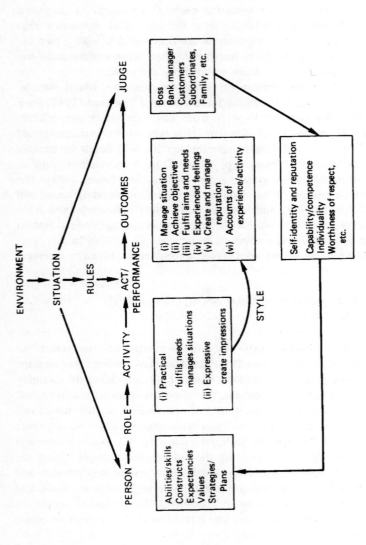

FIGURE 1.2 *The person–situation–act model*

SOURCE A. Branthwaite (1983) 'Situations and social actions: applications for marketing of recent theories in social psychology,' *Journal of the Market Research Society*, 25, 1, 19–38; E. Chell (1985b) 'The entrepreneurial personality: a few ghosts laid to rest?' *International Small Business Journal*, 3, 3, 43–54; R. Harré (1979) *Social Being* (Oxford: Blackwell).

comes, skills, etc. The role the person has adopted is linked to various functional activities to be performed in the situation. These are (a) a *practical* function to fulfil the individual's needs and manage the situation; and (b) an *expressive* function to create impressions.

Most activities are social in yet another sense; that is, they are performed in front of other people or with other people in mind. In this way how a situation is handled will contribute to the individual's reputation in the eyes of others. In order to execute an action effectively, it is necessary to understand the rules which govern the situation. Misunderstandings may occur where a context is misperceived, or perceived from a different perspective, such that an alternative set of rules are applied. How actions are executed is part of the individual's *style*, which also contributes to his or her reputation: i.e. 'It ain't what you do, it's the way that you do it!' Moreover, style may be enhanced by the person's dress; what he or she chooses to wear contributes to their reputation. Physical behaviour is also accompanied by verbal behaviour in which people give *accounts* of what they are doing, are about to do or have done. Accounts are used to explain, interpret or justify activities. They also demonstrate a knowledge of social rules and of what is required in the situation.

Does this model mean that the individual's behaviour is essentially role- or situation-determined? According to Harré (1979) there is both a motivational and a cognitive input made by the individual. Motivationally, the individual has goals which he or she aims to achieve through the situation. The general goals are, as we have seen, functional. Their purpose is a practical one of fulfilling the individual's needs and an expressive one of maintaining a reputation. However, there are also specific situational goals where individual differences may be apparent. Different people in the same situation may have different specific goals which are in conflict with one another. For example, management and union may both have the same general goals when sitting around the negotiation table – that is, of managing the situation effectively by achieving a negotiated settlement, and emerging from the situation with an unscathed if not enhanced reputation. However, each side's specific demands or goals may be incompatible.

The cognitive aspect of the person's input to the situation is their knowledge of relevant concepts and constructs. Such knowledge is important if the actor is to be able to negotiate situations smoothly and with ease – i.e. competently. Such concepts may be termed the 'jargon' of the situation. Further, to participate in any social situation certain skills are needed, for example, general social skills or more specialized, technical skills. It is apparent that there are strong similarities between Harré's analysis of person related variables, and that of Mischel (1973; 1981). Finally, in social situations, roles are played out and situations are handled in front of others or with various 'judges' in mind. Such knowledge in itself helps shape the individual's behaviour.

The implications of Harré's analysis for behaviour in organizations are these:

- It questions the utility of personality inventories for matching people to jobs. Rather, the ability to predict an individual's effectiveness in future job performance must be assessed in terms of the knowledge, skills and, experience of the candidate. The degree of competence and the motivation to apply him or herself to work situations will enable the individual to cope with the responsibilities entailed in the job and to execute them effectively and efficiently. The development of such a repertoire of skills will enable individuals to enhance their reputations and add to their future promotion prospects.

- There are implications for the management and control of employees through the identification of situations (in an industrial relations sense), the rules which govern these situations and the behaviours which are deemed appropriate.

- In two party or intergroup situations, different interpretations of the rules governing the situation, conflicting goals and expectations, may lead to misunderstandings and conflict.

- There are implications for social and technical skills training to equip individuals to cope effectively in work situations, for example, assertiveness training.

- In terms of enhancing their own promotion prospects, some individuals may be interested in learning how they can enhance their reputations.

- In general, managers, shop stewards and employees at all levels are attempting to manage situations in the work place and they will inadvertently or otherwise create impressions of what they are doing. The wealth of literature on management/leadership style suggests that how a person goes about their job is important. This model suggests that in order to be successful the manager must realize two things: (a) what it takes for successful *task* completion and (b) what is required to handle the *social* aspect of the situation. This means a two fold ability of being able to get the job done, fulfil task requirements and objectives, and secondly, an ability to create the right impressions in the eyes of others through one's own style of performance.

- In the micro-situation the meaning attributed to words may be shaped by the culture of the group (Marsh *et al.*, 1978); understanding the meaning and significance which other people give to situations is a fundamental part of negotiating the life course and of learning how to handle interpersonal situations effectively. Understanding does not, of course, mean accepting.

● This search for the meaning of situations renders much of social inter-action ambiguous. The meaning of a situation at one point in time may be reinterpreted at a later stage; impressions can be misleading; tables can be turned; and reputations can be both made and lost.

● As regards consumer behaviour, it may be a more effective marketing strategy to concentrate less on people's attitudes to a product and concentrate more on the demands of situations, that is, participation in certain social situations creates a need for particular goods and services (Branthwaite, 1983). This means in effect that by creating and manipulating situations it is possible to create demands for new products and open up new markets. Similar ends can be achieved by changing the rules for situations and by influencing the means to a good reputation.

THE CONSTRUCTION OF PERSONALITY

The constructivist theory of personality was both a reaction to trait theory and an attempt to develop a *social* psychological theory of personality (Hampson, 1982, 1988). The constructivist approach is an attempt to take into account three perspectives on personality – the personality theorist's, the lay and the self-perspectives. The personality theorist's approach assumes an *explicit theory* of personality, that is, an attempt is made to describe what personality is by inferring the structure of personality from ratings of behaviour. In contrast, the lay perspective assumes an *implicit theory* of personality which comprises descriptive and intuitive beliefs residing in people's minds. Also people have theories about their own personalities which act as a guide and enable them to manipulate and control other people through impression management. Thus, the self-perspective assumes the existence of *self* constructs.

Hampson argues that the personality theorist has shown no interest in either lay views about personality or in the beliefs which people hold about themselves. Moreover, there is an assumption of objectivity about the way personality theorists conduct their investigations which overlooks the fact that the personality theorists must decide which personality constructs to study in the first place! In preparing a psychological test, Hampson points out, the test designer relies upon his or her knowledge about behaviour–trait relations. Research has shown that people share a common understanding of the behaviours they believe to be associated with traits and also the co-occurrence relations between traits. For example, it might be expected that people who are sociable are more likely to be helpful, so that the traits 'sociable' and 'helpful' would be believed to co-occur. Further, Hampson argues controversially, 'personality does not have an *objective* existence independent of the human observer' (Hampson, 1988, p. 195). Behaviour is only understood as being socially meaningful once it has been *categorized* and *interpreted*.

To Hampson traits are categories for organizing and structuring social behaviour. People share a common set of understandings about the meaning of social behaviour and personality traits are used as a way of communicating this meaning (Hampson, 1984). This does not mean that 'personality is only in the eye of the beholder'. 'Socially constructed personality traits are assumed to be anchored in the real world' (Hampson 1984, p. 38). It is a socially arrived at consensus based upon the perception of patterns of actual behaviour which give a sense both of consistency and objectivity about the process. This cognitive approach to personality has quite a long history, as Krahé (1990) has recently shown.

The basis of Hampson's methodology is the concept of *prototypicality* put forward by Rosch and her colleagues in their model of object categories (Rosch *et al.*, 1976). It is assumed that most categories do not have clear-cut boundaries and that the criteria for inclusion are imprecise. Individual items are included or excluded from category membership on the basis of 'family resemblance' (Rosch, 1978). Thus categories may be conceived of in terms of *clear* cases which typify them. Hence, while nouns may be used to categorize people, traits categorize behaviours (Hampson, 1988). Thus, behaviours may be assigned to a trait category on the basis of their prototypicality.

The main conclusion to be drawn from Hampson's work is that personality can no longer be viewed as residing within individuals; rather, it is a product of social processes resulting from observer and self-observer perspectives. Constructivism would appear to imply that the psychometric method of assessment of personality used as the sole instrument is inadequate. Idiographic or even idio*thetic* methods of assessing personality characteristics may be usefully adopted (Krahé, 1990; Pervin, 1990). Indeed, for exploratory purposes, where the constellation of traits being investigated is not known in advance then idiographic/idiothetic approaches may be more informative. In a recent study to investigate the nature of the entrepreneurial personality an idiographic approach was adopted (Chell *et al.*, 1991). This method enabled the construction of a profile of the entrepreneurial type and indicated the existence of other types of business owner. While there is clearly a need for further research in order to establish the constructivist methodology, the investigation of the entrepreneurial personality indicated that in applied situations the method has much to recommend it.

ATTRIBUTING THE CAUSES OF BEHAVIOUR

How and why do people make attributions about other people's behaviour? Developing a conceptual framework to answer this question was the main concern of attribution theorists. In fact, attribution theory is a relatively new branch of social psychology – so much so that its origins can be traced back, essentially, to 1958 with the publication of Fritz Heider's book, *The Psychology of Interpersonal Relations.* Simply put, attribution theory concerns the assignment of causes to events; people, through curiosity and other motives, seek to explain significant events in their lives by being able to say what caused those events. Thus, attribution theory is about perception: perception of self, others and events.

There are two features of Heider's theory which are noteworthy – namely, 'common-sense psychology' and the 'naive analysis of action'. Heider made the point that as a matter of everyday occurrence people use a quasi-scientific approach to understanding other people's behaviour:

> In everyday life we form ideas about other people and about social situations. We interpret other people's actions and we predict what they will do under certain circumstances. Though these ideas are usually not formulated, they function adequately. They achieve in some measure what a science is supposed to achieve: an adequate description of the subject matter which makes prediction possible. (Heider, 1958, p. 5)

Fundamental to Heider's 'naive analysis of action' are the concepts of 'can' and 'trying'. In addition, he assumes that (a) people do not act as observers *simpliciter*; they seek to explain their observations in relation to other environmental happenings; (b) the features of the environment which hold the most significant explanatory power are other people's motives; they give meaning to experience, are perceived as such and reacted to on that basis. Thus, Heider's naive analysis of causality is simply that the results of an action depend on a combination of person and/or environmental factors (accepting that there may be occasions where either one or the other could have zero effect). Person factors are seen in terms of a power factor (ability) and a motivational factor (trying). The combination of personal and environmental influences determines whether or not someone *can* do something. In other words, she or he is able, willing (trying) and there is no situational or environmental obstacle in the way. Thus, in attributing causes to people's actions, the perceiver distinguishes between what is in the person's power to achieve, and the effect of environmental influences. Depending upon the distribution of causation between factors in any given situation, this is likely to affect one's perception and prediction of person's future behaviour. For example, where a person's motivation is seen to be high, we may say 'she's a trier'; or when we perceive her to have considerable skill, we may say, 'she's an able worker'; or when she is ill and underperforms, we attribute the underperformance, not to her inability nor necessarily to her lack of motivation, but to the environmental or situational factor, her illness, and not to her personally.

From this 'naive analysis of action' there have sprung numerous theoretical developments backed by considerable empirical support (see, for example, Eiser, 1979, 1980; Hewstone, 1983; Mower White, 1982). In the remainder of this section we will outline some of these developments and attempt to draw out the implications of this analysis for understanding behaviour in organizations.

Much of the work relating to attribution theory has investigated the conditions under which personal as opposed to situational attributions are made (Mower White, 1982). For example, Jones and Davis (1965) have put forward a theory of 'correspondent inference', which states that a *correspondent inference* is an inference about an individual's intentions and disposition which follows directly from their behaviour. In other words, the attribution of intentions and disposition is *consistent with* the behaviour. Two implicit rules appear to guide people in their attributions of others' intentions and dispositions. These are (a) the extremity rule and (b) social desirability cues. For example, in the case of (a) behaviour is a function of the personality of the doer if the action is *not* appropriate to the situation in which it occurs. Typical reactions to 'He broke the antique vase' might be 'He's a clumsy oaf!' or 'Nobody in their right mind would do such a thing.' However, if we knew that his hands were wet while handling the vase, this would put a different complexion on the matter. We might still, however, wish to say that it was silly to handle a valuable antique with wet and slippery hands. In the case of (b) where behaviour follows social desirability cues and is appropriate to the situation, it is difficult to make inferences about someone's personality. Thus, unusual or deviant behaviour is more informative. For example, he picked up the chewing gum dispenser and waltzed down the street with it (Marsh *et al.*, 1978).

Kelley's approach is perhaps more reminiscent of that of Heider in so far as it assumes that people make causal inferences about other people's behaviour in a quasi-scientific manner. More specifically, Kelley (1967) suggests that people use an analysis of variance model in order to draw causal inferences. Analysis of variance (ANOVA) is a statistical technique which can be used to indicate whether an independent variable (that which is presumed to be the causal agent) has had a significant effect upon a dependent variable (the reaction or response variable). Causal agents in Kelley's conception may be people, entities (things or environmental stimuli) and times (occasions and situations).

Kelley suggests further that there are four criteria which are applied to decide whether behaviour is attributable to personal or external (situational) causes. These criteria are: (a) distinctiveness, (b) consensus, (c) consistency over time and (d) consistency over modality. Behaviour is distinctive if it can be distinguished from the behaviour of other people in the same situation. If everyone runs for cover in a thunderstorm then there is nothing distinctive about any particular person's behaviour. However, if one individual puts up his umbrella and starts to sing and dance in the street, we might consider him eccentric. Again, if everyone observing our man dancing in the rain agrees that he must be eccentric then this adds weight to the assertion that his behaviour is attributable to personal causes. If this individual has been seen on a number of occasions dancing in the rain then his behaviour meets the criterion of consistency over time; that is, the same reaction is likely to occur on other occasions. Finally, the fourth criterion suggests that personal attributions are more likely to be made if a person is consistent over situations. For example, what other behaviours does the individual exhibit which might be considered eccentric?

While there is some evidence to support this theory (MacArthur, 1972), Kelley in a later paper acknowledged that often people have not the time to do a full-blown analysis before reaching their conclusions. Instead, they have, through experience, built up a 'storehouse of *causal schemata*' which they can draw upon to make a more expeditious judgement (Kelley, 1972a). However, if people are information processors, there must be numerous occasions where the incomplete data set points to several possible causes. In another paper, Kelley (1972b) suggests the principle of 'discounting' is employed to reduce the causes to the single most likely cause.

Jones and Nisbett's (1972) contribution is more controversial. They put forward the thesis that 'there is a pervasive tendency for actors to attribute their actions to situational requirements, whereas observers tend to attribute the same actions to stable personal dispositions.' Of the information available to actor and observer about an action, the point where divergence is most likely to occur is the actor's experience of the act. This information can be arrived at only by a process of inference. With regard to causes of the act, both actor and observer are able in principle to perceive possible environmental causes, although in practice it is unlikely that the observer has as complete knowledge as the actor 'only because of the likelihood that the actor is responding to events more extended in time than those available to the observer' (Jones and Nisbett, 1972, p. 84). Beyond this, it is also unlikely that the observer can have complete knowledge of the actor's intentions and his or her feeling states when performing the act.

Attentional cues are also a source of difference. For the observer, the environment forms a backcloth against which the 'figural' movement of the act is perceived. But for the actor almost the reverse is the case: unaided by mirrors or cameras, he or she must focus on the environment and cannot observe his or her own behaviour. Thus, the observer focusing on the actor's behaviour will suggest a dispositional account, whereas the actor will account for his or her behaviour in terms of situational demands. This account is taken a stage further when they argue that 'traits exist more in the eye of the beholder than in the psyche of the actor' (Jones and Nisbett, 1972, p. 89). The grounds for this contention are:

1. *Informational bias* – by which they mean that people are seen in only a few roles and in a biased sample of situations; it is therefore errone-ously inferred that their *role behaviour* is synonymous with their *personality disposition*.
2. *Information-processing bias* – people feel uncomfortable with incon-sistent information, and so cognitively they attempt to achieve consist-ency or balance in their perceptions. This need to achieve balance may act to distort perceptions of another person in order to make those perceptions of their behaviour 'fit' into their existing cognitive frame-work.
3. *Linguistic distortions* occur in so far as language facilitates the infer-ence of traits in that once we have labelled an action hostile, it is very easy to move to the inference that the perpetrator is a very hostile person. Furthermore, traits are associated quite strongly with each other, so that if a person is described as having trait X, it is assumed or inferred that he or she must also be Y.
4. *The rarity of disconfirmation* is also a feature of trait descriptions. The better one knows someone, the less likely one will apply a facile trait description. However, there are probably limits to this in that once a trait ascription has been made, people tend to construe other behaviours to fit the existing conception, and it is sometimes difficult to see in the face of this kind of bias what would count as disconfirmatory evidence. Possibly, the more damning the description the more difficult it is for the 'accused' to shake it off.

The controversial idea that 'traits exist more in the eye of the beholder' has been referred to earlier in this chapter. However, as Kenrick and Funder (1988) argue, the possibility of errors of judgement and bias creeping into the interpretation of another's personality does not of itself mean that 'personality' exists only inside people's heads. Furthermore, the notion of a 'mistake' or 'an error of judgement' does presuppose that a consensus can be reached on the basis of the available evidence. This underscores the point made earlier that there is a *social* dimension to gaining an understanding of personality (Harré, 1979; Hampson, 1982, 1988 – see above). What it is important to take on board is the possibility of error and the sources from which those errors might occur in real-life situations. In this regard, the four points made by Jones and Nisbett are a valuable contribution to our understanding of personality assessment.

1   Knowing One's Self

How do we become 'self-aware'? Bem (1965; 1967) has suggested that a person only becomes aware of the nature of his or her own actions and intentions after performing them; that the process of self-attribution is identical to that of other attribution in that the process is one of self-observation and inference. Thus, a person acts, perceives her own actions and describes the actions, attendant feelings and internal states by a process of inference. Bem's argument is that we as individuals are information processors and we make judgements about our own and other people's actions on the basis of an 'observational data input'. Furthermore, a person is in the same position as an outside observer much of the time, using the observed information about his or her own behaviour and its context to draw inferences about his or her inner state. A person is usually in a stronger position than other observers of their actions in that they may also access another data source: that of their own history; how they have behaved and felt in like situations. It is possible therefore to have a very accurate picture of one's attitudes and feelings most of the time, though a person may be mistaken about his or her own feelings, etc. People can 'con' or deceive themselves concerning what they are *really* like. This may be most apparent when people are acting defensively (refusing to recognize or 'face' reality) or are subject to conditions of stress.

The positions of Jones and Nisbett and that of Bem would appear on the face of it to be contradictory: on the one hand, Jones and Nisbett are arguing for a *divergence of perspective* by the actor and observer, while Bem appears to be arguing for an *identity* of perspective. Can these two positions be reconciled?

Mower White (1982) argues that Bem's thesis can be applied only if person does not know the causes of his or her behaviour. Thus in this situation, a person (P) has no special knowledge about the causes of his or her behaviour. They are, to all intents and purposes, in the same position as the observer (O). The only source of information available to P (and O) is that she has behaved in a particular way in a particular circumstance. P and O will thus *both* attempt to give a reasoned account of this behaviour (Farr and Anderson, 1983). Put another way, P is attempting to answer the question 'why did I do it?' and O 'why did she do it?' In this way, it is possible for O, on occasions, to give a more accurate or insightful account of P's behaviour, based on his or her more general or broad-based experience, while P may make a wrong attribution about her own behaviour.

There is another subtle difference which Farr and Anderson bring out. They argue that Jones and Nisbett and many subsequent attributionists have failed to capture Heider's original meaning in referring to P and O, but in fact have *reversed* that meaning: For Heider P referred to 'perceiver' (not person) and O to 'other' (not observer). When P is considered as perceiver then she becomes self-conscious or self-aware of her actions; we are in the phenomenal world of the 'I' and 'me' and not in the realm of cognition as such.

2 Attributing Success and Failure

What causes people to attribute to their behaviour the terms 'success' or 'failure'? This particular line of enquiry was pursued by Weiner and his associates (Weiner, 1974). They argued that such attributions could be 'internal' to the person or attributed to external causes. Usefully, Rotter's concept of 'internal versus external locus of control of reinforcement' (Rotter, 1966; Rotter *et al.*, 1962), suggested a variable behavioural mode (or personality trait) which organizes people's perceptions of particular aspects of their environment. This generalized expectancy is reinforced either by people's belief that what happens to them is a result of their own behaviours and attributes (internal control) or the result of luck, fate, chance or the influence of powerful others (external control). Thus ability and effort are properties 'internal' to the person, while task difficulty and luck are external factors (Weiner *et al.*, 1971, 1972). Other dimensions of this conceptual framework were the degree of stability of the causes. For example, effort is an unstable cause in that sometimes we may perceive ourselves as industrious, sometimes as lazy. In addition, Rosenbaum (1972) added the concept of intentionality. The upshot of this research was to demonstrate how the causal attributions of success and failure affected people's expectations of future success. Internal attributions, such as lack of ability, depressed one's expectations more so than when an external factor such as bad luck was ascribed. This framework was then used to explain achievement behaviour in the following way: when people high in achievement needs have been successful, they ascribe this outcome to internal factors (ability and effort). Hence, they experience pride in accomplishment. This attributional bias consequently strengthens the probability of subsequent achievement-related behaviour. People low in achievement needs, on the other hand, are much less likely to explain their success in terms of internal attributes and the feeling of success that they experience is thereby modulated. This in turn means that they are less likely to initiate achievement related activities.

As regards intensity of performance, persons high in achievement needs ascribe success to high effort and failure to lack of effort. The expenditure of effort is thus perceived as an important determinant of performance. Therefore high achievers work hard, since effort is seen as being necessary for success. Low-achievement persons do not perceive this link, however, and therefore display very little intensity of effort in achievement related tasks. Furthermore, persons high in achievement needs ascribe failure to a lack of effort on their part, while those persons who are low in achievement needs explain failure in terms of a lack of ability. The 'high achievers' even in the face of failure always maintain a glimmer of hope. However, further research (Weiner and Sierad, 1973) has shown that where people high in achievement needs are led to believe that their performance on a task is unrelated to their effort or ability, but controlled by some external factor, then their performance may be depressed below that of those individuals having low achievement needs and the same belief structure about environmental causes. Hence, by changing the causal ascriptions for failure it is possible to change the behaviour of persons high or low in achievement needs. This finding relates not only to work on achievement motivation, but also to work on learned helplessness (Seligman, 1975).

In the case of learned helplessness, where people are faced with adverse environmental conditions from which they cannot apparently escape, they will tend to abandon their attempts to overcome such conditions and adapt their behaviour to the conditions they find themselves in. Such behaviour has been related to the onset of depression. However, the implications of this for persons high in achievement needs are that their typical behaviour pattern can be changed (or even destroyed) where environmental conditions are sufficiently adverse such that their expectations of success are never realized and the only realistic assessment of their chances are those of failure.

3   The Implications of an Attribution Approach for Behaviour in Organizations

The management and supervision of others involves above all else the ability to maintain control, to exercise responsibility and judgement. The ability to control oneself and others arises from a knowledge of interpersonal relations. This means knowing how one is likely to behave in a given situation, how others are likely to behave and being able to give reasons for such behaviours. However, control does not arise solely as a result of those two knowledge inputs; it is also important to be able to specify alternative courses of action that are open to self and others. Furthermore, this suggests the need to develop an ability to assess what is the appropriate course of action under the circumstances and to carry it through.

In order to adjudge the *causes* of behaviour, information is needed about the *possible* causes, so that a judgement can be made about the most likely cause. In an everyday situation, misattributions may be made – people 'jump to conclusions' on the basis of the most scant evidence. Training in the analysis of causal attributions could enhance management's ability to exercise appropriate, reliable and considered judgements on the basis of a wider range of evidence; to be able to attribute responsibilities for actions to the rightful situational or personal causes. Such a skill, if it is acquired and exercised, could be an invaluable tool for developing solid relationships based on trust with the workgroup.

Attribution theory is not solely concerned with interpersonal attributions. It may also be applied to the nature of people's job performance. People can be differentiated into those who seek situations where they can achieve and those who do not. Such people attribute the causes for their success to different factors: the high-achievement seekers to personal factors about themselves such as ability and effort, the low-achievement seekers to features of the situation. Where high-achievement seekers find themselves in situations where the chances of failure are continually high, their on the job performance is likely to fall far below that of the low-achievement seekers. It is therefore important for management in situations of recession to buttress their 'high fliers' from such damaging situations. This may mean giving differential support, or different kinds of support, and actively trying to create opportunities for such individuals to continue to perform well. As a strategy it could be criticized on the grounds of being an 'elitist' philosophy. However, it is also a highly pragmatic one in that it is geared to the continued performance and survival of the organization.

SUMMARY

──────── The nature of personality has undergone many revisions over the past decade. The idea that personality is the expression of a set of underlying traits has been questioned on a number of grounds. In terms of (a) individual consistency; (b) the stereotyping implications of trait attributions; (c) the empirical difficulties of substantiating trait theory; (d) the concept of traits as linguistic devices; (e) the conceptual and contingent relations of trait ascriptions to various contexts; (f) epistemological problems with 'traits'; (g) the implications of trait theory for our view of human nature.

──────── An alternative to trait theory is that of interactionism. This gives more weight to the influence of situations, and the interaction of person within situations for shaping behaviour. Interactionism has been applied to the work situation. It may account for the interaction of workers with their work environment; attitudes to work, job satisfaction and so on, are a function of person and environmental factors and their interaction. The interaction is described in terms of how the worker perceives and defines his or her work situation.

──────── A well-researched area of person–environment interaction is that of stress at work. The factors in the work environment which may induce stress reactions are well understood. However, not all persons react to these factors in the same way. Those who are most susceptible can be identified by the patterns of behaviour they display when stressed. From knowing what causes stress for different kinds of people – Type A or Type B – it should be possible to develop optimal environments for them, so reducing their stress while maintaining high levels of performance.

──────── An alternative conceptualization of person–environment interactionism is the route taken by ethogenists such as Rom Harré. They stress the importance of the 'label' attached to the situation by the culture, the rules and norms associated with the situation and the role which the individual plays. Such fundamental features of situations, plus the individual's perception of it, give it *meaning*. The individual's objective then is to manage situations. In as far as this is done, impressions are conveyed to others and these build up to form the individual's reputation. There are a number of implications of this model for behaviour in organizations.

———— A further psychological approach to the conceptualization of a theory of personality is that of constructivism. Specifically, Hampson's theory of the construction of personality takes into account explicit and implicit personality theories; that is, on the one hand, theory and evidence gleaned explicitly from an *expert* perspective, and, on the other hand, evidence gleaned from *lay* and *self* sources. 'Traits' may be regarded as categorizing concepts and as such these different sources of evidence may be collected to assert the existence of behavioural tendencies. Constructivism questions further the possibility of a truly objective approach to understanding personality *at the individual level* and therefore questions the exclusive reliance upon psychometric measurement. One recent application of Hampson's theory has been in the investigation of the entrepreneurial personality.

———— Attribution theory is concerned with the assignment of causes to events. A number of theorists have contributed significantly to our understanding of the way person and situation attributions are made. They include a theory of how we come to know ourselves. Attribution theory is important to an understanding of organizational behaviour, not merely from the point of view of understanding interpersonal relations, but also from the point of view of job performance. How we attribute to ourselves the terms 'success' and 'failure' has important implications for our future behaviour. People differentiated in terms of their achievement orientation when successful tend to attribute different causes to their success. The nature of this attribution process determines whether they will continue to seek out situations where they can continue to achieve or not.

2 Developing People

From Chapter 1, the expression of personality, it would seem, results from various subtle sources of influence, both within the individual and in the situation. However, there are additional questions which can be asked of personality which were not covered in that chapter. These concern the extent to which personality develops during the person's life course. More specifically, does personality exhibit stability or change over the person's life span? And, what implications do either of these views have for the individual's career choice and development? In this chapter different approaches to, and perspectives on, the development of personality are reviewed, and their implications for understanding behaviour in organizations examined.

STABILITY OR CHANGE?

It has been suggested that there are three models of life span psychology (Gergen, 1977). These are stability, ordered change and dialectical models. Sigmund Freud's model of personality development represents both the stability and ordered change models; indeed, his theory defies precise categorization (Hampson, 1982). Freudian theory assumes that the personality is largely formed in childhood – by about the age of 6. In brief, there are three main stages of development – the oral, anal and phallic. Should an individual not have passed successfully through any of these stages, he or she is said to be 'fixated' at a particular stage. So, for example, a person fixated at the oral stage may continue to seek oral gratification by activities such as excessive cigarette smoking.

The person realizes him- or herself through interaction with the environment. This means, for Freud, that in daily life, people experience problems or difficulties which have to be overcome. The balance of elements or parts of the personality will determine how one overcomes and deals with those problems. For Freud, the personality comprises three parts – the id, ego and superego. The id is the impulsive, instinctual self; the ego is the rational, realistic aspect which realizes that immediate gratification of one's desires is not always possible; the superego may be thought of as the seat of the conscience, it is the individual's notion of right or wrong. A well-balanced person is someone whose different parts of their personality are in harmony and in which no one part is dominant.

What does it mean to say that the person expresses their *self* through interaction with the environment? The individual may be said to be striving always to understand him or her *self*, as, in a similar way, the person aspires to the *ego ideal* – the ideal self the person would like to become. The self-concept – who I am – is developed through interaction with others; becoming *self-conscious* is being sensitive to the perceptions and judgements of others of self. The situations people find themselves in, and the circumstances which they create, enable them to express those parts of themselves which were laid down in childhood. A personality in which the three parts are well balanced will approach situations in a way much different from that of an individual with an underdeveloped 'superego' or a dominant 'id'. However, whatever style of life a person leads, whether it may be considered a humdrum routine existence or a stimulating varied and full life, within   this spectrum of possibilities, most people at some stage experience difficulties which they have to sort out. Deciding how to handle such difficulties may cause them to experience inner conflict or tension which results in anxiety. The conflict is between inner impulses arising from the different aspects or levels of the personality. For example, if a person's boss is excessively unfair, should she react aggressively and give him or her a piece of her mind (thus allowing the id to dominate?) Or does reason eventually win through thus preventing her unleashing her wrath, and committing an act for which she is likely to be the ultimate loser? While her anger might well have been justified, the pragmatic part of the self dictates what is of practical value in the circumstances.

Freudian personality theory therefore assumes a stable, lifelong pattern to personality which *possibly* gives the appearance of change as the individual responds to different situations, but which in actuality is merely the acting out of a pattern laid down at a very early age in childhood.

It is important to consider Freudian thinking because of its enormous influence on later developmental theorists. Erikson, whom we shall consider next, was greatly influenced by Freud, but unlike Freud, he suggested that personality development continues into adulthood, and as such Erikson's theory is an example of incremental change.

INCREMENTAL CHANGE: ERIKSON

Erikson (1963) did not accept the notion that the personality was intractable after childhood. He believed that the personality could still be moulded and changed throughout an individual's adult life. In contrast to Freud, Erikson suggested that there are eight stages to development (see Figure 2.1).

STAGE	TIME FRAME	SUCCESS v. FAILURE CHARACTERISTICS
1. Early infancy	Birth to about 1 year	Basic trust v. mistrust
2. Later infancy	About ages 1–3	Autonomy v. shame and doubt
3. Early childhood	About ages 4–5	Initiative v. guilt
4. Middle childhood	About ages 6–11	Industry v. inferiority
5. Puberty and adolescence	About ages 12–20	Ego identity v. role confusion
6. Early adulthood	About ages 20–40	Intimacy v. isolation
7. Middle adulthood	About ages 40–65	Generativity v. stagnation
8. Late adulthood	About ages 65 and older	Integrity v. despair

FIGURE 2.1   *Erikson's eight stages of personality development*

SOURCE   E. H. Erikson (1963) *Childhood and Society* 2nd edn (New York: Norton).

Within each stage there is a juxtaposition of opposing forces; this indicates a critical point or crisis stage of development which the individual will successfully negotiate or not. Hence, Erikson assumes that the human personality in principle develops according to various predetermined steps, and with each maturational step this leads to the widening of the horizons of the individual and increasing social awareness. In order to enable the individual to successfully negotiate these critical points in his or her life, society is organized in principle to manage and maintain this development. This he terms 'the maintenance of the human world' and is exemplified in such rituals as the coming of age, ceremonial passages of rites, etc.

The first three stages are very much akin to the Freudian oral, anal and phallic stages. During the adolescent stages – industry versus inferiority, identity versus role diffusion – the adolescent is concerned with two development needs: doing and producing things in order to win recognition, gain experience and begin to shape up a career; seeking and determining his or her personal identity, discovering who he or she is and wants to be.

The first stage of adulthood is that of developing an intimate relationship with another human being. This *crisis* entails the problem of having sufficient confidence to be able to lose part of one's self in the merging with another. In the middle adult years the person tries to deal with the issue of generativity versus stagnation. This involves a meaningful look back at life in order to judge whether it has been meaningful and productive, or barren and without growth. The individual who has passed through this stage successfully will be in a position to readjust to a different role – that of mentor – stepping aside to enable younger people to assert themselves, while offering guidance and help from years of accumulated experience. In the final stage of adulthood, the individual attempts to consolidate and get a sense of integrity about his or her life; the alternative is a sense of despair that time is running out and not much has been accomplished.

Thus, each stage for Erikson involves a crisis which the individual has to work through and resolve before moving on to the next stage. The maladjusted personality is one which has not successfully resolved such a stage and whose development has thus been arrested or side tracked at or around one of these critical junctures.

AGE AND CHANGE?

As we have seen, Erikson has suggested that personality develops incrementally through discrete steps and that these steps or stages of development can be related to the chronological age of the individual. Other researchers have since adopted a similar approach. For example, Sheehy (1976) and Levinson (1978) have both stressed personality change at different stages of adulthood. Sheehy suggests that what happens to the adult is as a result of inner impulses and urges quite irrespective of external events. However, she acknowledges that many people at these purportedly different stages of their lives; are not necessarily aware of internal change or upheaval they tend rather to attribute their internal state of disharmony to some event which is going on around them. A major problem therefore with this kind of research is that of gathering data in such a way that the researcher can validly and reliably substantiate their working hypotheses.

Sheehy uses the term 'passage' to indicate a developmental stage; this terminology is largely to overcome the negative overtones of the term 'crisis' as used by Erikson. She has suggested the following *passages* of adult development:

1. Pulling up roots
2. The trying twenties.
3. Catch-30.
4. The deadline decade.
5. Renewal or resignation.

She describes these *passages* in the following way. The 'pulling up roots' stage occurs at around the age of 18–22. Here the adolescent is striving for independence and freedom. He or she may become physically and emotionally separate from parental influence and financially independent of them. This stage is often characterized by a brash show of confidence and the hiding of fears. It usually involves an identity crisis.

'The trying twenties' is a period of exploration of one's own identity. This phase is characterized by two strong urges; on the one hand, there is the urge to take on commitments, to build up a safe and secure base, and, on the other hand, to experiment, taking advantage of the opportunities open to the young person. The resolution of this particular stage will depend upon the individual's prior life history, family ties, values and beliefs about society's expectations of him or her.

The third 'passage' which the individual goes through occurs at the age of about thirty. Sheehy terms this stage 'catch-30'. It is described as a period of re-assessment and is characterized by an urge to burst out of the routine which has been established in the twenties. It is said to be a critical time for married couples, and for the single person, and also tends to be a time when decisions are made with regard to career and goal setting for the future. Often it is a case of watering down the idealism which typified past decisions and actions, and heralds a movement into a more down-to-earth, realistic stage.

'The deadline decade' occurs at about 35. Its onset is the result of the realization that the individual has reached the mid-point of his or her life. It therefore heralds a re-evaluation of the self, life, goals and orientation. Sheehy terms it an 'authenticity crisis'. In this phase, people discover parts of themselves of which they were unaware; this means a re-identification and a re-integration. The earlier sense of independence gives way to a sense of isolation and awful responsibility for one's actions and one's destiny. There is also a sense of 'last chances must be taken now'; this is the last opportunity to fulfil one's dreams. The individual thus becomes more self-assertive and this may manifest itself through the career.

In the mid-forties a new stability is eventually gained, through a process of renewal in the previous phase, or 'resignation' – a staleness which has resulted because the renewal has not been achieved. Either way this phase is usually characterized by the individual's greater personal happiness, an acceptance of their loneness, their friends and their privacy.

The appeal of such research is that most people, if they are asked, will acknowledge that they are 'not the same' at forty-five as they were as an adolescent. People perceive themselves differently, and are so perceived, at different ages. In this way, as Hampson points out, it is important to take into account both the lay and the self-perspectives in an understanding of personality development. However, the question still remains as to whether the individual has *really* changed, or is there that stable core of personality which persists throughout?

Hampson (1982) suggests that at different points in people's lives they are merely responding to changes in situations and changes in roles which need to be acted out and handled. Whilst there is a sense in which this is necessarily true, such an analysis does not allow for the fact that in making such *adjustments* the individual may acquire new skills (including social and interpersonal skills), new perspectives, new values and goals, all of which tend to affect the overall expression and presentation of self. Furthermore, it does not meet Sheehy's point that the *passages* she referred to were as a consequence of internal change, and were not primarily motivated from without.

LEVINSON'S THEORY OF ADULT DEVELOPMENT

Levinson has put forward a theory of adult development in which his central concept is that of *individual life structure* (Levinson *et al.*, 1978; Levinson, 1980). The life structure is shaped not only by personality development but also by the processes of socialization and adaptation. Life Structure (LS) is the pattern or design of a person's life; it is 'a meshing of self in the world' (Levinson, 1980). LS is shaped by both external and internal aspects, that is, by other persons, social systems and other outside realities and by the individual's values, desires, conflicts and skills. Levinson distinguishes himself from the psychologist who wants to look at personality development *per se*; his theory is one which takes into account both the psychological aspect of personality development and the sociological perspective. Thus, he says, LS stems from the 'engagement of self in the world; we put ourselves into the world and take the world into ourselves. Adult development is the story of the evolving process of mutual interpenetration of self and world'.

Thus, Levinson suggests that the *individual life structure* is shaped by three types of external event:

1. The socio-cultural environment where culture, norms, rituals and socially accepted rules dictate what behaviours are expected of an individual – the extent to which he or she conforms may profoundly affect the life course.
2. The roles one plays and the relationships one has – with family, friends, workmates, etc. – steer an individual's path in particular directions (for example, we talk about people being 'good' or 'bad' influences on someone, just as we evaluate their role performance: being a 'good' mother, unfulfilled in their job, a 'good' neighbour, etc.).

3. The constraints and opportunities which enable or inhibit the person from expressing and developing their personality, for example, events quite outside a person's control can present them with or deny them opportunities – a war, education cuts or a death in the family might be just some of the factors conspiring to deny someone the educational opportunity they aspire to.

For each individual there will be central and peripheral components of the life structure. For example, an individual's occupation and career may be central at one point in his life, but may later give way to family, community activities or whatever.

Despite these individual differences in experience and priorities, there is, Levinson suggests, a typical pattern to the LS which is true for all men (Levinson's research drew upon a sample of male subjects and in this sense is not necessarily generalizable to women). It evolves through an orderly sequence of periods during the adult years. This involves an alternating sequence of structure building and structure changing (transitional) periods. As was the case for Erikson, these periods of development are defined by the major tasks of building and shaping the Life Structure. For Levinson the stable periods may be from six to ten years in duration, while the transitional periods are up to five years. Thus both stable and transitional periods are major blocks of the individual's life cycle. *Specific* transitional events may occur within the transitional and stable periods. For example, an individual may be divorced, or a death of a loved one may occur in the family. Both types of specific event indicate the need for the individual to adapt and cope with the change in his or her life (see, for example, the work of Adams, Hayes and Hopson, 1976; and later section). Such specific transitional events must be kept analytically distinct from the major transitional periods included in Levinson's model.

There are four major *eras* in a man's life cycle (see Figure 2.2). These are *preadulthood*, which extends from birth to about the age of 22, and *early adulthood*, which lasts from 17 to 45. The period of overlap is marked by a transitional period – the *early adult transition*. This is the period of the termination of preadulthood and the initiation of early adulthood. At around the age of 40 early adulthood eventually gives way to *middle adulthood*, which lasts until approximately 65. Middle adulthood is initiated by the *mid- life transition* at approximately 40–45, a period of reappraisal for the individual before becoming a member of the 'dominant generation'. The final era of a man's life is that of *late adulthood*, which begins with the onset of the *Late Adult Transition* at around 60–65.

Within each of these eras are specific periods of development. Levinson

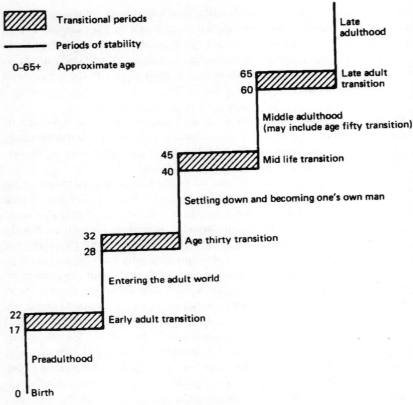

FIGURE 2.2 *Levinson's model of the life course*

SOURCE adapted from D. J. Levinson in N. Smelser and E. H. Erickson (eds) (1980) *Themes of Work and Love in Adulthood* (Harvard University Press).

arrived at a description of these periods through some empirical research he carried out in 1967. In this study, he interviewed 40 men from 4 diverse occupations: hourly workers in industry, executives, biology professors and novelists. These men were aged from 35 to 45. In essence he asked each of them to tell him the story of their life. Each life story was transcribed into up to 100 pages of script, from which Levinson reconstructed the individual life course, by looking for commonalities as well as differences.

The first period (age 17–22) – the *early adult transition* – the boy-man is faced with two tasks: (a) to terminate the adolescent life structure, and (b) to begin to explore the adult world.

The second period – *entering the adult world* (age 22–28) – is synonymous with Sheehy's 'trying twenties'. Here the individual becomes a 'novice adult'. He shifts his centre of gravity from the family of origin to establishing a home which is truly his own. During this period, critical events like establishing an occupation are important. It is a period of exploration; exploration of one's role which includes making choices among alternatives in the search for a more stable life structure.

The next period, which he terms the *age thirty transition*, constitutes a re-examination of oneself between the ages of 28 and 32. The initial choice of occupation is re-evaluated and the individual attempts to face up to the question of whether the life structure should be stabilized around the chosen occupation: should deeper commitments be made or should the individual 'break out' and make a change? This is a period for both men and women of moderate to severe crisis.

The next period is one of stability; it is called the *settling down* stage and lasts from about age 33 to 40. The major task is to build a second adult life structure. As the individual enters this period he is truly at the bottom rung of the ladder; his striving therefore is to become more authoritative, more competent and to be valued in his chosen field. Time at work, with family and other commitments tend to peak around this period.

This striving for authority, recognition and seniority brings the person up against a second phase of the settling down period – *becoming one's own man*. There is a feeling that no matter what, one has to become one's own man. In the work setting, the person may feel constrained by those in authority or by others whose influence is significant. There may be a feeling that superiors 'control too much and delegate too little'. To overcome this the individual will strive to 'make it on his own'. This may be accompanied by the aid of a mentor – a friend or colleague who acts as a role model to enable him to realize his ambitions, to give direction and advice when needed.

While in his late twenties and early thirties he was attempting to build a life structure in which he could realize his dreams and ambitions, the individual now realizes that he can no longer be looked upon as a 'promising young man'. He must turn those dreams into reality and move into a senior position in the world he is just entering. Thus, men strive during this period to realize their personal goals and ambitions. They will be fortunate if they do not stumble over many personal and work-related barriers. Such obstacles tend to lead to frustrations which bring the individual eventually up against the next stage – the mid-life transition.

There are three major tasks which characterize this period:

1. To reappraise the LS, that is, for the individual to ask himself whether
    or not the life structure that he has formulated and lived with over the
    past ten years is the one he wishes to continue to live with. This may set
    in motion a bout of questioning and soul-searching in terms of what
    he wants from the remainder of his life, his marriage, his family, his
    career, and so on. It may be exacerbated by the individual's sudden
    sense of his own mortality and the recognition that time is now limited.
2. A second task during this period is the need to come to terms with the
    polarities which exist in every person. At middle age the person feels
    both young and old; he feels both creative and destructive; he may
    identify the softer feminine and the harder masculine aspects of him-
    self; there is both an urge to feel attached to and dependent on others,
    and a need to feel separate and independent. The individual must come
    to terms with, and resolve these difficulties, and integrate them more
    fully into his personality.
3. The third major task is to modify the LS. The extent of alterations in the
    life course will vary from man to man; some may make quite dramatic
    changes both in career or occupation, and in their personal life. Such
    modifications signify that important changes have taken place in their
    character and the meaning of their relationships, their work and their
    life goals.

Some men pass through this stage with little difficulty and 'manage' the
transition with no major crisis. However, the majority experience inner
turmoil and struggle.

Behaviour associated with the mid-life transition includes that arising
from dissatisfaction with the job, marriage and family. It is a period when
men question many aspects of their lives and when rational, staid processes
often give way to seeming irrationality. For most men such a period cannot
be approached in a calm, self-controlled manner, but involves emotional
turmoil and personal upheaval. As a result, a person 'breaking out' may find
himself alone, abandoned by, or at least not understood by colleagues,
acquaintances and the broader occupational system in which he works.

The major task of *middle adulthood* is to build a new LS for middle age.
Again this structure is questioned at the *age fifty transition*. For many men
this transition is undramatic; they use it to make minor changes in LS, and
continue along the same general path. However, if the individual has not
gone through the crises and soul-searching of the *mid-life transition*, he may
well find himself faced with a relatively severe crisis at the age of 50–55.

Levinson's research has focused primarily on age-related life structures.
However, age linkages and life cycles become less definite as the individual
approaches old age. This may be due to different rates of physical degenera-

tion experienced by different individuals, unique work and social environments, and a divergence of post-work alternatives available to different members of society and different cultures. This is the 'autumn' of the man's life and a period of 'restabilization' characterized by a desire to regain control over the environment. It is important for the individual to begin the adjustment to his physical decline and transcend it. This is done by valuing wisdom as opposed to physical powers; socializing as opposed to sexualizing relationships; greater emotional flexibility, reducing vulnerability by shifting emotional investments from one person or activity to another; and resolving the problem of mental flexibility versus mental rigidity.

Finally, in late adulthood and the transition to old age, the older person becomes more apprehensive about the future. He is increasingly aware of his physical limitations; he may be confronted with the problem of maintaining status and be preoccupied with problems of future financial security.

Levinson's research can be criticized on a number of counts: the sample of men he interviewed was small and unrepresentative; it comprised male Bostonians from four different occupational groups. The research was conducted retrospectively, that is, the respondents were interviewed in their mid-forties and were asked to take a look back on their lives. This process presents problems of selective memory and the reinterpretation of past happenings: assigning a significance to events which was not apparent to the individual at the time, thus giving the impression of purposefulness and direction. Additionally, because the sample was all male, it is not clear that the model can be generalized to women. There are additional complications which may affect women's development, and these arise due to their biological function of childbearing. Apart from this, women's patterns of maturing do not seem to follow quite the same chronological age path as that of men. Thus, as Sheehy points out, a married couple who are of the same chronological age may find themselves drifting apart in their early thirties owing to quite different developmental needs. Furthermore, Hampson (1982) suggests that it is not always clear when one reads these biographically based pieces of research, whether the authors really are attributing the developmental change to internal urges and needs, or to a change in life style due to a career move or some external event generated by the social structure within which the individual operates.

There is inadequate discussion of the extent to which adult development is due to the way society is structured, thus imposing a series of tasks on its members as they grow older and the extent to which the tasks are the inevitable products of maturation. If the developmental stages of adult life are the consequence of the way careers and relationships are structured in a particular society or section of society then they are less interesting than if they can be shown to be universally true. (Hampson, 1982, pp. 243–44)

THE SEARCH FOR PERSONAL MEANING

Royce and Powell (1983) have put forward a comprehensive psychological theory of personality structure and change over the life course. This theory attempts to account for development and growth, individual differences in the way this growth manifests itself, and the significance and purposefulness of life for each individual. Each person's life, they suggest, is imbued with a quest to seek personal meaning and significance. Whereas some individuals will discover their own personal meaning in life, others may fail and withdraw from life.

Personal meaning in life comprises: developing a view of what the world is like – a *world view*; developing a *life style* through which one fulfils one's personal needs, values and goals; and the need to understand oneself, to develop *images of self* in relation to the world and life. Personal meaning is that part of the individual which is truly unique:

> Uniqueness in world views, life styles and self images is pervasive because the way in which individuals differ from each other psychologically are so pervasive. We differ, for example, in the acuity of the senses we possess and through which we pick information from the environment. We differ in the cognitive abilities that enable us to interpret, analyse and elaborate information that the senses take in. The differences extend to all important psychological domains – styles, values, affect, and motor skills. (Royce and Powell, 1983, p. 4)

Personality is organized on various levels and behaviour multiply determined. It is goal-directed as a result of this higher order activity, the quest for personal meaning:

> Personal meaning is not something that exists in the external world or confronts individuals from outside their skin. . . . It is a vision that each of us must create anew for ourselves. Moreover, this vision might underlie even the most mundane behavioural acts. (Royce and Powell, 1983, p. 8)

Personality is composed of six interacting systems – sensory, motor, cognition, affect, style and value – and is hierarchically organized (see

Figure 2.3). The most primitive parts of the system, dominantly under genetic control, are the sensory and motor systems at the base of the hierarchy. They are responsible for the inputs to and outputs from the individual. At the next level, cognition enables the individual to learn about the environment, affect to be aroused and to act. Style and value are the self-organizing or integrative aspects of the system. Information at this level is regulated in order to coordinate lower-order activities in order to achieve specifiable goals and meet the individual's needs. The higher-level systems thus control the activities of the lower-level ones, providing both feedback and direction. At each system level there are specifiable goals, all of which may be decomposed into strategies, tactics and actions. The highest goal in the system is thus the search for personal meaning and involves the integration of the three sub-goals – world view, self-image and life style – as indicated. Furthermore, there is interaction between the individual and the socio-cultural environment, for the individual searches for and maintains personal meaning not only through his or her own style and values, but also through social institutions, social norms, etc.

Over the life span there are different ways in which individuals change. For example, the sensory motor systems peak in late adolescence and from about the age of 20 there is a steady decline in this through to old age. However, this is not necessarily accompanied by a decline in the person's intellectual skills, and, as the person's goals change with age, they adapt successfully to the decline in motor or sensory skills. At the cognitive and affective systems levels the picture is somewhat more complex. While peaks may be perceived at around 20, the ability to conceptualize is not at its highest until age 40. Symbolizing, on the other hand, shows an increase over the last portion of the life span. Hence, the ability to think about and assimilate information, to derive meaning and significance from events, is represented in different modes which peak at different stages throughout adulthood. The affective system can also be thought of in terms of three subsystems: emotional dependence, introversion and emotional instability. All three aspects are high during adolescence, reflecting the more acute problems of growth, independence and integration that the individual in Western society faces at this point in his or her life. They dip during the middle part of life and then increase steadily towards old age. Style and value systems are less predictable because they rely less on heredity and more on environmental influences.

Style and value systems are very much influenced by the cognitive and affective systems and show similarities in their developmental trends. In general, however, it would seem that the individual's system of values and style grows steadily towards middle life and plateaus off thereafter.

42

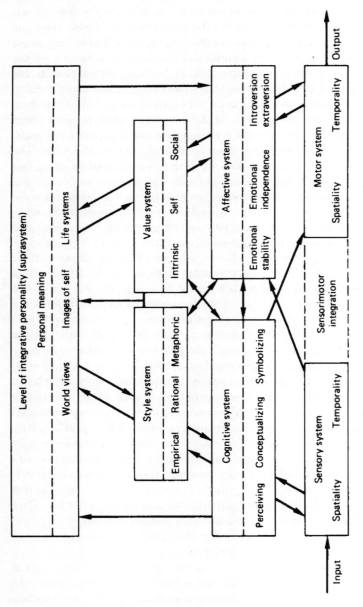

Figure 2.3   The six interacting systems of personality and their integration

Reprinted with permission of the authors and publishers from A. Powell and J. R. Royce (1978) 'Paths to being, life style, and individuality', *Psychological Reports*, 42, 937–1005, fig. 3.

What are the implications of this model for development over the life span?

In the infant the sensory and motor systems and the ability to perceive are all present. The cognitive–affective systems do not develop until late childhood and adolescence. On the other hand, while the value and style systems have begun to be differentiated prior to adolescence, they become increasingly more apparent in the post-adolescent period. The development of these systems and functions increases the need for integration. This process of integration is carried out by the value and style systems. The integrative goal becomes the maintenance of personal meaning, and style and value occupy a central role in the coordination of the rest of the system to meet this goal. In old age the personality structure once more becomes reduced. Now there is no longer a sharp distinction to be made between the cognitive and sensory systems on the one hand and the motor and affective systems on the other. Accordingly, the interaction between the individual and the outside world is lessened. The integrative goals at this stage tend to be those of constructing images of life, the approach to death and a general integration of self.

As these various biological and psychological changes take place within the individual, goals or decision problems also undergo evolution over the life span. Thus, over the course of life, the individual is faced with different decision problems that must be successfully resolved before there is growth. Regression is a reversion to earlier decision problems. So, for example, neurotic reactions arise from an individual's 'temporary loss of values'. Individuals may go through 'existential crises' in which they revert to a lower level of integration. The nature of *personal meaning* also changes over the individual's life, not only because of the emergence of different biological systems and their growth and development, but also due to cultural and self influences. With the emergence of new systems, new ways of conceptualizing and perceiving the world occur. Furthermore, with the shift in dominance and the peaking of different systems at different times, what is meaningful to the individual will change over time. In adolescence developing thought processes and arousal states dominate, but at the same time there is the gradual unfolding of the individual's value system. Adolescents question parental and other value systems in order to sort out their own; and they experiment with different styles in order to develop their own style more fully. At this stage, the interaction between the cognitive value systems results in the development of cults, ideologies and religious beliefs.

The focus of adulthood and the second half of life shifts increasingly towards a 'quest for meaning' and a 'living out of one's thoughts, feelings and values as well as a struggle with various existential crises' (Royce and Powell, 1983, p. 247). The focus shifts towards greater emphasis on self-completion and life style: 'Thus, there is an increasing assertion of self without regard for the consequences, in combination with a retrospective analysis and summing up of one's life.' This 'quest for the meaning of life' is either resolved or further revised during the last phase of life. It involves the integration of self, world view and life style. Here 'existential *angst*' probably reaches a peak as the individual takes a long look back on his or her life, assessing it in terms of whether it has affirmed or failed to fulfil 'life's meaning'. In general, there are five broad phases to the life span as indicated in the summary table (see Table 2. 1). What is noticeable in the adult is the increasing emergence of the 'self'. Thus, direction in adulthood is a 'complex outcome of heredity, environment and "self" '. It is a time when people have most freedom to choose their own personal life style, their career and so on. Structure and choices made for one may give a sense of security and comfort; freedom to determine one's own destiny is accompanied by anxiety and awe in many people.

APPLICATIONS OF THE PERSONALITY CHANGE MODELS TO BEHAVIOUR IN ORGANIZATIONS

How can the organization apply knowledge of personality development in order to gain an understanding of, and manage better, the behaviour of its employees? The simple lesson is that people at different stages in their life cycle will have different motivations. The implications of this are that, for instance, young people in their early twenties may be anxious to prove their worth, although their commitment to a particular organization may be superficial. Commitment comes with age and experience, when one has had the opportunity to reappraise the course one has taken. In one's early thirties the realization that one can progress through the organizational hierarchy may be sufficient motivation for some to work hard, while for others, outside commitments due to mortgages, a young family and so on, may be the spur to advancement. In the middle years, many people experience the 'mid-life crisis', which may be exacerbated by the lack of opportunity for change at work. One's performance may fall off, behaviour may become erratic if not irrational and ability to hold the job down may be impaired.

From the organization's perspective, management must develop insight into the characteristics of the job, the organization and career paths within it. At the selection and recruitment stage they must be able to diagnose the long-range growth potential of a person and be able to integrate recruitment/selection activities with those of job placement and early supervision (Schein, 1978). If they can do this successfully, then they will overcome the problems of early disillusionment and labour turnover. The new recruit may present a threat to supervisory and middle management. Therefore, the training, and choice, of supervision of new recruits is critical to the induction of new staff. Sensitivity to personal change will enable the organization to ease its managers through an appropriate career path. Career blockages, at any stage but particularly at the mid-life transition, can heighten the sense of frustration and deepen the problems of transition. Organizing periodic discussions with managers at different levels about their careers, their job and so on, is one way of attempting to pick up signs of problems and to demonstrate a caring attitude on the part of the organization. Sending managers on training courses periodically is another traditional way of looking after their development. However, there may be a point where the manager challenges: 'training for what?' If there is no sign of advancement then, motivation to do further training may be shunned.

The Royce–Powell model also emphasizes other aspects of personal development which are either not included or are given a place of less central importance by the other theorists. This psychological model stresses the importance of individual differences and the uniqueness of the self. The implication of this is that managerial tactics or solutions to problems may be effective with some employees and not so with others. The manager must be flexible in order to respond to differences in individuals. Allied to this is the strengthened development in adulthood of the self-concept and the need for personal meaning in life. Personal failure in this regard will result in estrangement from self, others and life. Thus, in terms of organizational behaviour, employees at whatever level in the organization, seek meaning through their work, as well as outside work. Organizations which fail to fulfil such needs should not be surprised if they have a disillusioned, disaffected and apathetic work-force on their hands. Work can become meaningful to individuals if they are enabled to take a pride in the company they work for, in the product they help produce and in the job they do.

Thus, there is not one simple solution for the organization to take. People are all different and what may fulfil one person may not fulfil another. Jobs may be redesigned to enable workers to use more of their capacities. Different forms of participation and consultation may also be used so that employees can have a say in how the job is done and to enable them to

TABLE 2.1 *Summary comparison of the transformations of personality during various phases of the life span*

Phase of the life span	Quantitative	Differentiation	Personality transformations Integration	Integrative goals	Self-direction
Infancy	Greatest changes in sensory and motor areas; style and value at their lowest	All systems and sub-systems differentiated	Little or no personality integration	Adaptive sensory-motor integration	Minimal
Childhood	Greatest changes in the areas of cognition and affect	Subsystems and their components and higher-order factors further differentiated	Integrative action largely through affective processes	Adaptive cognitive-affective constructions	Slight
Adolescence	Greatest changes in affect, style, and value, but all are changing; sensory system at its peak	Emergence of styles and values; articulation of them increasingly important	Cognition and affect are the integrative systems	Emotional, or cognitive-affective balance; *social* value and *empirical* style dominant	Phase of initial formulation of life goals

Phase of the life span	Personality transformations				
	Quantitative	*Differentiation*	*Integration*	*Integrative goals*	*Self-direction*
Adulthood	Period of relative stability; some growth in styles and values, with slow decline in sensory, motor, and cognitive subdomains of perceiving and conceptualizing	Greatest differentiation in styles and values; articulation of one's life goals of central importance and a continuing process	Styles and values operate as distinct systems that organize or integrate personality	World view, life style and self-image are the focus of further growth and development; *intrinsic* value and *rational* style dominant	Phase of maximal self-direction; generally stable period, although great change is possible
Old age	Period of even greater decline in cognitive conceptualizing and perceiving, with continued increase in symbolizing abilities; further declines in sensory and motor	A variety of functions of personality begin to consolidate in order to compensate for decline in sensory, motor, and cognitive abilities	Increasing importance given to style and value commitments and the 'interiorization' of personality	Images of life, integrative self, and an approach to death; 'completion' is main theme throughout; *self*-value and *metaphoric* style dominant	Self-direction impaired by one's failing body and by social reactions to aging

SOURCE   J. R. Royce and A. Powell (1983) *Theory of Personality and Individual Differences: Factors, Systems and Processes* (Englewood Cliffs, New Jersey: Prentice-Hall).

exert some control over decisions which affect them (Chell, 1985a; Wall and Lischeron, 1977; and Chapter 9 of this volume). At higher levels of management, there may be more scope to enable employees to develop their potential and express themselves and their individuality through work. Periodic assessment by informal discussions and the assessment centre method will enable the organization to better place its managers; it may enable the organization to arrive at options other than promotion where frustrating career blockages exist.

Growth, development and change can be painful and so the organization should be sensitive to the needs of its managers. On the one hand, there will be young, career-minded people attempting to establish themselves, while on the other hand there may be people who have reached middle age and are attempting to come to terms with the fact that they have not 'made it'; they have not realized the dreams of their youth. Here older, experienced employees may be invaluable in helping guide their colleagues through difficult periods. A well-balanced age profile, therefore, is one way of enabling this to happen; another is to develop a caring attitude to new recruits and to extend this throughout their careers. This could well be one of the best investments the organization makes to secure its future.

CHANGE AND TRANSITION

The problems of transition, of coping with change, cannot be attributed entirely and exclusively to the natural unfolding of the life course. Major events such as marriage, the death of a close relative or friend, a change of job, moving house, etc. are for most people the causes of disruption to an established pattern of life and which engender the need for adjustment and the assumption of new or different patterns of behaviour.

Adams *et al.* (1976) put forward a general model which prescribes the pattern of behavioural/affective change in the individual during the process of adjustment to a major event. Not every change that a person experiences will trigger the 'transition cycle', two conditions must be fulfilled:

1. The individual must be aware of a discontinuity in their life space.
2. A new pattern of behaviour responses is required in order to handle the new situation.

There are different forms of transition; the characteristics of which rest on two key dimensions: whether they are predictable or unpredictable and voluntary or involuntary. The essential point, according to Hopson and Adams (in Adams *et al.*, 1976), is that

> whether a change in one's daily routine is an intentional change, a sudden surprise that gets thrust upon one, or a growing awareness that one is moving into a life stage characterized by increasing or decreasing stability, it will trigger a *cycle* of reactions and feelings that is predictable. (Adams *et al.*, 1976, p. 9)

Figure 2.4 shows the changes in self-esteem which occur during the seven stages of the transition.

Stage 1 they term *immobilization*. This has been variously described by other researchers as a state of shock, the consequences of which are an inability to plan or to reason things through. Some changes may be viewed positively, while others may be characterized by negative expectations and

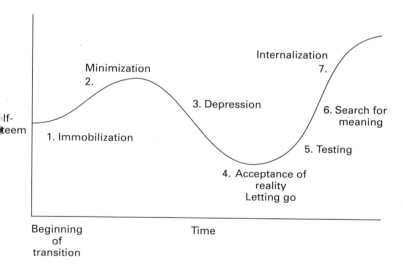

FIGURE 2.4   *Self-esteem changes during transitions*

SOURCE   Adams, J. S., J. Hayes and B. Hopson (1976) *Transition: Understanding and Managing Personal Change* (London: Martin Robertson).

some may be familiar or not so familiar. The nature of the expectations and the degree of familiarity with the situation will all affect the depth of feeling of the individual at the outset of the cycle.

Stage 2 – *minimization* – shows the individual changing or attempting to minimize or trivialize the reality of the change which is taking place in their life.

Stage 3 shows the onset of *depression*, that is when the reality can no longer be denied; they are, effectively, beginning to acknowledge the fact that a change has taken place.

Stage 4 is described by the term '*acceptance of reality*'. The individual begins to 'let go' of the past and their psychological involvement with it and to accept the new reality with renewed positive feelings. This starts the shift out of the depression to:

Stage 5 is where they typically commence *testing* themselves in the new situation. This can be a difficult stage, not only may the person be stereotyping reality, but they may experience feelings of irritability and anger.

Stage 6 is termed '*search for meaning*' and is predominantly cognitive, that is, the individual attempts to understand all those feelings experienced in stage 5. This conceptualizing gives way to:

Stage 7 is where the meaning is incorporated into their behaviour, that is, *internalized*.

In general, moving through the transition cycle as described is rarely a smooth process and is typically stressful for the individual concerned. There are, however, ways of coping with the transition which may lessen its impact and duration. For example, an attempt to shape and anticipate the nature of the change in advance suggests an attempt by the individual to gather as much intelligence about the forthcoming change. Clearly this can only occur where the change can reasonably be anticipated. Hopson and Adams (in Adams *et al.*, 1976) outline in some detail the kinds of tactics an individual may initiate in order to manage the transition, distinguishing between *proactive* and *reactive* strategies.

A proactive strategy may be to delay various decisions until the person feels they can cope with them, to create personal stability zones and/or to seek support from others. Examples of reactive strategies are withdrawal or 'opting out' and disengagement from the real problem. Being proactive is not always the more appropriate stance to take; just occasionally it helps to sit back and let others take decisions for one.

Building upon the work of Adams *et al.*, and other researchers in this specific field, Nicholson (1990) has put forward his own model of the transition cycle which he describes as non-normative. It is intended as 'a systematic general framework to allow interpolations and interpretation of the full range of extremely different experiences we know people to encounter in transition' (Nicholson, 1990, p. 87).

Nicholson's work on work role transitions is a precursor of his model of the transition cycle (Nicholson, 1984). He sees the transition cycle as having three guiding principles. They are recursion – that is, continuous movement; disjunction – the ability to identify distinct phases or stages in the cycle; and interdependence – the influence of one stage on another.

An individual may react either positively or negatively towards a transition and this will clearly affect how they negotiate the change (see Figure 2.5.).

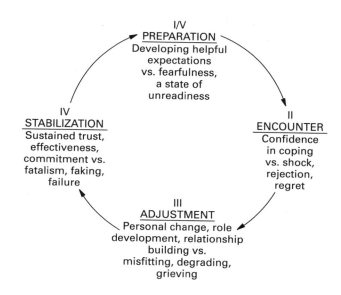

FIGURE 2.5   *The transition cycle* (after Nicholson, 1990)

SOURCE   Nicholson, N. (1990) 'The transition cycle: causes, outcomes, processes and forms', in S. Fisher and C. L. Cooper (eds) *On the Move: The Psychology of Change and Transition* (Chichester: Wiley).

Phase I is termed *preparation*. The person may be able to achieve a realistic state of readiness, developing clear and realistic expectations of the anticipated change. On the other hand, a change may occur unexpectedly with little time to prepare.

Phase II – *encounter*. Being well prepared is likely to enable the individual to cope with the change successfully; this in itself will build confidence. On the other hand, unpreparedness may result in shock and an inability to handle the situation one finds oneself in, and result in feelings of disquiet, rejection and regret that one allowed onself to become involved.

Phase III – *adjustment*. An individual is adjusted to a situation when consonance has been achieved between personal change and role development. Resistance to change will result in a misfit between the person and their environment and may be accompanied by their grieving for their lost past or forgone opportunity.

Phase IV – *stabilization*. Successful adjustment will tend to lead to a successful stabilization phase in which both personal and organizational goals are achieved. This will facilitate and deepen relations of trust and commitment to others and enable the individual to realize their personal potential. On the other hand, the corollary to a poor adjustment phase is the development of dysfunctional relationships with colleagues with underachievement and other performance problems.

There are a number of clear practical implications of this analysis in terms of individual career accounting and the adoption of strategies for managing the transition cycle. At the preparation stage it is clearly crucial to maximize readiness. For an organization, this means giving consideration to recruitment procedures in order to reduce 'mystification, misinformation and mismatch' (Nicholson, 1990, p. 91). Too heavy a reliance on psychometric assessment on the one hand, or impressionism on the other are likely to be an inadequate basis for selection. At the encounter stage an individual needs to feel equipped to explore in safety the new situation. This may mean persons taking the initiative themselves, or others anticipating such a need and enabling it to happen. At the adjustment phase the individual needs support to prevent them sinking into any of the negative feelings which are readily associated with personal change. Positive, constructive yet realistic feedback will facilitate the management of this phase. The stabilization stage requires a level of vigilance and responsiveness which will enable small adjustments to be made in order to sustain effective performance.

Nicholson (1990) identifies further four facets of change *per se*. These are changes of (a) context, (b) relationships, (c) status and (d) function. The cycle itself may also vary along nine identifiable dimensions. They are:

I *Speed* or rate at which the transition occurs – this may mean not only how quickly an individual moves through the transition but also the frequency of transition cycles that occur and which have to be managed.

II *Amplitude*, that is the extent of novelty or radicalness of the change or transition.

III *Symmetry*, that is the 'shape' of the cycle and the differential lengths of time spent on each phase.

IV *Continuity* This has to do with the succession of transition cycles, whether they follow logically or in an arbitrary, incoherent fashion.

V *Discretion*. This dimension is about the scope of the person to determine the content and scheduling of experiences throughout each phase.

VI *Complexity* varies according to the range of demands made on the individual and hence the number of adaptations and adjustments which are required.

VII *Propulsion* has to do with the source or instigator of the cycle; it is both related to individual freedom and self-determination, and moderated by situational/environmental factors including labour market position.

VIII *Facilitation*. This raises the issue of where help may come from to enable the individual through the transition cycle. For example, in terms of socialization at the place of work there may be established novitiate/ or mentoring systems.

IX *Significance*. What are the long-term consequences of the transition cycle, both for the individual and the organization in personal change terms and in terms of role/organization development?

Using the four facets of change and the nine dimensions of the transition cycle, it is possible to profile different types of transition event such as a promotion, a career change, retirement, etc. Such profiles may then be used as a basis for developing clear strategies for choice and action.

ORGANIZATIONAL CONSTRAINTS AND ADULT DEVELOPMENT

Change – not merely of circumstances, but also of behaviour – is thought to typify adult life (Nicholson, 1990). Some changes may have lasting effects, establishing new patterns of behaviour which manifest themselves in changes in the adult personality. An adult's search for meaning in life may be achieved through work/career experiences. On the other hand, the work-leisure pattern of a life may merely offer a 'backdrop', a structure which for the most part is assumed, taken for granted.

The task of enabling individuals as employees to cope with the many and various changes which will happen to them may be dealt with informally or formally within the organization. Small to medium-sized organizations are unlikely to have a personnel function or formally developed human resource management (h.r.m.) policies and practice. The care taken of individual employees may therefore be a matter of chance. Procedures for recruitment may be inadequately grounded in organizational objectives; this, along with poorly founded impressions of the candidate's personality and abilities are likely to prove a poor basis for the decision taken. Even in larger organizations which support a personnel department, there is no guarantee that employee development will be part and parcel of policy and practice.

Organizational constraints are determined in part by h.r.m. policy and practice, and what might broadly be termed organizational culture. Organization culture develops over time as a consequence of the values, beliefs and established practice of the members; the degree of organizational change which is instigated within the business, and how it is managed also shapes the culture. People may self-select different types and styles of organization culture and management. The more information they are given at the recruitment stage, the better able they are to understand what will be required of them and to adjust to the new job and organizational demands. Exchange of information at this crucial stage – recruitment – is important for both parties.

After recruitment, the job and the individual are both likely to change over time. The idea that people should fit the job is now dated as a deliberate employment policy; rather, the idea of role development to enable the job to fit the specific characteristics of the person is thought to be more desirable on some counts. It can be more difficult to manage and may be one reason why in the past it was not a prevalent practice.

Argyris (1957) would appear to have anticipated such developments in organizational behaviour. He assumes that each person is attempting to realize their full potential – to self-actualize – but that the organization does not always facilitate this process. Each individual, he suggests, in becoming part of the adult world is striving to:

- develop from a state of *passivity* to one of increasing *activity* as an adult;
- develop from a state of *dependence* to one of *independence*;
- *increase* their skills, abilities and repertoire of behaviours;
- move from *shallow* to *deep* interests;
- develop from having merely *short-time* perspectives to much *longer-time* perspectives;

- rise from a *subordinate* position to an equal or *superordinate* one;
- develop an awareness and control over *self* as an adult.

Argyris thus assumes a concept of personality which can mature and develop throughout life. It is not so much that the roles and environment cause fluctuations in behaviour, but rather that the personality finds both expression and the ability to change in response to the environment. Moreover, this model of personality development suggests that there is a reciprocal influence between personality and career development. The individual who is ambitious and career-minded will attempt to realize his or her personality development through the career path, and the career path will enable the individual to grow and mature.

However, there are some problems. For example, Argyris points out that the fulfilment of individual needs and formal organization requirements are often incompatible. Whilst the individual may be striving to realize his or her full potential, the organization may not provide the opportunity for this to happen: there may be little opportunity for individual expression and flair; or there may be no vacancy for promotion. Thus individual effort and striving may be frustrated, and so may the maturing person.

In such circumstances, employees may regress to becoming dependent, cease to take initiatives, become submissive, passive, alienated and bored. The sorts of employees that the organization may have developed may not be the ones which senior management would have wished for (Schein, 1978). Therefore the organization must adopt a strategy which will enable it to tap the full potential of its employees. Promotion, perks and pay rises may provide only a temporary solution. An alternative way forward which will enable the individual to develop and mature with the job is likely to involve some reorganization of work and responsibilities.

The advent of new technology presents management with just this issue. The job can be made meaningless or it can be enriched so that the operator assumes greater responsibility. Two examples may serve to illustrate this issue. Word-processing equipment in the office poses such a dilemma for management. On the one hand, the secretarial job can be changed *quantitatively*. The secretary can be asked to produce more of the same; the job can be made repetitive and boring. On the other hand, it can be changed *qualitatively*: the secretary can be required to do a greater variety of jobs and, in effect, become an important part of the management team (Mattes, 1984). On the shopfloor, we may be witnessing the gradual 'bleaching of the blue collar' (Blandy, 1984). Boddy and Buchanan (1984) provide an example from the baking/confectionary industry. Traditionally, the master baker, doughmen, and a supervised team of operators manually mixed the various ingredients to produce biscuits. When computerized mixing was introduced most of the traditional functions were carried out by machine, the recipe now being contained on a paper tape.

> The doughmen (renamed mixer operators) were left with only a small number of residual tasks. They found the job boring, monotonous and lacking in responsibility; management found that the operators had become careless, irresponsible and unsuitable for promotion. (Boddy and Buchanan, 1984, p. 177)

In contrast to this, the installation of electronic weighing equipment enhanced the job of the *ovensmen* by enabling them to have constant updated records of the packet weights displayed on a video screen near their work place. This accurate information enabled them to make small early adjustments in the baking process, so producing the correct weight of biscuits, and enabling the ovensmen to do their job better.

SUMMARY

——————— There are various models of personality which assume that the personality exhibits either stability or change over the life span. Freud's theory of personality development defies precise classification, although his assumption that the basis of personality is laid down in childhood suggests an underlying stability.

——————— Erikson (1963) does not believe that personality development is intractable after childhood. He has suggested an eight-stage model in which the individual at each stage must resolve a particular 'crisis'. The outcome, if successful, is growth; if unsuccessful, regression.

——————— Erikson's stages are characterized by a task to be worked through; this particular idea has been assumed by later theorists. Both Sheehy (1976) and Levinson (1978) further refined the adult stages of development. Sheehy suggested five 'passages' or stages which occur between adolescence and the mid-forties. Levinson's model suggests an individual 'life structure' comprising stable and transitional periods in which change, heralding further personal growth, takes place.

——————— Criticisms of the Sheehy and Levinson models include the problem of identifying whether it is personality as such which has changed or whether what one is witnessing is the adaptation and modification of behaviour to cope with changing circumstances and situations.

The Royce–Powell model is a highly comprehensive theory of personality structure which also accounts for change over the life span. Personality is conceived of as a hierarchy of sub-systems of increasing complexity and lessened genetic control. The need for interaction and integration of the different systems creates complex behaviour patterns. The pinnacle of the structure is the need to imbue actions with personal meaning and significance. Such meaningfulness derives from the life style and world view that individuals develop over the course of their lives. As different systems are at different stages of emergence during life, behaviours that were meaningful at one stage are superseded by different activities which are more nearly in tune with current higher-order activities and goals.

The extent to which change in the life course unfolds as a natural part of the life course is debatable. Adams *et al.* and Nicholson have put forward models of the transition process which describe a train of events with which individuals, dealing with change in their lives, must cope. The practical implications of these models for counselling, selection and recruitment, monitoring processes and the organization of work etc. are apparent.

Awareness and sensitivity to personality development will enable the organization to develop methods of increasing employee commitment, motivation and work effectiveness. Opportunities for change may be created through the introduction of new technology. This means the redesign of work to create qualitatively improved jobs and greater participation and consultation to increase involvement and responsibility and to make jobs more meaningful. It will also enable employees to grow and mature with their jobs.

3 Controlling People

INTRODUCTION

One of the major problems facing management today is that of understanding what motivates people. In order to be able to control people it is necessary to understand what makes them *move*. For some it will be the offer of more pay, for others higher status and prowess, but there is no one single thing which will satisfy all people for most of the time. It is these facts – that all people are different and have different wants and desires and that motives are complex and dynamic – which make it difficult to predict people's motives with any frequency or reliability. However, by studying motivation we can gain some insights, draw some conclusions and arrive at some useful generalizations, all of which will make the process of controlling others that bit more effective. In this chapter therefore we will be looking at *what* motivates people as well as *how* to motivate them. In addition we will also be examining management styles which play an important part in influencing employees to pursue goals and derive job satisfaction as a consequence.

UNDERSTANDING *WHAT* MOTIVATES PEOPLE

1 Need Hierarchy

People's reasons for acting in the way that they do are intimately and complexly part of their personality. This particular assumption was at the basis of Murray's and later Maslow's theory of human needs. Whilst Murray suggested the existence of a multiplicity of needs, Maslow attempted to narrow the field, to develop general categories into which all needs could be subsumed. These general categories of needs fall into a hierarchy, from the lower-order, most basic needs at the base of the hierarchy, through to the higher-order, growth needs at its pinnacle (see Table 3.1).

The mechanism of movement is governed by the principle of prepotency. This means that an unsatisfied need becomes the dominant motivator. Once it has been satisfied then the next need in the hierarchy is activated. Thus, the idea is that a person is primarily most concerned to satisfy his or her *physiological* needs for food and drink, warmth, shelter, sex and so on.

TABLE 3.1   *A comparison of the basic need theories proposed by Maslow, Alderfer, McClelland and Herzberg*

Maslow (1943) (hierarchy)	Alderfer (1969) (implied hierarchy)	McClelland (1961)	Herzberg (1959) (implied hierarchy)
1. Physiological needs			Working conditions
	Existence needs		
2. Safety needs (material)			Salary and benefits
Safety needs (interpersonal)		Power	Supervision
3. Social, love or belongingness needs	Relatedness needs	Affiliation	Workgroups
4. Esteem needs (feedback from others)			Recognition
Esteem needs (self-confirmed)			Advancement Responsibility
	Growth needs		
5. Self-actualization		Achievement	Job challenge Accomplishment

SOURCE   E. H. Schein, *Organisational Psychology* (1980) 3rd edn (Englewood Cliffs, New Jersey: Prentice-Hall).

Once these needs are satisfied, people next look to make themselves more *secure*: the shelter must not only keep them warm and dry, but also safe. Having secured themselves, they seek to satisfy their *interpersonal* needs, to belong to a group, to have friends, to be loved and cared for. The need for *self-esteem*, to gain respect from others and to have self-respect now dominates the individual's being. And finally, they seek to become all that they can become, that is, to *self actualize*.

This conception of human needs was popularized by McGregor in the 1960s. It has an intuitive appeal and attractive simplicity. However, it gave the impression of rigidity, for it was clear that some people did not always attempt to satisfy their basic needs before their higher order needs. Maslow himself was aware of cases like that of Mahatma Gandhi, who fasted for political as well as religious reasons. But perhaps it was such exceptions that proved the general rule? However, it was clear that different people might have different priorities and that any purportedly general theory must accommodate this fact. Furthermore, it is also possible for several needs to be activated simultaneously: people can be hungry and attempt to satisfy that need, while being proper and careful how they eat; they can make polite conversation and command respect while dining.

The traditional shape of the need hierarchy was that of a triangle, with physiological needs at its base and self-actualizing needs at the pinnacle. This suggests the greater importance of the basic needs. However, need this be so? It has been suggested (Hersey and Blanchard, 1982) that this particular version of the model might be applicable in those countries struggling to feed their people, whereas an inverse triangle might be typical of some groups of people in the more developed nations. Between these two extremes the most dominant need might occur at any point. For instance, for some, *social* needs may invariably be the greatest motivator.

Conceptually, self-actualization is not that easy to grasp. It has been taken to mean the realization of a person's potential in so far as they might become a footballer, a writer, a lorry driver, a mother, a craftsman, etc. To confine this concept within occupational bounds seems very restricting. It is true that an individual may fulfil much of their potential through such an occupation, but still not become all that they might become, as was the essence of the original definition. Self-actualization is what the person strives for, but may never fully achieve. They may misidentify their potential and frustrate their development by concentrating effort in inappropriate directions. They may never know when they have 'arrived' and suffer the dissatisfactions of never feeling fulfilled. They may identify several sources of strengths within themselves and have to make choices. Social and organizational constraints may dash any hopes of self-fulfilment of this type. In this way, the concept of self-actualization can be linked to individual career structure and the idea of deriving personal meaning through work, as was discussed in Chapter 2.

Apart from the problem of conceptual clarification, there was the additional problem of finding empirical support for the theory (Hall and Nougaim, 1968; Lawler and Suttle, 1972; Wahba and Bridwell, 1976). Largely owing to these problems, Alderfer (1969, 1972) suggested a 'new' theory of human needs (see Chell, 1985a). Essentially, he collapsed Maslow's five categories into three conceptually distinct ones and called them *existence*, *relatedness* and *growth* needs (see Table 3.1). Thus, existence needs included Maslow's *physiological* needs plus the need for safety from physical harm. Relatedness needs included Maslow's *social* or *belongingness* needs plus the need to feel secure among family and friends and the need to receive respect and esteem from others. Finally, growth needs comprised feelings of self-worth and accomplishment, personal development and self-actualization. Although there is an 'implied' hierarchy, Alderfer has allowed for greater freedom of movement between the categories. He has also tested empirically his theory in a number of organizations and other settings.

2 Need, Expectations and Incentive Value

An alternative approach to understanding *what* motivates people has been developed by McClelland (1961) and Atkinson and Birch (1979). McClelland suggested that there are three needs which are closely related to managerial behaviour. These needs he identified as *achievement, affiliation* and *power* needs. People have all these motives in different, measurable strengths. However, in order that such motives be aroused, people assess the likelihood of attaining the goal or object and its associated incentive value in different situations. Thus, people with a high need for achievement will weigh up the difficulty of the task and the various risks associated with it; they will also consider whether there will be any personal sense of accomplishment and satisfaction to be derived from having successfully completed the task. Accordingly, high-need achievers tend to choose tasks of moderate difficulty levels, which present a challenge and which realistically can be achieved. People low in this particular need or who fear failure will rather tend to choose tasks which are either ridiculously easy or difficult. In this way, they are either sure of succeeding or they are in a situation where no one would expect them to succeed and they are effectively 'let off the hook'.

High achievers tend to be individualistic and highly productive people; however, without additional training they do not always have managerial skills. They are hard-working and have personal goals and standards which they work towards. In team situations they often expect others to work as hard as they do and have a tendency to be impatient and irritable when people do not match up to these expectations. They like to take personal responsibility for finding solutions to problems and to receive rapid feedback on their performance. The incentive for them is the feelings of accomplishment at having achieved their targets in the knowledge that their effort and strivings were worthwhile.

The need for affiliation is often a very strong need in many people. It affects their relationship to the workgroup and its leader. People with a high affiliation motive strive for friendship, group cohesion and conformity.

This motive is not necessarily associated with productivity and managerial effectiveness, unless the cohesion and conformity are linked to organizational goals (Klein and Ritti, 1984). However, as a managerial attribute, concern for other people's feelings and the need to understand others, it is useful in that it contributes to increased interpersonal competence and results in solid working relationships between superior and subordinate (Litwin and Stringer, 1968).

Need for power is also an interpersonal need. It is a need to influence others and to make others behave in ways in which they would not have otherwise behaved. Individuals high in need for power enjoy 'being in charge'. They strive for influence over others, accumulating all the symbols and emoluments of power. Accordingly, they prefer to be placed into competitive and status oriented situations and tend to be more concerned with gaining influence over others and with their prestige than with effective performance. McClelland (1975) has identified four stages to the power orientation: (a) drawing inner strength from others, (b) strengthening oneself, (c) having an impact on others, and (d) acting as an instrument of higher authority. Thus, the first stage is to be a loyal follower and serve powerful others. Next, the individual collects symbols of status, plays the game of one upmanship and begins to dominate situations. Progressing to stage three – self-assertiveness – he or she becomes more aggressive and attempts to manipulate situations in order to control other people's behaviour and to use others in pursuit of his or her own personal goals. Both stages two and three tend to cause interpersonal conflict and may lead to resentment, communications problems and coalition formation. Stage four represents the pinnacle of the socialization of the individual on this dimension. Here they tend to subordinate their own personal goals and use their power in pursuit of organizational goals. This represents a legitimate use of power through established authority systems, particularly when compared with the personal dominance and marginal legitimacy of power needs as expressed in stage three.

3   Herzberg's Motivation–hygiene Theory

Maslow, as we have seen, conceived of needs as fundamental to the personality. McClelland and Atkinson both saw the need motive as part of the personality but that it is triggered by environmental factors. The emphasis of Herzberg, in contrast, is on identifying those aspects of the work environment which will motivate workers. In his initial study (Herzberg *et al.*, 1959) he carried out extensive interviews with some 200 engineers and accountants from 11 industries in the Pittsburgh area. The interviewees were asked about the kinds of things on the job which made them unhappy or dissatisfied and those things which made them happy or satisfied. When he had analysed the results of this survey, he drew the conclusion that there were two different categories of factor that affected how employees felt about their jobs. When they were dissatisfied, these respondents tended to blame environmental factors, whereas when they felt satisfied they put this down to the job itself. Herzberg termed the first category of factors *hygiene* or *maintenance* factors because by maintaining the job environment at an acceptable level feelings of dissatisfaction could be avoided. The second category of factors he termed *motivators* because they effectively motivated people to superior job performance.

What precisely were these factors? Company policy and administration, supervision, working conditions, interpersonal relations, money, status, and security were all identified as maintenance factors. They are not an intrinsic part of the job but are all related to the conditions under which the job is performed. Motivating factors, on the other hand, involve feelings of achievement, professional growth and recognition, increased responsibility and the satisfaction of accomplishing a challenging job. It is clear that Herzberg's model fits rather well with the other need theories discussed so far (see Table 3.1). For instance, *extrinsic* factors such as the working conditions (canteen facilities, cleanliness, temperature, etc.) are synonymous with Maslow's *physiological* needs; salary and benefits (such as pension) provide for the individual's *material safety* and supervision for *interpersonal safety*; interpersonal relations with fellow workers fulfil employees' social needs; while recognition, advancement and responsibility meet their self-esteem needs. Finally, personal growth, the sense of achievement and accomplishment from a challenging job, provides for the employee's self-actualization needs.

In terms of the implications for managerial behaviour, it is clear that once the extrinsic factors are of an acceptable standard then employers should concentrate on the motivators in order to increase productivity and efficiency. The suggestion is that instead of merely *enlarging* the job so that employees are essentially doing more of the same kinds of things, the job should be *enriched*. This means expanding the job vertically so that greater responsibility, job challenge and recognition are included. Examples of enriching jobs were included in Chapter 2: a secretary asked to do repetitive work on a word processor means merely that the job is enlarged quantitatively. Alternatively, the time which is saved through the greater efficiency of the new technology could be used to involve the secretary in managerial jobs with increased responsibility.

One of the practical problems is the ability of management to redesign jobs so that all workers are provided with a challenge. This is particularly so of assembly work. However, with increased automation this particular problem may cease to exist in quite this form (see Chapter 8).

In conclusion, Herzberg's motivation–hygiene theory has been subjected to extensive criticism largely due to various methodological difficulties associated with the original study. It has received corroborative support from several independent studies (Broedling, 1975), however, and provides a more concrete way of expressing, for instance, Maslow's need hierarchy.

One of the problems with all the need theories discussed so far is that they do not deal adequately with individual differences and they have not been linked sufficiently to models of adult development (Schein, 1980). They also tend to be expressed at a high level of generality, and this fact makes them very difficult to use in practice. Furthermore, there appears to be a false logic to the argument that underpins need theory. The argument goes something like this: if management successfully identifies and caters for employee needs then this will result in their increased satisfaction and a more highly motivated workforce. The upshot of this will be an increase in productivity. However, the problem is the logic of the assumption that generally held feelings of satisfaction will necessarily lead to enhanced job performance (Fisher, 1980). The relationship is neither a necessary one nor is it simple. The question rather is, What specific aspects of job performance lead to increases in worker satisfaction and productivity? Examination of need theories alone is unlikely to reveal a complete answer. Rather, part of the answer lies in how the employee is handled, and not simply in the satisfaction of his or her wants.

HOW TO MOTIVATE OTHERS

Managers cannot rely solely on understanding *what* motivates their subordinates; they must know *how* to motivate them. There are several distinct theories which may be applied to this aspect of the problem. The issues which these theories address can be put quite simply:

1. If employees are doing what I want them to do, how can I get them to do it again? If they are not doing what I want, how do I get them to change their behaviour and methods of working?
2. How do I get my subordinates to assume organizational goals and direct their behaviour and effort towards achieving those goals?
3. What expectations do my subordinates have of me, the job and the organization? And how can I fulfil those expectations in such a way

that they *want* to put effort into the work and do the job well, while satisfying their own goals and needs through their work?

1 Reinforcement

The use of reinforcement and punishment present ways of controlling and shaping other people's behaviour. Reinforcements are simply things that have positive personal value, and as such people seek reinforcements which are perceived as rewards. Punishments are events that are painful – physically or psychologically – and therefore people try to avoid punishment. Behaviours that are apt, correct or approved of by superior, subordinates or peer group, are likely to be rewarded. Such positive reinforcement means that an individual will probably repeat those behaviours in the same or similar circumstances in the future. This is known as *generalization* and enables the establishment of consistent patterns of behaviour, such as working hard and receiving rewards.

Punishment may also be used to control people's behaviour. Some people may behave correctly in order to *avoid* punishment. This is termed *negative reinforcement*. For example, they may do something which they do not enjoy in order to avoid being reprimanded for not having done it. *Punishment* per se, as a means of controlling behaviour, differs from negative reinforcement: it is the giving of something unpleasant as a consequence of undesired behaviour. It indicates what the individual should not do. Therefore if punishment is used to promote desirable behaviour it is likely to be ineffective.

Incentives become associated with rewards. Incentives are things of value which people strive for. When people are offered rewards for working hard, they come to expect these rewards in the future. The rewards then become an incentive to work hard. Hence incentives are said to motivate behaviour because the behaviour is considered *instrumental* to attaining the rewards. However, because people have different needs or wants, the meaning and significance of the rewards to each of them varies. Therefore, people's motives, desires or wants modify the effectiveness of the incentives.

If rewards (i.e. incentives) are attached to achieving work goals, then it is the rewards not goal attainment *per se* which the employee is interested in. Therefore, if there are costs involved in goal attainment (for example, working harder and longer hours), this will provide a disincentive to goal attainment and the desired behaviour may not occur. Thus employees will not pursue organizationally defined goals if there is insufficient incentive to do so, or if the rewards for doing so are offset by considerable costs.

What are the conditions which link reward systems to performance? Lawler (1977) has identified the following:

- The need for a good measure of performance.
- The ability to identify which rewards are important to particular individuals.
- The ability to control the amount of rewards an individual receives.
- The need to enable employees to perceive the relationship between performance and rewards.
- The need to establish a climate of trust whereby employees may justifiably believe that rewards will be given for good performance.
- The need for flexibility in the administration of rewards.
- The need to be able to administer rewards frequently and so sustain extrinsic motivation and satisfaction.

The key characteristics are therefore: *importance* to individuals, that is, rewards must be valued; *flexibility* by presenting choices to individuals as to what kind of extrinsic rewards will suit them; *frequency* in order to sustain motivation at a high level; *visibility* to enable employees to perceive the connection between performance and rewards received; and *cost* of sustaining frequent or high levels of rewards as measured against organizational effectiveness.

What are the factors that influence the effectiveness of performance pay plans? Again Lawler (1977) has made several useful suggestions. Importantly, he reaffirms the 'no one best way' approach, that is, 'no one pay performance plan represents a panacea' (ibid. p. 197). In deciding upon organizational policy with respect to a reward system, a contingency approach is desirable. That is, the effectiveness of a pay plan or reward system will depend upon a number of situational conditions:

A plan that works well for one organization often is unsatisfactory for another, for a whole series of reasons. Thus, although it is tempting to say that a particular approach to pay administration is always best, it is wiser to consider the factors that determine which kind of plan is likely to be best in a given situation. (Lawler, 1977, p. 197)

The first consideration is whether or not it is appropriate to have an individual versus group- or organization-wide plan. Where jobs are independent it is possible to differentiate between individuals as regards the extent of their effort and their contribution to organizational performance. However, many jobs are interdependent; they require cooperation between individuals in workgroups or teams to coordinate activities and to ensure a steady flow of work. Hence, group-based payment schemes would be most appropriate. For similar reasons, it is often difficult to assess objectively an individual's performance, whereas it may be possible to measure quantitatively, and therefore objectively, a group's performance. This raises two issues: (a) What activities constitute performance for an individual or group? (b) Is it possible to measure performance? In some jobs there are no objective ways of measuring performance and it may be necessary to resort to a subjective form of assessment. In this circumstance, it is essential that there is a high degree of trust between superior and subordinate or workgroup. Indeed, Lawler suggests that there is a linear relationship between trust and objectivity of the performance measures used. 'Even with the most objective system, some trust is still required if the individual is still to believe in the system. [Moreover,] unless a high degree of trust exists, pay plans based on subjective criteria have little chance of success.' (Lawler, 1977, p. 199)

Is the employee able to influence the criteria upon which his or her performance is being evaluated? A profit-sharing scheme, for example, may have little to do with an employee's effort and in this sense may have the opposite effect of that intended, i.e. low motivation and low job satisfaction. Furthermore, how frequently should employees be rewarded? There are two basic schedules of reinforcement: fixed or variable. The research evidence is equivocal. Claims have been made, as a result of the research of B. F. Skinner, that variable-ratio schedules are the most effective in motivating and sustaining performance at a given level. Lawler (1977) argues against this method on the grounds that it neither increases organizational effectiveness nor enhances the quality of working life. The temptation is for an organization to adopt it as a way of spending less money. But this would be counterproductive, contributing most certainly to employee dissatisfaction. However, if it is merely used as a different means of distributing the same amount of reward, it could be that some individuals do prefer the variable ratio schedule, in which case the optimum solution would be to run two schemes based on fixed and variable schedules. In that way everyone would have the plan they want and this should increase organizational effectiveness at the same time.

There are several criticisms of operant or reinforcement theories. They include the apparent emphasis on *extrinsic* rewards, and the implied model of human nature, viz. that of a mechanical, predictable person whose cognitive apparatus plays no part in determining levels of motivation. A more detailed account of this controversy is given in Chell (1985a). A number of points are worthy of emphasis. Hamner (1979), in defence of

behaviourist programmes, argues that self-reinforcement programmes operate in such a way that the feedback (i.e. source of motivation) can be either
externally or internally mediated. Hamner *et al.* (1978) have advocated a
more integrated approach to human motivation. They have suggested a
general model which combines both reinforcement and cognitive approaches.
This line of argument has been developed by Fedor and Ferris (1983), who
have re-examined the divergence of perspectives between the cognitive
theorists and the behaviourists. They argue that from a pragmatic point of
view, there is a need to integrate a cognitive orientation with a behaviourist
perspective. For instance, there are obvious benefits for the manager of
focusing upon overt behaviour (as opposed to making inferences about the
employees' underlying psychological states). However, there is also a case
for considering how a participative approach to handling employees affects
their behaviour within an existing organizational behaviour (OB Mod)
reinforcement programme. This approach could be further integrated with
the idea of employee involvement in setting their own performance levels,
compared with the use of unilaterally assigned goals.

2 Social Learning

Recently, Davis and Luthans (1983) have distinguished an alternative approach to the OB Mod technique. This is the *social learning* approach.
Social learning theory is also a behavioural theory. However, there are
some distinct differences between the two approaches. First of all, the
dictum that 'behaviour is a function of its consequences', which underpins
behavioural or operant approaches, is condemned as being too limiting.
Rather, behaviour is in reciprocal interaction with the cognitive processes
of the person and the environment. The cyclical nature of this process is
such that, for instance, a person may conceive the consequences of their
proposed behaviour, decide among alternative courses of action, behave
accordingly and thus modify the environment in which they are operating.
This environmental modification creates a new situation which may suggest
new alternative behaviours among which the individual can again exert
choice. In essence, there are three major differences between social learning
and operant theory. They are:

- The role of vicarious processes or *modelling*.
- The effects of covert *cognitive* processes.
- The part played by *self-control* processes.

People not only learn by experiencing the consequences of their actions; they are also capable of learning by observing the actions of other people, that is, by role modelling (Bandura, 1969, 1977). This process has important managerial and supervisory training implications (Goldstein and Sorcher, 1974). In addition, cognitions or thought processes mediate between the situation and how the person will subsequently behave. People filter incoming stimuli; their past experiences affect the way they categorize later experiences. They have the ability to imagine different scenarios and act them out in their mind and to talk about and represent symbolically different behavioural possibilities away from the immediate stimulus situation. Furthermore, people, through accumulated experience, understand the consequences of various actions in different situations. These consequences provide a means of self-regulation; they act as standards of self-control; of what in effect is appropriate behaviour in specifiable situations. They enable the person to evaluate their performance against a desired performance level in the absence of any external reinforcers. This ability to exert self-control and self-direction is fundamental to organizational behaviour (Luthans and Davis, 1979).

An application of social learning theory is that of behavioural self-management (Davis and Luthans, 1983). This requires the development of an awareness of the contingencies which regulate behaviour through self-observation and self-monitoring. The idea is to establish a new behaviour, increase or maintain an existing behaviour or reduce or eliminate a behaviour. Two possible strategies may be adopted. They are (a) *stimulus management* and (b) *consequence management*. Stimulus management means exerting control over the extent to which one is subjected to particular situations, for example cutting down on paperwork to free oneself to do other things, reducing committee work or avoiding conflict-ridden situations. Consequence management, on the other hand, requires a person to evaluate their performance and administer self-rewards or punishments. This is a process of self-determination, which constitutes setting one's own goals and targets which are achievable but not easily so, and administering a small reward for goal attainment. Such rewards might constitute less take-home work or simply an extra coffee break. Important environmental variables which would facilitate such behaviours are:

● The nature of the trust relations between superior and subordinates.
● The extent to which management are prepared to delegate authority and responsibility for task accomplishment.
● The extent to which individuals and work groups are allowed to be autonomous, to set their own targets and administer their own rewards.

FAIRNESS AND JUSTICE

When rewarding or punishing an employee it is important that the manager or supervisor be seen to be fair. Does this mean that all employees and workgroups should be treated equally, and if not what is to be the basis of this process of distribution? Adams (1965) has suggested that *equity*, not equality, should be the criterion. The conceptual basis of equity theory is that of social exchanges in which people respond to each other, giving and taking, influencing and being influenced through social interaction. Such exchanges are characterized by *reciprocity* and *social comparison* processes, in which people expect to receive something in return for effort or a favour given and where they compare their good fortune or lack of it with that of others. Notions such as these can be applied directly to workplace relations. An employee who works hard might expect the employer to recognize this and pay them accordingly. It would be judged unfair or unjust if the employee were being underpaid, and a 'cushy number' if they were being paid in excess of what they could claim to be earning. No attempt is made by employees to assess *objectively* how much effort they are putting into their work, or how much they are receiving as their 'dues', in terms of pay, job satisfaction, perks, etc. What *is* important is how the exchange is *perceived* by the two parties. In addition, *inputs* and *outcomes* to the exchange process must be recognized as legitimate and relevant to the exchange relation. Whether such an exchange is perceived as fair will depend on comparisons made by the employee with a *reference group*. In asking themselves whether it is fair that they should work so hard and only receive a pittance, they must make some sort of comparison with a *relevant other*.

1 Definition of Inequity

Adams used two terms to help define inequity: person (P) is any individual for whom equity or inequity exists, and other (O) is any individual:

1. with whom P is in an exchange relationship; or,
2. with whom P compares herself when both she and O are in an exchange relation with a third party (such as an employer); or,
3. with third parties who are considered by P as being comparable (such as employers in a particular industry or in a particular geographical location); or,

4. O may be P in another job or another social role; or,
5. P and O may be representative of groups of workers, rather than individuals, for example, toolmakers, firemen, nurses, etc.

Inequity exists for P whenever he or she perceives that the *ratio* of his or her outcomes to inputs compared with the ratio of O's outcomes to inputs are unequal:

$$\frac{O_p}{I_p} > \frac{O_a}{I_a}, \text{ or } \frac{O_p}{I_p} < \frac{O_a}{I_a} .$$

Op – Outcome for person; Ip – Input of person; Oa – Outcome for other; Ia – Input of other.

In industry, a group of workers may compare the skill and experience they put into a job with the pay and prestige they obtain as rewards, in comparison with some other workgroup, usually located in the same company. The maintenance of, and disputes over, differentials involves precisely this process, and the fact that there are such disputes suggests that the relative importance of different kinds of inputs and outcomes are not viewed in quite the same way (Eiser, 1980).

Adams's simple formulation of the exchange relationship has been criticised and alternative formulations offered (Walster *et al.*, 1976; Anderson, 1976). Both of these alternatives are discussed more fully in Chell (1985a), Eiser (1980) and Mowday (1979). Suffice it to say that Walster's formulation suggests that an individual compares his or her *net* gains with those of O, whereas Anderson suggests that an individual compares their *proportionate* share of the rewards relative to the proportionate share of the inputs. Whatever is the most apt formulation, the problem for the individual suffering inequity is the same. Inequity for P will result in feelings of dissatisfaction, guilt or anger. These feelings create tension and in this way motivate P to reduce or eliminate them by creating an equitable situation. How do they – how should they – cope with an inequitable situation? There are several options open to them:

● Alter inputs, for example by restrictive practices or by improving the quality of one's work.
● Alter outcomes, for example by bargaining for more pay or better conditions, or accepting a drop in pay.
● Distort inputs and outcomes cognitively; that is, the rewards received

may be perceived in such a way that a person may *believe* that they are being treated fairly. Leave the field, in other words resign, obtain a transfer or absent oneself from work.

● Act on O for example, by attempting to alter or cognitively distort O's inputs and outcomes, or by trying to force O to leave the field.

● Change the object of comparison, an option which may be appropriate if P has changed jobs or received a promotion.

2   Modes of Inequity Reduction

Clearly, an employee has a choice among modes of inequity reduction. However, in certain circumstances, some modes of inequity reduction may not be open to P psychologically. They will therefore aim to choose the mode of inequity reduction that will cost them the least. Some guidelines are that:

1. They will attempt always to maximize their rewards.
2. They will attempt to minimize inputs that are effortful and costly.
3. They will resist real and cognitive changes in inputs that are central to their self-concept and to their self-esteem.
4. They would rather change the way they think about O's outcomes and inputs than their own in order to maintain their self-concept.
5. They will only 'leave the field' when the perceived inequity is too much to bear and there is no other way of dealing with the situation, otherwise absenteeism will occur more frequently.
6. They will resist changing the object of their comparison once it has become a fixed and stable part of their way of thinking about themselves, their pay and conditions.

Although a number of researchers have criticized Adams's theory on a number of counts (see Chell, 1985a, and Mowday, 1979), there is nevertheless considerable support for the basic propositions of the theory (Lawler, 1977); this is particularly so in the case of *underpayment*, while in the case of *overpayment* there is a tendency for employees to rationalize their excessive rewards (Mowday, 1979). It has been argued that equity theory does not necessarily stand on its own; rather its role in determining employee behaviour can be brought into sharper focus if it is incorporated into a more broadly based theory. It is therefore to a description of the latter that we now turn.

EXPECTANCY, INSTRUMENTALITY AND VALENCE: AN UMBRELLA THEORY

At work, employees are buffeted by a multitude of incoming stimuli. Many of them may be long-serving and know the 'setup'; others may not have been with the firm too long, but believe they know the 'score'. What is it they think they know?

- They know, or think they know, what the boss wants them to do – how many 'widgets' to produce by teatime, but why bother?
- They know what they need to do to produce so many widgets by teatime, or do they?
- They know what they will be paid if they produce so many widgets, but is that important to them?
- They know what each member of the group wants; why produce more?
- They do not want to change their way of working or their productivity rates; why should they?

These are some of the *real* problems that face managers and foremen when they feel productivity should be higher but are not quite sure how to deal with employees' beliefs about what is expected of them, and how to change those beliefs. To start with it is not clear that the employees' goals are necessarily in line with those of management. Any apparent satisfaction they experience seems to bear no relation to their job. They enjoy the company of their workmates, and they look forward to receiving their pay at the end of the week; that would seem to be all. How should management persuade these workers that a higher target of productivity is worth their extra effort? Is simply paying more the answer to increased productivity?

If we start from the simple premise that people will direct their effort towards the achievement of outcomes which are desirable to them, how will this enable us to develop a comprehensive theory of motivation? Outcomes which are desired are related to an individual's needs at a particular point in time. Can on the job performance lead to outcomes which fulfil an individual's needs and motivate him or her to produce more, at a faster rate and/or of better quality? As we have seen, need theories *per se* do not suggest how the manager should handle such a problem, expectancy theory does. It suggests that the manager should (a) diagnose the needs and wants of individual members of the workgroup; (b) ensure that there are outcomes from successful job performance which will fulfil those needs; (c) show how subordinates can attain those outcomes; (d) link successful job performance – high productivity, good quality, etc. – with desired outcomes; (e) show how effort will lead to the required level of performance.

It was Vroom (1964) who initially developed expectancy or valence–instrumentality–expectancy (V.I.E.) theory. The three components of this model can be explained as follows. Instrumentality is the belief that if we do one thing it will lead to some other outcome. For example, a student who works hard is likely to do well in exams. Vroom differentiates between first- and second-level outcomes. So, hard work or effort may lead to a superior performance (first-level outcome), which in turn may lead to a promotion, a reward, an increase in pay or whatever (second-level outcome). Usually people are not neutral with respect to such outcomes; they set a particular value on them. Valence (or value) can range from – 1, where an outcome is not desired, through zero, where a participant is indifferent to it, to + 1 – a positive attitude to a highly valued outcome. In Vroom's model the valences of the outcomes are summed. Expectancy is the probability (ranging from 0 to 1) that a particular action or effort will lead to a first-level outcome.

One of the important features of this model is the feedback mechanism. People assess whether or not they have achieved their desired goals through successful task performance. Clearly, net dissatisfaction will act to reduce the employee's motivation to perform the job with the same level of efficiency. More recently, Porter and Lawler have developed the Vroom model. The basic ingredients of this model are that a person's motivation is a function of:

● Effort to performance expectancies.
● Performance to outcome expectancies.
● Perceived valence of outcomes.
● Perceived instrumentality of first-level outcomes leading to second-level outcomes.

The model is summarized in Figure 3.1. Although it is expressed slightly differently, this basic model is essentially the same as that of Vroom. Where Porter and Lawler differ is in conceiving of a set of contextual factors which could mediate at various linkage points in the model and thus influence the extent of an employee's motivation. For example, effort towards successful task accomplishment can be self-defeating if the person has not the skill or ability to do the job. Indeed, where personal characteristics are important, these too will affect task accomplishment. Role perceptions, such as understanding the full extent of the part one has to play to ensure effective task performance, will detract from an employee's ability to achieve that first-level goal if the role is unclear, ambiguous or conflict-

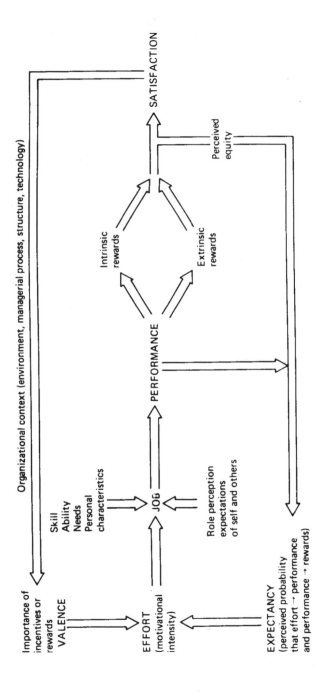

Figure 3.1 *The Porter–Lawler model of the process of motivation*

Source L. W. Porter and E. E. Lawler III (1968) *Managerial Attitudes and Performance* (Homewood, Ill.: Irwin-Dorsey).

ridden. Second-level outcomes may take the form of intrinsic and/or extrinsic rewards. Whether or not such rewards result in feelings of satisfaction for the employee will depend upon the intermediate step of weighing up whether they are equitable. Where the rewards are perceived as being fair for the job performed, the resultant feelings of satisfaction will enhance the value of the reward and influence his or her perceptions that effort does indeed result in the attainment of desired rewards. Clearly, perception of inequitable rewards will result in feelings of dissatisfaction, and depress the employee's motivation to put effort into job performance. In this circumstance, his or her attitude will be tantamount to 'why bother?' It is the job of management to ensure that the circumstances which lead to such attitudes do not occur.

What then are the implications for managers of this model? Nadler and Lawler have set out a list of seven factors:

- Work out what outcomes each employee values.
- Determine what kind of performance you desire.
- Make sure desired levels of performance are attainable.
- Link desired outcomes to performance.
- Analyse the total situation for conflicting expectancies.
- Make sure that second-level outcomes constitute a sufficient reward.
- Check the system for equity.

Such a managerial strategy assumes that various policy decisions consonant with that strategy have been made organization-wide. The policy implications for the organization of implementing such a theory have also been outlined by Nadler and Lawler (1977). They are:

- To design pay and reward schemes which reward performance and effort.
- To design jobs in a flexible way so that employees' different needs are fulfilled.
- To know when to link rewards to group performance.
- To train managers to be more sensitive to the effect of groups on individuals' expectancies; and to be able to align these expectancies with organizational goals and objectives.
- To train supervisors in motivational management, enabling them to set clear and achievable targets linked unambiguously to appropriate rewards; to enable the supervisor to administer rewards, thus giving him or her the power to create positive motivation through positive reinforcement in the workgroup.

- To regularly monitor motivation throughout the organization.
- To individualize organizations, ensuring that there is sufficient flex- ibility built into the system to ensure choice for employees in areas such as reward systems, fringe benefits, job assignments, etc.

It should now be clear that expectancy theory embraces all the preceding models of motivation and also presents management and organization with a strategy for action. Is the theory valid? There have been a number of critical reviews of empirical research carried out to try and validate the theory (see Chell, 1985a, for a brief account of these). The problems lie in being able to operationalize the concepts in such a way that appropriate variables, such as 'effort', 'job performance', 'satisfaction' and 'reward', can be measured in a particular organizational context. Apart from this academic question, there is also the pragmatic question of whether this model does constitute a useful management tool which enables managers to think clearly about job performance, reinforcement contingencies, etc., and enables them to effectively raise productivity and their employees' job satisfaction. This, after all, is the real 'acid test' of such a theory.

A MOTIVATING MANAGERIAL STYLE

The implications of adopting an all embracing theory of motivation such as expectancy theory suggests that management should adopt a style of handling the workforce which will optimise its potential benefits. McGregor (1960) described two management styles which were underpinned by contrasting assumptions about human nature. These he termed Theory X and Theory Y. These assumptions are listed in Table 3.2.

Theory X assumes that most people prefer to be directed and controlled, do not want to assume any responsibility and want safety and security above all else. In addition, they are motivated by money, fringe benefits and the threat of punishment. Managers holding such assumptions structure, control and closely supervise their employees, believing them to be largely ir- responsible, unreliable and immature people. One problem with this par- ticular style of management is that it tends to be self-fulfilling, and it only satisfies the most basic, lower-order needs. It is therefore questionable as to whether it is a correct view of human nature.

Theory Y assumptions tend to be more compatible with an expectancy theory approach to motivation. They assume that people are not by nature lazy and unreliable and that people can be self-directed and creative if properly motivated. People have considerable *potential*, if only man-

TABLE 3.2 *The assumptions underpinning Theory X and Theory Y*

Theory X

1. The average human being has an inherent dislike of work and will avoid it if he or she can
2. Because of this human characteristic of dislike of work, most people will be coerced, controlled, directed, threatened with punishment to get them to put forth adequate effort toward the achievement of organizational objectives
3. The average human being prefers to be directed, wishes to avoid responsibility, has relatively little ambition, wants security above all

Theory Y

1. The expenditure of physical and mental effort in work is as natural as play or rest
2. External control and the threat of punishment are not the only means for bringing about effort toward organizational objectives. Man will exercise self-direction and self-control in the service of objectives to which he is committed
3. Commitment to objectives is a function of the rewards associated with their achievement
4. The average human being learns, under proper conditions, not only to accept but to seek responsibility
5. The capacity to exercise a relatively high degree of imagination, ingenuity, and creativity in the solution of organizational problems is widely, not narrowly, distributed in the population
6. Under the conditions of modern industrial life, the intellectual potentialities of the average human being are only partially utilized

SOURCE   D. McGregor (1960) *The Human Side of Enterprise* (New York: McGraw-Hill).

agement would recognize this and adopt a strategy which would unleash it.

Theory X and Theory Y are views or implicit attitudes towards employees. However, there may be a difference, even an inconsistency, between attitude and behaviour. Argyris (1971) has suggested that there are sets of behaviours which tend to be more closely associated with Theory X or Theory Y assumptions. These he terms behaviour patterns A and B. Behaviour pattern A, which he suggests is more closely associated with Theory X, consists of individuals who do not own up to their feelings, are not open, are unadventurous, and do not help others engage in these behaviours. They tend to be closely supervised and their activities are highly structured. Behaviour pattern B contrasts markedly with that of A. These people are open, supportive and facilitating; they show concern for each other and for each other's individuality; and the group atmosphere is characterized by a high degree of trust.

XA and YB are usually associated with each other, but not necessarily so. There may be circumstances when it is expedient for managers to adopt the opposite behaviour, as when a manager wants to train an immature workgroup so that eventually it may become autonomous, responsible, hardworking and trusting. What is needed is a diagnosis of the organizational environment, knowing when it is appropriate to adopt a particular style, not to become facilitative and supportive overnight when the workgroup is used to – and expects – XA-type behaviour.

SUMMARY

———— The major challenge for management is in understanding *what* motivates and *how* to motivate subordinates.

———— Several theories deal with the issue of *what* motivates people; they are termed *need* theories. It is management's job to identify employees' needs; to attempt to provide working conditions and design tasks in such a way that they can satisfy these needs. The effect is purported to be a motivating environment in which employees feel satisfied on the job and obtain the rewards they want, while the organization should benefit from increased productivity and the smoother running of its activities. The problem is that there is no necessary connection between employee satisfaction and increased productivity. It is therefore important to consider *how* to motivate employees, not merely to give them what they want.

Positive reinforcement in the form of rewards is one way of giving incentives to employees to work hard or be more productive. Pay is an important source of reinforcement, but there are several factors which management should consider before introducing a pay plan or reward system. These include linking the rewards to a good measure of performance, being able to identify rewards that are valued and controlling the administration of rewards in such a way as to sustain motivation and satisfaction. Developments in thinking in this area suggest a need to integrate reinforcement and cognitive theories. Such a move would provide the opportunity of considering how to involve workers in setting their own performance levels and using participative leadership styles.

An alternative approach to reinforcement theory is that of social learning theory. Although this too is a behavioural theory, it differs from reinforcement theory in three ways: it suggests that new behaviours and attitudes can be learnt through *modelling*; it stresses the importance of *covert cognitive processes* and of processes of *self-control*.

When rewarding an employee it is important that the manager or supervisor be seen to be fair. The basis of distribution of such rewards is that of equity. An employee will consider a situation inequitable when he or she compares the ratio of his or her inputs and outcomes to that of some comparison other or standard. Under conditions of inequity, the employee will attempt to change aspects of this relation in order to restore the situation. This is particularly so in the case of underpayment, but in the case of overpayment a tendency to justify or rationalize high rewards is common.

Expectancy theory tends to embrace need, reinforcement and equity theories. It assumes that people will direct their efforts towards the achievement of outcomes which are desirable to them. It attempts to demonstrate the links between effort, performance and rewards contingent upon that performance, and shows how the manager should behave in order to establish those links in the minds of his or her employees.

It is important for managers to adopt an appropriate, motivating managerial style. Two styles are examined: Theory X and Theory Y. It is wrong to think of one style as being the 'best way to manage'. Each style will depend for its success not simply on its compatibility with an expectancy model of motivation but also on the nature of the workgroup, their behaviour, their maturity, their acceptance of management and the style of management.

In the ensuing chapters, the management of workgroups and teams will be examined in more detail, and some of the ideas on the nature of the group and the leadership style will be developed more fully.

4 Working with Groups

The ability to work effectively with groups of people is a fundamental and necessary skill of management. Groups pervade organizational life, and fulfil many different functions at both a formal and informal level. But how can managers galvanize groups of people into action? How can they influence groups to accept organizational goals as their own and to be productive and perform at an acceptable standard? It is because answers to questions such as these are so fundamental to the process of management that developing an understanding of what groups are, and how they may be influenced and directed, is critical to effective, satisfying and productive group functioning. In this chapter we attempt to examine group structure and process as they affect group discussion, group problem-solving and group decision-making. In the two chapters that follow we concentrate on how to build effective teams and the process of team leadership.

DEFINITION AND PURPOSE OF GROUPS

From a psychological point of view, a group is not simply a collection of individuals. A manager who spots a crowd of workers outside the factory gate may or may not be perceiving a group. The crowd may have arrived early and be waiting for the gates to be opened. So while they may have a common *purpose*, they may work in different parts of the factory and thus 'not knowing each other' they do not *interact* or *perceive* themselves to be a group, nor are they in any sense *interdependent*. Different circumstances, such as a picket on the gate, would transform the crowd to a group situation. The picket fulfils all the criteria of what constitutes a *psychological* group.

TYPES OF GROUP

How groups are classified is usually a function of the nature of their task or purpose, their structure and the relative degree of permanence of the group. Groups may be brought together to fulfil a particular task; to the extent to which this is true, they may be termed *formal* groups. In the coffee break, at lunch or dinner time, people chat and relax, play cards or sports to pass the time, and in effect form *social* groups. People on the same shift and in the same workgroup will tend also to fulfil their social needs together; *proximity* therefore is important in the formation of social groups at work. The more the workgroup has to interact in order to complete a task, the more the interdependence among group members. Here homogeneity of common values, beliefs and goals is basic to the smooth functioning of the group. The greater the homogeneity, the greater the sharing and acceptance of similar ideas and the more cohesive the group. Such a group must agree how best to achieve group goals, how to go about completing the task effectively and be able to fulfil the needs of its members. Effective, interacting groups are characterized by a high degree of cooperation among their members.

In *coacting* groups, these conditions do not apply to the same extent. A coacting group is one in which members may carry out different or similar tasks independently of each other. The requirement is for effective co-ordination of member activities at a later stage, and to this extent some cooperation is required. Jobs in the service sector, such as insurance and banking, provide numerous examples of coacting workgroups.

Counteracting groups, on the other hand, are groups with opposing aims which may be 'locked into' a power struggle in their endeavours to compete for scarce resources. The groups are usually internally cohesive and homogeneous with respect to their own group's aims and values, and need to be agreed on the best method for achieving their purposes. The problem is largely that of handling the relationship between such groups.

Not all groups are permanent; they may have been formed to do a particular job. Once the task has been completed, the group may be disbanded. Project groups, special taskforces and working parties fall into this category.

GROUP FUNCTIONS

Within the organization, the *formal* function of the group is to fulfil organizational goals. This might mean the completion of routine tasks efficiently and speedily. The issues here might be: Who sets the targets – does the group have any say about what tasks it should complete? And how should the job be done and at what pace should they work? The problem for management is how to ensure commitment to such organizationally defined goals. Where the job is non-routine the issue is rather different. Lack of clarity in instructions and expectations of group members of what needs to be done in order to accomplish the job to the required standard causes anxiety and stress. A different approach by management in order to reduce anxiety and alleviate potentially stressful situations is clearly needed.

Groups have several advantages over individuals. These are:

● The ability to work on complex, interdependent tasks.
● The means of generating new ideas and creative solutions to complex problems.
● Superiority for purposes of liaison and coordination.
● To facilitate the implementation of complex decisions.
● Greater suitability as vehicles for change.
● To enable the socialization and training of new members.

In addition to these *formal* functions, groups also fulfil various social needs. For example:

● They fulfil affiliation needs for friendship, love and support.
● They define the individual's sense of identity and maintain their self-esteem.
● They enable individuals to establish and test social reality through discussion, questioning and talking about events and coming to share perspectives about how those events should be defined.
● They reduce feelings of insecurity, anxiety and a sense of powerlessness by reducing uncertainty and providing each other with social support.
● They enable members to solve problems and accomplish tasks through the group.
● They are a means of entertainment, alleviating boredom and fatigue, boosting morale and personal satisfaction.
● They provide a means by which members can counter managerial power.

This functional analysis suggests that there are two primary objectives of the organizational group. They are effective task completion and member satisfaction. How might the system within which the group operates affect these two important outcomes? Research by Burns and Stalker (1961) suggested that organizational structure which they typified as being either 'mechanistic' or 'organic' was related to innovativeness. Meadows (1980a) has taken these ideas and applied them to the small group. Innovativeness is the ability to generate and implement new ideas and to cope with change whether that be in new technology, work practices or developing new products. How does group structure enhance or detract from this ability to innovate? Table 4.1 outlines the characteristics of mechanistic and organic systems.

Meadows found that not only was innovative activity associated with organicness in small group structure and operation, but so too was member satisfaction (Meadows, 1980b). This research highlights the need for greater flexibility in management practice to handle workgroups sensitively, particularly in problem solving situations. However, there are further implications of the 'organic' workgroup. They are:

1. To enable 'logical' or natural groups to emerge; this means exercising control over the technology, the physical environment, location factors and bureaucracy.
2. Being *flexible*, knowing when it is appropriate to use groups.
3. Being able to compose an effective group in terms of the representation and balance of a pool of appropriate skills, knowledge and abilities, comprising people who can work well together, who are agreed on the goals to be achieved, have similar basic values and beliefs and are able to communicate effectively together.
4. The status of various members must not get in the way of frank and open communication and exchange of information.

The problem, however, is not simply one of structure but also one of how the group goes about trying to fulfil its aims. There are two key aspects to this process issue: they concern the internal dynamics of the group and the way the group is handled and led. Clearly the two are not independent of each other. In this chapter it is intended to concentrate upon internal dynamics, while in subsequent chapters consideration will be given to leadership style.

GROUP DYNAMICS

The underlying normative structure of the group guides member behaviour. 'Norms are rules of conduct established by members of the group to maintain behavioural consistency' (Shaw, 1981, p. 279). Groups develop accepted standards of behaviour and take every opportunity to reinforce those standards. Some norms may be counterproductive from the organization's perspective, for example restrictive practices, whereas other norms such as the desire to do a job well may help the organization maintain quality of output. There are several distinct characteristics of norms (Hackman, 1976; Shaw, 1981):

● Norms are social products and tend to mediate between attitudes and behaviour (Fishbein and Ajzen, 1975).

TABLE 4.1 *The characteristics of mechanistic and organic systems*

Mechanistic systems	Organic systems
1. Tasks are broken down into functionally specialized jobs	Individuals contribute their special knowledge and experience to the common task
2. Separate jobs are performed by functionaries as ends in themselves	Individual tasks arise from the problem situation
3. Individual tasks are defined and coordinated by a formal hierarchy of superiors	Individual tasks are adjusted and continually redefined through interaction with others
4. Rights, obligations and methods for each job are precisely defined	Rights, obligations and methods are not precisely prescribed; problems may not be posted upwards, downwards, or sideways as someone else's responsibility
5. Responsibility is determined by rights, obligations and methods	Commitment to the task and the organization goes beyond any technical definition
6. There is a hierarchical structure of control, authority and communication	There is a network structure of control, authority and communication

Mechanistic systems	*Organic systems*
7. Knowledge about, and control of, the task are located towards the top of the hierarchy	Knowledge about, and control of, the task may be located anywhere in the network
8. Communication is vertical rather than lateral	Communication is lateral, rather than vertical; participation and consultation rather than command
9. Operations and behaviour are governed by instructions and decisions from superiors	Leadership is facilitative and advisory; members are involved; behaviour is not governed by instruction or dictat
10. Loyalty and obedience are mandatory	Commitment to the 'technological ethos' is more highly valued than loyalty and obedience
11. Greater importance and prestige are attached to 'local' rather than 'cosmopolitan' knowledge, experience and skill	Importance and prestige are attached to affiliation and expertise related to the industry, skill or profession rather than to the organization

SOURCE T. Burns and G. M. Stalker (1961) *The Management of Innovation* (London: Tavistock).

- They cannot be imposed from outside the group; they must be accepted by a majority of group members, although external social norms do influence group decision-making (see later section).
- They are not developed about every conceivable situation; they are formed with respect to things of significance to the group.
- They usually apply to all members of the group, though not necessarily so; this may depend on the role particular group members play.
- They vary according to the degree of acceptance given them by the group.
- They differ with respect to the amount of deviation that members will tolerate.
- In one sense, they simplify the group influence process and may facilitate the process of leadership and control.
- They apply to group *behaviour*, not members' thoughts and feelings.
- They tend to develop and change slowly.
- Some members have the latitude to deviate from group norms, but usually this privilege is reserved for high-level or high-status members – in other words, legitimacy is an important criterion of acceptance of normative behaviour.

There are four general classes of factor which influence conformity to group norms; these are:

1. *Personal*, including individual needs and the personality characteristics of group members.
2. *Interpersonal*, arising from the composition of the group, the homogeneity of its membership in terms of shared values, ideology, beliefs and goals, and the extent to which the group members feel secure.
3. *Social* factors such as the need to produce group outcomes and achieve group goals, the need to maintain group credibility, the need to fulfil members' expectations and desires to be a member of the group, and the extent to which the group is open or closed.
4. *Situational* factors, such as the type of problem facing the group; structural factors such as group size, differences in role and status and the mechanistic versus organicness of group structure.

Norms create expectations in the minds of members as to what behaviour is required in various circumstances. These have been termed *horizontal* or interpersonal norms (Paicheler, 1976). Such norms may establish standards as in the case of maintaining a particular level or quality of output. This was clearly demonstrated in the case of the Bank Wiring Room of the Hawthorne

Works, where the group had agreed a particular level of output, and deviations from this were discouraged by 'binging' (Mayo, 1949). Members who produced above the agreed level were termed 'ratebusters', while members who produced below the requirement were termed 'chisellers'. Another example of the maintenance of standards by the group is the quality control circle. Such standards are significant when (a) members value the conditions the standard has been established to support; and (b) members believe that adherence to the standard will help maintain this condition (Zander, 1982). In this sense, it is important that group members understand and accept the reasons behind the standard so that there is not simply blind adherence to it and the reasons why the group will benefit from it. In order to achieve this end, it is essential to create commitment among group members. Thus an attempt is made to increase cohesiveness in the group, so mustering support for the standard. This is done by choosing persons who fit well together, explaining what people might get out of belonging to the group, demonstrating to new recruits that the group will meet their needs, and showing that they will derive more satisfaction from this group than from others (Zander, 1982). Another important way of achieving commitment is by involving members in discussion, so enabling them to shape group norms and standards; that is, group norms or standards are not fixed or static as Zander's analysis implies. Finally conformity to standards is encouraged by offering rewards or giving punishments.

A potential problem is that a lack of competing demands on the individual may mean further immersion in the one group. Some groups may even attempt to eliminate individualism so that members are encouraged to lose interest in their own needs and put group needs first. Being a member of more than one group will tend to obviate this tendency, although it can present other problems, for example that of conflicting interests.

Pressure on members to conform can cause other sorts of problems where (a) there is incompatibility between a member's personal goals and those of the group or organization; (b) there is no sense of pride from being a member of the group; (c) there is a desire to attain one's own ends rather than those of the group; (d) the member is in a peripheral position in the group and is not recognized as a fully fledged member; (e) the price of conformity is perceived as being too high, for example, if it will damage her career, is against the law, will harm her health, etc.; (f) an individual may refuse to conform because colleagues' efforts to influence her are not compelling, or she may feel that the group's decision in this instance is not sound. A deviant can, in some circumstances avoid punishment: (a) if she is an influential group member; (b) by withdrawing temporarily from the group or not taking her share of the load; (c) by being a member of a very large group in which her deviancy goes undetected; (d) by deviating on non-critical matters; and (e) where the group supports rather than shuns deviants.

It is clearly easier for members to conform to group norms and standards, but is it possible to oppose them without fear of punishment, personal strain, feelings of guilt or loss of self-esteem? The following recommendations for action are based in part on Zander (1982):

● Know your own mind; what beliefs are important to you, what goals you want to achieve and where you think the group should be heading.
● Decide what effect the inducements and coercions of colleagues have upon you. Consider whether it is possible to accept or ignore their appeal.
● Consider whether it is possible to respond to some of the urgings of colleagues without losing sight of one's own goal, or giving the appearance that one has capitulated.
● Ask yourself whether you have the courage of your convictions. If so, do not give up personal preferences merely to prevent disharmony in the group.
● Recognize when you have lost interest in a group because this reduces the threat of being rejected.
● Hold out against social pressures by concealing from others what you think.
● Recognize like-minded members and join forces with them; this will not only give you psychological support in the realization that you are not the only person to hold those views, but also enable you to develop plans to jointly oppose the group if necessary.

It may need a strong-minded individual to resist the pressure to conform. Such undue pressure towards uniformity of view can have serious consequences for effective group problem-solving. This desire for unanimity can, for example, lead to premature decisions, that is, decisions taken before enough information has come to light to allow an optimal or even an adequate decision to be reached. Group members who disagree with the majority view may withold their opinions because they do not wish to be different or because they believe that everyone else in the group agrees with the majority (Schanck, 1932). Furthermore, the pressures towards uniformity may prevent members of the group from seeking additional information or consulting outside experts (Janis, 1972). This points to one of the more serious consequences of pressure towards conformity – that of *group think*.

1 Group Think

Group think refers to 'a mode of thinking that persons engage in when *concurrence-seeking* becomes so dominant in a cohesive ingroup that it tends to override realistic appraisal of alternative courses of action' (Janis, 1971). Group think-type conformity tends to increase as group cohesiveness increases. 'Group think involves nondeliberate suppression of critical thoughts as a result of the internalization of the group's norms'. In sum:

> The more amiability and *esprit de corps* there [are] among group members of a policy-making ingroup, the greater the danger that independent critical thinking will be replaced by group think, which is likely to result in irrational and dehumanizing actions directed against outgroups. (Janis, 1971)

There are eight main symptoms of group think:

- Members share an illusion of *invulnerability*; this leads to overoptimism and a willingness to take extraordinary risks.
- Victims of group think collectively construct *rationalizations* in order to discount warnings and other forms of negative feedback, which if taken seriously might lead group members to question the assumptions underlying past decisions.
- Victims of group think believe unquestioningly in the inherent *morality* of their ingroup; this belief inclines the members to ignore the ethical or moral consequences of their decisions.
- Victims of group think hold *stereotyped* views of the leaders of enemy or opposing groups; the stereotype is so powerful that members come to believe that genuine attempts at negotiation with the outgroup are unwarranted.
- Victims of group think apply direct *pressure* to any member who even momentarily expresses doubts about any of the group's shared illusions or who questions the validity of the arguments supporting a policy alternative favoured by the majority.
- There is a tendency towards *self-censorship*, when victims of group think avoid deviating from what appears to be group consensus; they keep silent about their misgivings and even minimize to themselves the importance of their doubts.
- Victims of group think share an *illusion of unanimity* within the group concerning almost all judgements expressed by members who speak in favour of the majority view; silence is interpreted as concordance.

● Victims of group think sometimes appoint themselves as *mindguards* to protect the leader and fellow members from adverse information that might break the complacency shared about the effectiveness and morality of past decisions.

The consequences of group think are poor decision-making and inadequate solutions to problems being dealt with. The reasons for this are as follows:

1. The group limits its discussion to a few courses of action.
2. The group fails to re-examine the course of action initially preferred by the majority after they learn of risks and drawbacks they had not considered initially.
3. The group fails to spend time evaluating 'rejected' courses of action in terms of non-obvious gains or ways of reducing prohibitive costs suggested by these alternatives.
4. No attempt is made to obtain information from experts to aid in this process of evaluation of alternatives.
5. There is selectivity of attention: members show positive interest in facts and opinions that support their preferred policy; they ignore facts and opinions that do not.
6. The group fails to work out contingency plans for dealing with setbacks that might jeopardize the overall success of the course of action they have chosen.

It is difficult to tease out quite what the motives are for members to be so unquestioning and so ready to acquiesce to the dominantly held view. Socially, people do have a strong need to conform, as has been amply demonstrated (Asch, 1956). Indeed, the normative social influence in such cases appears to be underpinned by a collectively bolstered belief in the group's own power and importance. It is in large part, I would suggest, a politically motivated action. This does not mean that the group must be composed of politicians – although Janis's original groups were – because any group in an organization which is trying to manoeuvre itself into a favourable position *vis-à-vis* other groups may be said to be politically motivated. There seem to be two conditions which facilitate such strong conformity: (a) where the group is jockeying for position and calls on its members to 'toe the line'; and (b) where the group is already in a powerful position, and possibly has a charismatic leader who reaps the dues of having put the group in that position by demanding further allegiance.

If the consequences of group think are undesirable, are they nevertheless inevitable, or are there steps which can be taken to counter them? Janis suggests the following measures:

- The leader should encourage critical evaluation of ideas, including his or her own.
- High-status members of the group should initially adopt an impartial stance in order to encourage an open enquiry.
- The organization should set up external policy-planning groups to look into the same questions under different leadership, in order to prevent the insulation of an ingroup.
- The leader should encourage members to discuss the group's deliberations (where confidentiality is not a problem) and report their reactions to the group.
- Outside experts should be invited to group meetings and encouraged to challenge group views.
- The group should spend time considering the opposition's strategy, taking on board warning signals from these rivals and considering all possible alternative scenarios.
- When considering the feasibility and effectiveness of various policy decisions the group should divide into subgroups and consider the issues separately under different chairpersons, come back together again and hammer out the differences.
- After a preliminary decision has been reached, a further meeting should be held in order to enable members to express any lingering doubts they might have.

Janis was concentrating his attention upon top policy-making groups, but what about lower-level decision-making groups in organizations? How can managers carry their workgroups along with them and ensure that a sound decision has been reached? Let us go back to thinking about Meadows's research. The study was carried out in two research and development departments, where the primary objective was technical innovation. Meadows found that an organic system of operating was far more conducive to innovative activity than a mechanistic mode of working. But what of the individual actors in this type of situation; how might they behave? Research by Norman Maier (1970) demonstrated how managers could elicit the best from their workgroup to ensure effective problem-solving behaviour. To innovate, to discover that the company needs to move in new directions in order to survive or to decide how best to design work schedules for greater efficiency and productivity are just some examples of the sorts of problems which face management in competitive industries. Sometimes managers are unable to solve such problems on their own, because (a) they have insufficient information to do so or (b) they need to carry the group along with them. In such circumstances the manager needs to adopt a participative management style. In this way they can ensure substantial control over subordinates and increase the probability of arriving at an optimal solution to the problem at hand. The specific behaviours that the leader should engage in are these:

- Share the problem with group members, presenting whatever information is at the leader's disposal at the time.
- Ask for members' views, concentrating particularly on reticent members.
- Prevent dominant personalities from having a disproportionate influence.
- Try to ensure cross-communication within the group.
- Minimize blame-oriented statements.
- Redirect unfocused discussion back to the problem at hand.
- Encourage the generation of alternative solutions.
- Delay the evaluation of alternatives until all have been presented.
- Guide the process of screening alternatives and selecting the optimal solution.

This 'recipe' for effective management behaviour in group problem-solving situations is clearly compatible with Meadows's notion of 'organicity'. In addition, managers who adopt this approach will avoid 'groupthink' situations arising. Furthermore, managers are not assumed to be born with skills such as these; they can acquire them through training. In sum, decision effectiveness for Maier is a function of (a) the degree to which the solution meets the objective economic and physical requirements of the problem – the *quality criterion* – and (b) how far the decision is acceptable to subordinates – the *acceptance criterion*. Through the participative process, existing knowledge and expertise of subordinates can be tapped, so improving the quality of the decisions. Furthermore, participation may act as a palliative, either by reducing pockets of resistance to new ideas or by readily ensuring acceptance for the implementation of the decision. Indeed, a further endorsement of the Maier-type approach is apparent in recent research (Tsosvold, 1991) which argues strongly for a team management approach, suggesting that this, in most circumstances will enable an organization to gain a competitive edge.

Maier's 'recipe' looks useful *if* the manager or group leader already knows what the problem is, and the group can recognize and accept her definition of the problem. This is not always the case (Sims, 1979). In such instances, the initial phases of the problem solving process may be identified as these:

- Problem recognition; do people in the group recognize that there is a problem that needs to be dealt with?
- Problem definition; do people understand what the problem is and what are its causes?
- Problem formulation; do people identify the same elements in the situation as being relevant to the problem, as this will affect its formulation?
- Context of the problem situation; what elements of the situation can be manipulated to solve the problem to good effect without creating unacceptable ethical implications or side-effects?

It can take a great deal of time, discussion, argument and political manoeuvring before consensus is reached on what constitutes *the problem*. Drummond (1991a), for example, offers some graphic illustrations of the problems which may arise with problem recognition, definition and understanding. The subsequent stages in this process are then:

- The search for action alternatives to solve the problem.
- The evaluation of action alternatives.
- The implementation of the decision.

Perhaps one should say 'implementation of *a* decision'. In most discussion situations there is generally more than one course of action open to the group (apart from the 'do nothing' option). Problem-solving situations may depend on the gathering of facts and information. However, the extent to which scanning the environment for information occurs in practice is also questionable, particularly in a small firms context where available resources for such an activity are in short supply. Nor do all decision situations have a simple fact gathering basis to them; there are still choices to be made and the actual decision is based on expert *judgement* as to what is the right thing to do in the circumstances. Leading a company, and making investment decisions of various sorts, are typical examples of decision activities which require this kind of expert judgement. But is a group of people more likely to make a better decision than an individual on his or her own? Conventional wisdom has led us to believe that the group would tend to make the better decision because of the pooling of a larger number of ideas and a better mix of abilities and skills among the membership. Maier (1970), as we have seen, devoted a great deal of research effort developing training techniques to enable leaders to elicit optimum decisions from their workgroups. Moreover, it was thought that any tendencies towards extreme judgements by individuals would be countered in group situations, where extreme judgements would, in effect, cancel each other out. It seemed therefore counterintuitive when a piece of research was carried out which threw considerable doubt on such conventional wisdom. This research was carried out by James Stoner (1961) and the phenomenon he demonstrated became known as 'risky shift'.

2   Risky Shift

The research paradigm was one where the average decision made by individuals prior to group discusssion was compared with the average group decision after discussion. In each case, they were asked to consider a range of possible outcomes to a series of hypothetical situations. The research instrument used is known as the 'choice dilemma questionnaire' (CDQ). The CDQ consists of twelve hypothetical 'real-life' situations in which a fictitious person must choose between a risky or conservative course of action. For example, an electrical engineer may be faced with a choice between (a) remaining in his present job, with a modest salary but very low promotion prospects, and (b) joining a new firm which has a highly uncertain future but which offers the possibility of sharing in the ownership of the firm. The respondent's task is to indicate what the odds for success would have to be before he or she would advise the fictitious person to take the risky alternative. In order that the decision can be quantified, there are five different probabilities of success of the risky venture: 1 in 10, 3 in 10, 5 in 10, 7 in 10 and 9 in 10. In addition, the respondent has also the option of taking no chances. Once people have individually made their choices about what odds they would minimally hope for before recommending the risky course of action, the completed CDQs are collected up, fresh ones are administered and the individuals form a group. In the group situation, they are instructed to arrive at a decision through consensus about what should be done in each case. The difference in the degree of risk-taking between the average position of the group members before discussion and the decision eventually reached defines the magnitude of the risky shift.

The not inconsiderable research carried out subsequently, to demonstrate the prevalence of 'risky shift', has been summarized elsewhere (see for example, Cartwright, 1971; Chell, 1985a; Dion *et al.*, 1970; Fraser and Foster, 1984; Vinokur, 1971). In essence, several explanations were put forward. They included the *diffusion of responsibility explanation* – a process said to make risk-taking more facile for group members; the *persuasion explanation*, which suggested various ways in which group members would be more easily persuaded by risky options; the *familiarization explanation*, which held that increased familiarity with the arguments underpinning the risky alternative led to an increased willingness by group members to commit themselves to that option; and, finally, the *cultural value explanation*. The latter explanation suggested that risk was valued in the American culture. Group members who would want to be seen adopting the more socially desirable option would therefore opt for what they thought was a risky preference. When in a group situation they realized their option was not more risky than the average, they would shift their preference in the 'risky' direction. For some time the latter explanation seemed to be convincing; however, it lost favour when it was realized that (a) for any issue discussed there had to be assumed an associated universally held value; (b) for every group decision that was taken it had to be assumed that risk was an overriding criterion of decision acceptance; (c) social comparison was the key mechanism explaining shift; and (d) groups tended towards making extreme judgements in choice situations where relative riskiness of the decision outcome was not a factor.

The latter finding was first demonstrated by Moscovici and Zavalloni (1969) and was termed *group polarization*. Group polarization describes the situation where the average post-group response tends to be more extreme in the same direction as the average of the pre-group responses (Myers and Lamm, 1976). Polarization thus refers to an increase in the extremity of the *average* response of the group; it does not, as is the usual connotation of the term, refer to a *split* within a group of people. Polarization also refers to shifts towards the already favoured pole, whereas *extremization* refers to movement away from neutrality regardless of direction. Two other interesting observations may be made about group polarization:

(1) It need not apply to individuals; a three-person group with scores of + 3, + 1 and − 1 on a + 3 to − 3 attitude scale might all put down + 1 after discussion (Fraser *et al.*, 1971), but at the group level a slight move to extremity has occurred in the shift from a mean of 0.67 to + 1. None of the individuals is more extreme than prior to the discussion, in actual fact members have typically converged (Myers and Lamm, 1976).

(2) Where is the *psychological* mid-point of an attitude scale? Evidence suggests that it is not the mathematical mid-point.

The generality of the group polarization phenomenon over a wide range of situations was demonstrated. The problem then was that of attempting to find an explanation which took into account all the observed facts. There were three candidates proposed: (a) the group decision rule explanation, (b) the interpersonal comparision explanation and (c) the informational influence explanation.

The group decision rule explanation suggested that the observed shift was in fact a statistical artefact, and no actual psychological change needed to be postulated. This explanation predicts a shift towards the dominant pole when the majority favours that direction and when there is skewness in the distribution of initial choices. This means that the deviant minority of individuals in the tail of the skewed distribution shift in accordance with the majority view. There is considerable plausibility about this explanation, but available data tends to contradict it (Myers and Lamm, 1976). The real crux of the matter is that

> Even if statistical prediction by a model should prove to be quite accurate, this does not necessarily constitute a psychological explanation of the dynamics of actually producing change in individual subjects. (Myers and Lamm, 1976, p. 613)

The second type of explanation – that of interpersonal comparisons – is a form of *normative social influence*. Normative social influence has been defined as 'influence to conform to the positive expectations of another' (Deutsch and Gerard, 1955; see also, Chell, 1985a; Eiser, 1980; Fraser, 1978). The essence of this explanation is that mere exposure to the preferences of others is a necessary and sufficient condition for shift. It means that group members formulate three normative concepts on a decision item: (a) that of the group norm; (b) their own position; and (c) their ideal position. Regarding their own position, they select one which is in line with that of the group norm, but is thought by them to be slightly more extreme than the group norm and is also socially desirable because it conforms with supposed peer preferences. This tendency for group members to conform to the normative expectations of self and others does appear to be an important group dynamic (Asch, 1951, 1956; Chell, 1985a; Eiser, 1980). However, whether it is both a necessary and a sufficient condition for group polarization effects to occur is a moot point. It suggests that the source of the message and not the content is important. In the examples of 'group think' discussed previously there does appear to be substantial evidence of normative social influence being both necessary and sufficient for group polarization to occur (Janis, 1971).

The third explanation of group polarization is that of informational influence as a result of cognitive learning arising from exposure to arguments during discussion. Informational social influence has been defined as 'influence to accept information obtained from another as evidence about reality' (Deutsch and Gerard, 1955). The idea is that discussion generates arguments predominantly favouring the initially preferred alternative, and for any given group member, some of these arguments are likely to be persuasive. Learning occurs in the already favoured direction and responses are modified accordingly.

Several mathematical models have been formulated of this mechanism of informational influence. It is assumed that the amount of group shift will be determined by three factors: direction, persuasiveness and originality of each argument (Myers and Lamm, 1976). Hence, in discussion, the potency of an argument will be zero, either if the rated persuasiveness is zero (i.e. the argument is trivial or irrelevant) or if all group members have considered the argument already prior to discussion. As regards direction, although it is claimed to be 'an excellent predictor of shift' (Myers and Lamm, 1976), care must be taken in evaluating its effectiveness when considering depolarization effects.

Despite the apparent success of informational influence theory, cognitive learning in producing group polarization is not a complete explanation in itself; the importance of the *social* dynamics of the process have become quite apparent. This is because active discussion generates more change than the passive receipt of information. But why is this additional process necessary? Surely if the participants merely received the arguments and new information via a tape recording, then their revised opinion would still generate the same degree of shift? Apparently not. Myers and Lamm (1976) point out that what in effect is happening in the group is a process of attitude change. Merely attending to and comprehending arguments is insufficient to cause an attitude change, as Kurt Lewin's classic work on the differential effects of discussion group and lecture format amply demonstrated (Lewin, 1947). In other words, group members listen to the arguments, take them in, and actively reformulate the information into terms that they themselves can understand and express. Once the arguments are part of their own cognitive framework they rehearse them, so committing themselves publicly to a particular position. This increased sense of involvement also appears to be typical of group polarization.

The social motivation for conforming to the preferred position of the majority is that of presenting oneself in the most socially desirable light, of preserving, if not establishing, an image of self which is acceptable to the majority of group members. The deviant individual who holds out and will not move on an issue, is put under a great deal of informational and normative social influence so to do (Fraser, 1978; Chell, 1985a).

Both the interpersonal comparisons and the informational influence explanations have been criticized by Fraser and Foster (1984). The problem as they see it is that such explanations tend to be predominantly individualistic, whereas what is required is an explanation which is truly social. A possible way forward is the normative explanation initiated by Moscovici and Lecuyer (1972). Their initial starting point was to consider whether or not group norms emerged or were changed within an existing group. This led to the consideration that in laboratory or established groups considering novel ideas, norms would emerge during the course of discussion, while in established groups norms would be shaped or changed (Chell, 1985a; Fraser 1978). The reason for polarization would then be accounted for in terms of a shift by the minority towards the majority. The advantage of this normative explanation is that it emphasizes the fluidity and dynamism of group processes.

It could still be argued that this process too is highly atomistic and individualistic. Indeed, Moscovici and Lecuyer (1972) did draw on the social (inter-individual) comparison processes explanation. A further level of sophistication is therefore provided by considering norms as operating at two levels – horizontal and vertical (Paicheler, 1976, 1977, 1979). What this means is that there is both interpersonal normative social influence (the horizontal level) and an interaction between group members and external social norms (the vertical level). This raises a further query: What are the conditions within the group which structure the balance between a predominance of interpersonal social influence and the impact of external social norms on group thinking? For instance, this explanation could account for group think; group think results from a heavy concentration on interpersonal normative social influence processes, blocking out as far as possible a consideration of external factors in terms of both informational social influence and external norms. However, interpersonal normative social influence processes are insufficient to explain group think; it is also necessary to consider factors shaping group structure such as status expectations and power position among the membership (Chell, 1977, 1985a). Groups which are so inward-looking may be reacting to external (or even internal) threat (as may be instanced in cases of depolarization). Outward-looking groups are likely to be more robust, able to defend their actions and accommodate new ideas, opinions and ways of thinking. Thus, the extent to which a group is open or closed is a function of the perceptions of group members of personal and group security and affects the operation of vertical social influence processes.

Another condition may be that of the degree of organicness or organicity within the group (see earlier section). Mechanistic groups tend to be rule-bound, with established norms for making decisions; movement outside those guidelines is difficult. Here external social norms are unlikely to stretch beyond organizational boundaries, the culture of the organization dictating how bureaucratically operations shall run. Organicity, on the other hand, enables new people bringing ideas from outside the organization to have influence and shape decision-making. By contrast, only when there is environmental 'turbulence' may mechanistic structures find themselves in need of adapting and considering new ways of doing things.

COPING WITH POLARIZATION EFFECTS

The question has been posed as to whether polarization does occur in real as opposed to laboratory or 'nonsense' groups as Fraser and Foster (1984) prefer to call them? The answer is a cautious and qualified 'yes', but there are other processes – depolarization, extremization, group think, averaging, etc. which also occur. The problem is what conditions *cause* these group processes? Some caution must be exercised here, but it does appear likely that in ambiguous or novel situations an *essential* condition for group polarization effects to occur is the absence of an already established norm, rule or procedure to which it may refer and by which process it would *normally* resolve an issue. In the discussion which ensues, role and status factors may play a part in influencing the direction of the debate (Chell, 1985a). Where status equality exists, then other factors such as the inherent persuasiveness of the arguments may be salient. On the other hand, in making decisions about organizational issues such as the introduction of new technology or working practices, what marketing strategy to adopt in order to deal with external competition, new lines in product development, etc., external norms may play a large part in swaying a group decision in one way or another. What is happening in the company or the industry as a whole may be one external norm which holds great sway. But, none the less, small groups have often been known to resist strongly external pressure of any sort to change. This suggests that another condition which affects a polarization or depolarization of attitudes may be the presence of at least one influential member within the group, or that over a period of time, with the input of new information, a 'critical mass' of like-thinking individuals may 'push' the group norm in a particular direction.

Given such possibilities, the manager has two questions to ask him or herself: (a) Do I have sufficient 'clout' to win the arguments and carry the majority of the group with me? (b) If I am not confident of my own position power to win over the rest of the group, what is the general direction of the rest of the group's feeling on the issue; are they likely to polarize in mine or some other direction? If the group feeling is in the desired direction, then group discussion will be a useful strategy for reinforcing that position. If not, then the manager should either control the communication content so as to elicit desired arguments, or simply introduce the action as a *fait accompli*. In the latter eventuality, the manager must be sure that she will obtain the group's acceptance of her action.

An alternative strategy which the manager might take is that of avoiding group discussion. There are several methods which enable her to do that, namely statistical aggregation and the Delphi and nominal group techniques (Delbecq *et al.*, 1975; Murnighan, 1981). Statistical aggregation is confined to quantitative problems: several people make individual estimates of the best answer to a problem. The estimates are collected, and the average or median response is used to determine the final solution. If averaging is used, then an extreme response would sway the estimate in a particular direction. This might encourage members to 'play the system'. However, once it was realized what was going on the futility of this would be apparent, because extreme estimates in opposite directions would tend to cancel each other out.

The Delphi technique extends this procedure a little further. Again the group does not need to meet, which is a considerable advantage to persons who loathe committee meetings, or to a multi-national company with plants spread over a wide geographical area. The problem or issue is stated in writing as clearly and as unambiguously as possible and the chairperson/ administrator sends a copy to each member of the Delphi panel. Potential solutions are returned to the chair, who summarizes them and feeds them back to the panel in a questionnaire format which seeks their reactions to these initial recommendations. The preferences of the panel are collated and again fed back with additional queries. The procedure continues until a clear solution emerges. If a consensus does not emerge, voting can be used. This technique has the advantage of being able to involve a very large number of people, but it also has a clear disadvantage: that of time. It is possible that using computer aids rather than the conventional mailing of questionnaires and awaiting responses could be used to speed up the process. Even then it is unlikely that one could get instantaneous answers, for the obvious reason if nothing else that busy executives will not always be at a terminal or be available to respond personally to every problem which issues forth via their modem. However, the potential for increased efficiency is clearly there.

The nominal group technique (NGT), unlike the above two techniques, does require that the group meets. The problem is posed to the group, and each member individually generates as many ideas and alternative ways of tackling the problem as he or she can think of. These are written down on a notepad placed in front of each member, and after about fifteen minutes each presents one idea in round robin fashion. As the ideas are being presented, the chairperson records them on a flip chart in full view of the group. A discussion of the ideas ensues, mainly for purposes of clarification, and then the voting procedure begins. This can be achieved by either of two methods: (a) each group member might vote for her five preferred alternatives, ranking them from one to five; (b) each of the ideas can be rated on a ten-point scale. Voting or ratings are done privately. The chairperson tabulates the votes and announces them to the group. If there is a clear-cut winner the session ends. Otherwise, where there is a small set of possible solutions, discussion ensues and a second vote is held. This procedure continues until a solution is found.

Murnighan (1981) has made a useful comparison between these group decision-making techniques. For example, NGT is less costly than the Delphi technique in terms of both time and money; it increases the commitment of group members and their cohesiveness as a group; it is open to some degree of conflict and social pressure but this is controlled and reduced by the way the discussion is restricted.

Table 4.2 shows an evaluation of six different decision techniques using a list of critical criteria. This is based on Murnighan's research, but also included for comparison is Norman Maier's group problem-solving technique – a technique which it would appear compares very favourably with the rest. The ordinary group technique describes the situation where a meeting is called, the group is presented with a problem and it is discussed in a fairly unstructured, free-flowing manner. It is, as we have seen, vulnerable to all kinds of social pressures and, although sometimes it can work well, there are many ways in which it can go wrong. The Maier technique should score low on social pressure if (a) the leader is sufficiently skilful at handling the group, and (b) he or she does not attempt to prematurely sway the group towards his or her preferred solution. Indeed, in this and most of the other group techniques, effective group leadership means avoiding blatantly advocating a particular position. Conflict should be kept to a minimum by firm chairpersonship using the Maier approach. Participation in the discussion of possible solutions and the cross-wise interaction which is encouraged in this type of group should result in increased commitment to the agreed outcome and help make the group more cohesive. Brainstorming, which Murnighan also includes, is dismissed as an enjoyable process

TABLE 4.2 *An evaluation of six different decision-making techniques*

Criteria	Ordinary	Brainstorming	Aggregation	Maier	NGT	Delphi
Number of ideas	Low	Moderate	NA	High	High	High
Quality of ideas	Low	Moderate	NA	High	High	High
Social pressure	High	Low	None	Moderate to low	Moderate	Low
Time/money costs	Moderate	Low	Low	Moderate	Low	High
Task orientation	Low	High	High	High	High	High
Potential for interpersonal conflict	High	Low	Low	Moderate	Moderate	Low
Feelings of accomplishment	Higher low	High	Low	High	High	Moderate
Commitment to solution	High	NA	Low	High	Moderate	Low
Builds group cohesiveness	High	High	Low	Moderate to high	Moderate	Low

NA: Not applicable.

SOURCE Adapted from J. K. Murnighan (1981) 'Group decision-making: what strategies should you use?', *Management Review*, February, 55–62.

for group members, while research has shown that it does not generate as high a number of good-quality ideas as was once supposed. This finding clearly limits its usefulness in most management situations.

SUMMARY

———— Members of a psychological group have a common purpose; they interact and perceive themselves to be a group. There are different types of group arising from degree of formality, task structure and the extent of dependency between members. Such variables distinguish between interacting, coacting and counteracting groups.

———— Groups may have formal functions to perform, but members also have their own needs which they strive to fulfil through the group. This creates a problem for management of eliciting from the group commitment to organizational goals.

———— The environment or system within which the group operates is important because it affects group functioning in terms of effective task completion, innovative activity and member satisfaction.

———— The underlying normative structure of the group underpins member behaviour. Norms are implicit rules of conduct adhered to by the majority of group members for a greater proportion of group interaction in order to maintain behavioural consistency. There are four main factors which influence conformity to group norms; these are personal, interpersonal, social and situational.

———— 'Horizontal' or interpersonal norms help maintain group standards. An important variable is that of creating commitment to the standard. This can be achieved through increased cohesiveness and member participation in formulating standards.

———— Conditions which help increase the pressure on the individual to conform are dependency and the elimination of individualism. Such pressure to conform can cause numerous problems for individuals and there are few circumstances which will enable the deviant member to avoid punishment for non-conforming behaviour. Some suggestions have been put forward by Zander (1982).

———— A serious matter for concern is the extent to which undue pressure towards conformity in an already cohesive ingroup will lead to group think. The behaviours which are symptomatic of group think are well documented (Janis, 1971), the main consequences are poor decision-making and inadequate solutions to problems. There are some measures which can be taken to avoid group think occurring in the first place. Indeed, sound decision-making can be enhanced by a participative management style (Chell, 1985a; Maier, 1970). However, one problem which may arise is that of identifying the problem and achieving group recognition and acceptance of what the problem is (Sims, 1979).

A further consideration is whether groups can make less extreme, less risky decisions than individuals. Research on risky shift suggested that they cannot (Stoner, 1961). Attempts were made to explain this phenomenon, but it was superseded by a more global phenomenon termed 'group polarization' (Moscovici and Zavalloni, 1969). Attempts at explaining polarization effects (the tendency for the mean decision after discussion to shift towards the preferred pole) were numerous and protracted over time (Fraser and Foster, 1984). The currently preferred explanation, which appears to account for a variety of polarization effects in real as well as laboratory groups, operates at two levels: that of interpersonal normative and informational social influence and vertical normative behaviour (Paicheler, 1976, 1977, 1979).

5 Team Building

Both the notion of, and concern for, team building has sprung primarily from the camp of the 'organization development' specialists and consultants. Their specific aim is the development of the total organization in order to fulfil the twin objectives of realising organizational goals and satisfying individual needs (French and Bell, 1978; Schein, 1980). This process of development may take place at different levels within the organization – organization, group and individual – although each cannot be thought of as being totally independent of any other level. Team building is clearly a group level activity, although the effectiveness of a team is not exclusively a 'group phenomenon' but depends very much on the activities and behaviours of individual team members. In this chapter we will commence pragmatically with the question why organizations might need to spend time, effort and resources on developing effective teams. Next, we will consider what the crucial ingredients of such teams are, and finally we will examine some tried and tested methods of team building.

THE IMPORTANCE OF TEAM BUILDING

A primary consideration for any organization is that of whether its management team, departmental units, workgroups and other specialist groups operate effectively. This raises the question – and it is not first and foremost an academic question – of what constitutes effectiveness. From a managerial perspective, this is usually measured in terms of outputs – enhanced performance, increased productivity, etc. There is, however, a school of thought which suggests that not all organizational activities should be assessed by these criteria alone (see, for example, Knights *et al.*, 1985). Whatever disagreement there exists as to what constitutes the products of an effective group, there is a level of interpersonal operations within a group which is essential for it to function properly. Such interpersonal and intragroup processes lead to what McGregor (1960) has termed the 'atmosphere' of the group. Table 5.1 lists the contrasts between the atmosphere of an effective and ineffective group.

According to McGregor the effective group is cohesive, relaxed and friendly; discussion is open and disagreement possible. Effectiveness is a function of group members' orientation and attitude, and not simply the

TABLE 5.1 *Contrasting behaviours in effective and ineffective groups*

Effective groups	*Ineffective groups*
1. Group atmosphere is informal, comfortable, relaxed; no obvious tensions; no boredom; a working atmosphere of people who are both involved and interested	1. The atmosphere reflects indifference boredom or tension. The group is not challenged by its task or genuinely involved in it
2. Lot of discussion which is task relevant and in which everyone participates	2. A few people dominate the discussion and contributions are frequently off the point with no attempts made to keep the group on track
3. The task or objective of the group is well understood; it has been arrived at through discussion and all members are committed to it	3. From what is said, it is difficult to understand what the group task or objective is; people have different, private objectives which they are attempting to achieve in the group, there is no common objective
4. People listen to each other and ideas are freely expressed	4. People do not really listen to each other and ideas are ignored or overridden; people leave such meetings having failed to express their ideas and feelings, being afraid of ridicule or undue criticism
5. Disagreement is expressed not suppressed or overriden by premature group action, those who disagree do so genuinely and expect to be heard	5. Disagreements are generally not dealt with effectively; they may be suppressed for fear of open conflict; where they are not suppressed, there may be 'open warfare' of one faction attempting to dominate another; there may be 'tyranny of the minority' in which an individual or sub-group is so aggressive that the majority accedes to his or its wishes in order to preserve the peace or get on with the task
6. Decisions are reached by consensus, but the group does not allow apparent consensus to mask real disagreement, formal voting is minimized, as it tends to be divisive; the group does not accept a simple majority as a proper basis for action	6. Decisions/actions are often taken prematurely before the real issues are examined or resolved; a simple majority is considered to be sufficient, with the majority expected to go along with the decision; this creates resentment and a lack of commitment to the decision by the minority
7. Constructive criticism occurs and is not of a personal kind	7. Criticism creates embarrassment and tension; it is often personal and destructive
8. People are free to express their personal feelings as well as their ideas	8. People hide their feelings; they are not considered an appropriate area for discussion
9. When action is taken, clear assignments are made and accepted	9. Responsibility for action when it is taken is unclear, and there is a lack of confidence that individuals who have been so designated will carry out their responsibilities.
10. The chairperson does not dominate discussion, rather leadership shifts depending upon the issue under discussion	10. The leadership is fixed and resides in the chairperson who sits at the 'head of the table'
11. The group is self-conscious about its own operations; whether the problem is procedural or interpersonal, the group will try to resolve the problem before proceeding	11. There is no discussion in the group about its own operations or maintenance functions
12. Power struggles as such do not occur in the group; the issue is not who controls but how the job gets done	

SOURCE D. M. McGregor (1960) *The Human Side of Enterprise* (NewYork: McGraw–Hill).

behaviour of the leader. Zander (1982) adds to this by pointing out that a *discussion* group serves five purposes:

- It helps members recognize what they do not know but should.
- It is an occasion for members to get answers to questions.
- It enables members to seek and obtain advice on matters that bother them.
- It lets people share ideas and derive a common wisdom.
- It is a way for members to learn about one another as persons.

The discussion group therefore does not necessarily meet in order to take decisions which lead to actions, or to solve organizational problems; rather, as indicated above, it serves both an educational and advisory purpose. To this end, the leader may have a particular role to play under the following set of circumstances: where members (a) are reluctant to take part in discussion, (b) lack ideas and (c) fail to give and take.

Groups, as was made apparent in Chapter 4, do not operate in isolation, and there is one salient dimension of organizational climate which shapes members' behaviour in discussion groups: that is, whether the organization is *achievement-* or *help*-oriented. In the former case, people place value on achieving their own personal ends, getting ahead, competing with peers, and so on. In other words, members are *individualistic* and put little store in group concerns. The help orientation contrasts markedly to this as members endeavour to help their fellows grow as persons; they ask, listen and seek understanding, explain and increase mutual comprehension of issues, and withold judgement of others (Zander, 1982).

The discussion group is, of course, by no means the only type of group that must be effectively managed. A type of organizational group which is assuming greater importance is the innovative project group, the multidisciplinary research team or project-planning group (Meadows 1980a; Thomsett, 1980). The way such teams operate cannot be divorced from the prevailing culture and value systems with which the organization is imbued (see Table 5.2).

In order that the project team be effective there are additional factors to be considered, such as the roles people play in the group and whether a 'natural group' is allowed to develop (Schein, 1980; Thomsett, 1980).

The following set of roles were identified as possible leadership functions by Thomsett (1980). Where the team is multidisciplinary, members will be experts in their own field and may well assume leadership when issues pertinent to them are raised. They are:

TABLE 5.2   *Two prevailing organizational paradigms*

Old paradigm	New paradigm
The technological imperative	Joint optimization
People as an extension of the machine	The machine as an extension of people
People seen as interchangeable spare parts	People seen as an asset to be developed
Maximum task breakdown, division of narrow and single skills	Optimum task grouping; interdisciplinary teams; multiple, broad skills
External controls (supervisors, specialist staffs, procedures)	Internal controls (self-regulating subsystems)
Tall organization chart, autocratic style	Flat organization chart, participative style
Competition, gamesmanship	Collaboration, congeniality
Information hidden for use as power	Information shared to facilitate cooperation
Alienation	Commitment
Low risk-taking	Innovation

SOURCE   Based on R. Thomsett (1980) *People and Project Management* (New York: Yourdon Press).

- Chairperson/moderator.
- Spokesperson/liaison/gatekeeper.
- Organizer/manager.
- Group maintenance person/ social leader/ 'den mother'.
- Technical leader/theoretician.
- Entrepreneur/planner.

   While it is undoubtedly true that individuals may play different 'if not key' roles in a group, this list of types of role generated by Thomsett gives the appearance of ad-hockery. There is no fundamental analysis of why these roles are critical or if indeed they are critical under all circumstances. In a later section, a more systematic approach to the analysis of team roles is explored. However, there is one role which has been systematically researched and it is that of *integrator*. While project teams may be assumed to work closely together on a shared task, multifunctional teams of various sorts may have a less permanent or regular existence. They may be formed to solve particular problems and are likely to represent different departments, interests and values. The composition of such a team may well be crucial. This means not only selecting people with appropriate characteristics in order to fulfil group goals and carry out necessary tasks and functions, nor does it simply mean bringing people together who are assumed to be able to work well together; it also means the need to integrate people of different backgrounds, skills, abilities, persuasions and affiliations, who, in terms of their technical know-how, speak different languages.

This problem of integration was studied by Lawrence and Lorsch (1967a, b) in R & D-intensive organizations. The problem as they saw it was the difficulty of reconciling the need for specialization (differentiation) with the need for tighter coordination (integration of effort). Integration was unlikely to occur naturally. There was therefore the need to create a special functional role, that of *integrator*. This role was said to involve 'handling the non-routine, unprogrammed problems that arise among the traditional functions as each strives to do its own job'. It also involves resolving interdepartmental conflicts and facilitating decisions (Lawrence and Lorsch, 1967a, pp. 142–3). We are not concerned here with *inter*group issues, as they are beyond the scope of this chapter (but see Lorsch and Lawrence (1972) and Chell (1985a) for two contrasting approaches to this problem). Rather we are concerned with the need to bear in mind such 'macro' dimensions as organizational structure, culture and objectives as they impact on the functioning of groups and individuals. In terms of the problems for the organization of innovation and change, Kanter suggests the need for 'integrative thinking' within organizations to ensure team-oriented, cooperative environments in which change is facilitated and innovation flourishes (Kanter, 1984, p. 27 *et seq.*). Further, the issue must be a concern for any modern organization which has adopted a matrix structure (Dyer, 1977).

There are a great many other reasons why an organization needs to take groups seriously, but essentially it must always question the assumption that a group of employees will work effectively as a team without any assistance. So far we have talked about project teams and innovative groups. Such concepts suggest particular sorts of organization – technologically based perhaps, although this need not necessarily be so in the case of project teams. They also suggest the ideas of growth and development. However, in the climate of the 1980s the watchwords for many organizations were rationalization, redundancy, derecruitment and so on (Chell, 1985c). In such a climate, groups may be formed to plan for and execute a change in the organization against a backdrop of anxiety, fear and emotional turmoil. Krantz (1985) has provided convincing evidence of the way teams may operate under such circumstances. His argument (based on the conceptual framework of Bion (1961)) is that intrapsychic structures (individual fears, anxieties, etc.) are made manifest in the social structure and culture of the institution. There is apparent regression to more primitive modes of thinking, underpinned by subconscious defence mechanisms of denial, fantasy, paranoia, and so on. The upshot is one of irrational behaviour and illogical decision-making at a group and not simply at an individual level. The general lesson therefore is that teams must be developed to deal effectively with all eventualities; only then can organizations escape ad-hockery, defensiveness, factionalism, unhealthy agreement and so on.

Tsosvold (1991) has offered a constructive alternative to the ineffectiveness and/or neuroticism of the group. He has fleshed out the characteristics of group culture in two contrasting organizations: 'Stagnate', where people operate on an individualistic, competitive basis, and 'Dynamic', where the company has developed a team organization. Team organization motivates and energizes people in a group towards effective action. The team model comprises five steps:

- Envision.
- Unite.
- Empower.
- Explore.
- Reflect.

Each team needs a vision which will unite its members in a common effort, direction and purpose. The team must feel confident that it has the power to realize its vision. Even with these ingredients, not all group interaction goes smoothly; there are issues which arise and which must be dealt with. This means that an effective team must be able to explore such issues constructively. The continuity of an effective team cannot be taken for granted: team members must work continuously at group improvement. This suggests the team should reflect upon what it is doing, build upon achievements and carry out regular monitoring.

Tsosvold assumes that the team can be inculcated with a desire to work cooperatively; that is, that such recognition can be cultivated among team members that what can be gained by means of cooperation is of more value than the dysfunctional effects of individualism, competitiveness and the pursuit of self-interest.

Cooperation is not based on altruism, but on the recognition that, with positively related goals, self-interests require collaboration. Cooperative new product team members want each other to develop useful ideas and work hard to create a new product that makes everyone successful. (Tsosvold, 1991, p. 46)

This marks the difference between a win–win organization culture and a competitive culture where there is always a loser or losing group.

This model raises a number of issues, not least of which is that of the leader's role: does the leader have a vision? Where has the vision come from, and how does it articulate with the organization's wider objectives? In an entrepreneurially led organization, or a family business, how realistic is it that the vision be evaluated by the team? A further problem arises, owing partly to the prescriptiveness of the model; this gives a sense of the imperative to many of the actions. It is not difficult to envisage how, under certain circumstances, there might be a tendency towards escalation of commitment to a particular vision or set of ideas. Such circumstances may range from the desire of the leader not to lose face to the absence of anyone within the team who is willing, able, or perhaps powerful enough to evaluate and think through the ideas which have been put forward (Drummond, 1991a).

In summary, effective teams in organizations rarely occur by chance, but require various conditions to be met in order to ensure their existence. One such condition assumes the importance of commitment at all levels to the ideas of team development, as it is related to the culture and atmosphere which permeates the whole organization. Within the group, it can make the difference between being able to communicate well with other specialist team members, playing an appropriate and useful role in the group, being able to appreciate multiple perspectives on a problem and arriving at high quality, acceptable solutions. Finally, it is argued that while it is necessary to (a) establish the need for effective groups and (b) establish an organizational climate and structure within which such groups can operate, these two conditions alone are insufficient to ensure that a group will operate effectively. In the next section of this chapter we consider further how groups of people can be made into effective teams.

GROUP AND TEAM DEVELOPMENT

It is clearly important to think of what type of group one is dealing with and the sort of task(s) it has to perform. A highly generalized way of distinguishing between workgroups is to think of them as being either *family* or *special* groups. The family group is the basic workgroup, characterized by a degree of permanence and stability of membership and task function. The special group, on the other hand, may be a task force or committee set up specifically to tackle a particular problem. Whatever the type or purpose of the group, there are two general problems associated with the dynamics and maintenance of the group as a group. These are the degree of comfort that people experience as group members, and the processes by which the group becomes more cohesive and effective over time.

There are several considerations which face the manager before deciding to implement a team development programme. The first is to be able to articulate the reasons why such a programme should be instigated at all. A further consideration is that of being able to select an appropriate programme, and a third is the problem of who is to be included as part of the team. In addition to these issues, there are others such as the length and location of the programme, the need for an external consultant and the relationship between manager and consultant (Dyer, 1977).

A basic, simple team development programme has been suggested by Dyer (1984). It consists of the following:

1. Take at least one day off for team building and get away from the work site so there will be no interruptions.
2. Ask each person to write his or her answers to the following questions and be prepared to share them with others at the meeting:

   (a) What keeps you from being as effective as you would like to be in your position?
   (b) What keeps the staff (unit or department) from functioning as an effective team?
   (c) What do you like about this unit that you want to maintain?
   (d) What suggestions do you have for improving the quality of our working relationships and the functioning of our department?

3. At the meeting, have each person read or present his or her responses to the above questions as someone writes them on a blackboard or flipchart. There will be four lists: (a) blocks to individual effectiveness, (b) blocks to team effectiveness, (c) things people like and (d) suggestions for improvement.
4. Ask the group to list according to priority the problems they want to address. This forms the agenda for the meeting.
5. Permit the group to begin work on achieving the goal of the team development session: to eliminate as many obstacles as possible. This may include changing assignments, clarifying roles, clearing up misunderstandings, sharing more information, or making other innovations. The point is to engage the team in a regular examination of its

own effectiveness and the development of solutions to its own problems. If a consultant is used, his or her role is to keep the team looking at its processes as it works on its problems.

The conceptual basis to a programme such as this is that of the team building cycle (Dyer, 1977). The elements of such a programme are:

1. Someone recognizes that there is a problem or problems.
2. Data are gathered to determine the causes of the problem. This stage may include the consultant carrying out interviews with members of the group individually. However, this has to be handled carefully because it has been known for individuals in group situations to deny their own interview data! An attractive alternative to this is that of open data sharing (as utilized in the programme outlined above). This means in effect that individuals only raise those issues which they honestly feel they can handle through open discussion.
3. Diagnosis and evaluation of the data consists of a process of summarizing and prioritizing. Examples of summary categories are those such as (a) those issues we can work on in this meeting, (b) those issues that someone else must work on (identify the individuals concerned) and (c) those issues that apparently are not open to change and we must learn to live with.
4. The problem-solving and planning stage occurs as the group focuses upon the issues identified in the previous stage and attempts to find a solution to them. In this context the manager acts as group leader, while the consultant acts as observer/facilitator, concentrating his or her attention on the process by which the group arrives at its conclusions (Schein, 1969).
5. Implementation and evaluation is the stage where actions planned during the team building session are put into practice. This requires commitment on the part of the manager, and in this respect too the consultant may play an invaluable part (Dyer, 1977).

DESIGNING MANAGEMENT TEAMS

Dyer's approach consists largely of developing *existing* teams of managers. Belbin (1981), in direct contrast to this, has taken the concept of team building a stage further back. He and his co-workers have conceived of team members as resources, and then asked the question: What combination of personnel is required to make a balanced and effective team? This route led to an analysis of the roles which were necessary to make such teams. The rigorous developmental and analytic work which went into the management team concept was carried out over a period of nine years by the Industrial Training Research Unit at Cambridge and the Administrative Staff College, Henley-on-Thames. Further work was also carried out at the Staff College, Melbourne, Australia.

The feature which differentiated Belbin's work from that of many other researchers in this field was his express intention to measure not only the output of the teams but also the input. In other words, what exactly were the human resources which went into the construction of the team, and what was the relationship between input and output?

Team members were given a battery of psychometric tests that had been specially selected and devised. These yielded data on the personality characteristics and mental ability of each member. This meant that different combinations of personnel could be grouped together and their effectiveness measured. One test situation utilized was an Executive Management Exercise (EME). The resource inputs of each team had already been measured; now it was a matter of observing the process by which the participants interacted. Trained observers were used to record the type of contribution each member was making at half-minute intervals. Indeed, this type of observation technique has a long research tradition (Bales, 1950; Chell, 1976, 1985a). On this occasion, seven categories of behaviour were observed: asking, informing, proposing, opposing, delegating, building and commenting. The numerical scores for each participant on each of these categories revealed who was doing the most talking and the nature of the interventions which were typical of each member. Then, relating these process data to the input measures enabled one to show whether, for example, the person doing the most proposing was one of the cleverer members, as measured by the tests, or one of the more ebullient, as measured by the personality inventory.

The EME was a computer-based game which placed emphasis on analysis and calculation, and a modelling approach to business generally. A different game was devised to assess other skills. This team game – 'Teamopoly', based on Monopoly – achieved the purpose of bringing home emphatically the reason for team failures – either faulty team composition or poor use of team resources. Team success was measured in terms of financial outcomes which indicated the teams' effectiveness in meeting their objectives.

Several experiments were carried out in a systematically planned attempt to determine the composition of a successful team. Initially, they attempted to form a high-powered management team composed entirely of clever people, that is, people who had scored high on the mental ability tests. The rationale for this think tank-type situation is self-explanatory, but, the results were far from what was expected. These 'Apollo teams', as they were known, invariably came last! The problem was to explain this 'Apollo Syndrome': why were they so ineffectual? Observers noted the unsatisfactory nature of the group process. There was a great deal of abortive debate and a lack of coherence in decision-making; several pressing jobs were neglected; members acted independently; and there was a lack of coordination of action.

A further experiment was to compose teams of similar personalities. This, in one sense, was a very real attempt to assess the problems of *elective homogeneity*, that is, the tendency of top management teams to 'clone' themselves. Using measures of personality, they composed four types of team: *stable extroverts* (SE), *anxious extroverts* (AE), *stable introverts* (SI) and *anxious introverts* (AI). In general, extroverted *companies* performed better than did introverts. In terms of planning activities, SEs found it difficult to concentrate, and so diversions like snooker became far more attractive. However, on the positive side, such teams had good communications, they tended to operate in pairs and so there was built in flexibility of operations, they were able to deal effectively with others, and they used the record sheets of the observers in order to modify their company style. There were clear weaknesses inherent in all these companies. The SEs were prone to making small errors, and because they were so easy-going, they failed to notice or to attempt to rectify them. The natural balancing qualities in the teams were noticeably absent, although the style of operation clearly suited all members; however, whether it continued to do so in the light of continued failure of the teams is a question to which the answer can only be speculative.

Finally, in this run of team experiments, Belbin composed 'pure' teams entirely of one type of team worker. This team member was identified and labelled *company worker* (CW). CWs are disciplined, conscientious and aware of their external obligations, they have a well-developed self-image and possess a degree of internal control, they are tough-minded, practical, trusting, tolerant and conservative in the sense of being respectors of established conditions and ways of looking at things. They are *not* 'organization men' in the William Foote Whyte sense. The experimental groups were composed of teams high in CWs and low in CWs and high and low in mental ability. The results were largely negative, reflecting the limitations of the CW teams. The CWs lacked any real ideas, they were inflexible, strongly committed to achieving group goals and worked well towards that end. However, they invariably failed to get good results.

Such experiments as these underlined what were, in effect, the limitations of 'pure' teams: they developed a style and quality of their own such that if the situation matched the style it was possible for the company to excel. However, there was no guarantee that any particular situation would continue in that form, and such teams had not the variability in resources to respond effectively to new and different situations:

> The longer a management team is exposed to the problems of the real world the greater is the need to be prepared for a full range of problems and situations, and to have a team ready to meet them. (Belbin, 1981, p. 29)

Earlier in this chapter, and in the book in general, we have discussed the issue of innovation particularly as it pertains to R & D management. It is therefore pertinent to consider the role of creativity in the team and the sorts of insights which Belbin's work can offer. Surprisingly perhaps, he suggested that the number of ideas proposed in the team was not as highly correlated with success as might have been expected. The problem was the lack of ability to utilize the ideas produced, not the generation of ideas *per se*. In fact there are drawbacks of encouraging everyone in the group to become creative, in particular the problem of disposing of unwanted ideas. The search for a compromise then becomes political and a matter of appeasement. An alternative strategy is to get the team to understand and make better use of the individual talents of its members: to harness those talents and to reduce the 'noise' of all ideas that can be produced.

Using Cattell's formula for *creative disposition*, creative individuals having a distinctive set of personal qualities were identified. As part of the continued experimental work, individuals who scored highly on the mental ability test and on creative disposition were selected and 'planted' into separate companies. The plants (PLs) (as they were termed) or 'ideas people' not only dominated in this department as was expected, but also skilfully manouevred themselves into positions where they could get their ideas across and accepted. Thus the notion of having a creative person in a team was well borne out. However, it is interesting to note that companies with more than one PL fared no better than companies with none!

Another creative individual who could be distinguished from the plant was termed the *resource investigator* (RI). The RI was more extrovert than the PL; he or she was of average ability and valued versatility, and was sociable, enthusiastic and low on anxiety. RIs were people for whom new ideas were a focus of interest. Yet, rather than standing out as originators they were more inclined to pick up fragments of ideas from others and develop them. They were particularly adept at exploring resources outside the group. Liaison work gave them just the right opportunity to come back with some new proposition which could often transform company plans. Whereas the PL tended to be a loner, an oddball with a very original mind, the RI preferred close involvement with people and was skilful at using resources. Contrariwise, the more the PL fulfilled his/her role, the less he or she looked like a manager; whereas the more the RI fulfilled his/her team role, the more he or she did look like a manager. Clearly, a team could benefit from possessing both types of innovator.

A role which is crucial in any team is that of its leadership. One aspect of this role is that of being able to skilfully use resources as typified by the roles enacted by different team members. Whether the leader has gained members' acceptance or is appointed rather for his or her effectiveness is a moot issue in the leadership debate. However, in most management teams leaders must primarily be effective, and so a critical question for this investigation was to ask what are the characteristics of someone who adopts the role of effective team leader.

The role of chairperson was demonstrably a critical one; however, there were some interesting if not surprising features of the successful chairperson. It seemed that successful chairpersons were not *on average* more mentally able or creative than their unsuccessful counterparts. Nor were they far ahead of their colleagues on mental ability, either. In terms of personality they are trusting, dominant, calm and unflappable in the face of controversy; they possess a practical realism and basic self-discipline; they are naturally enthusiastic and have an extrovert capacity to motivate others; and they are prone to detachment and distance in social relations (that is, not pure extroverts). In addition, they tend to be positive thinkers, who are approving of others and they like people who are lively and dynamic. In a nutshell, they are 'someone tolerant enough to listen to others but strong enough to reject their advice' (Belbin, 1981, p. 53).

A good chairperson profile was a good predictor of *company* success. Such a person was characteristically able to make the best use of the resources in the group; he or she was highly adapatable when it came to people and never lost his or her grip on a situation. He or she is well able to make a judgement based on an assessment of what is needed in practice and is well able to intervene at critical points in the exercise. Meetings are never allowed to get out of hand and are infused with a sense of direction and purpose. But why does the chairperson score only averagely on mental ability? Belbin suggests that this feature facilitates communication with colleagues. In contrast, less clever chairpersons cannot follow the drift of arguments, do not appreciate the alternatives open to them and give the appearance of indecision. The very clever chairperson, on the other hand, tended to pursue his or her own ideas which were liable to be based on arguments which team members could not always follow. Communication tended to break down and the intellectual authority, enhanced by status considerations, tended to discourage any prospective opponents or advocates of caution.

The role of chairperson was not the only leadership role; there was another, which Belbin and his co-workers termed *shaper*. Shapers abound with nervous energy; they have a strong need for achievement and are challenging; they tend to argue, disagree and are impatient; and for them winning is all important. Characteristically, they tend to overreact to disappointments or annoyances. In a group they are a disruptive force, but may also galvanize the team into action.

There was also the *Apollo chairperson* who appeared to have characteristics in common with the classic chairperson and shaper. Unlike the shaper, the Apollo chairperson had no desire to lead from the front. While unlike the classic chairperson, who had the ability to draw out the potential of the group, the Apollo chairperson was 'a tough, discriminating person who can hold his(/her) ground in any company; yet he(/she) never dominates' (Belbin, 1981, p. 63).

So far the research had revealed five key team roles – company worker, plant, resource investigator, chairperson and shaper. While these were necessary within an effective management team, they were insufficient to present a well-balanced team. What, therefore, were the team roles that were missing? Firstly, there was the problem that a team containing a PL and RI may well find itself faced with several conflicting ideas. There was therefore a need for someone with sufficient capability to be able to evaluate conflicting proposals. This role was labelled *monitor-evaluator*. The ME is clever, detached and has a 'built-in immunity for enthusiasm'. He or she makes shrewd judgements and prides him or herself in never being wrong. In addition, MEs have low drive, which enhances their ability to judge, increasing their impartiality. The role of ME is quite the opposite of 'seat-of-the-pants' management.

There is always the danger in any team that a particular member or members will be unable to play the role for which they are best suited because of the competitiveness of other members. It is useful therefore to have someone in the team who is able to intervene in order to avert possible friction and enable members to use their skills to positive ends. Such a person 'has a special part to play in making a team successful, especially when it contains one or more individuals with outstanding talent but who are unable to work with colleagues' (Belbin, 1981, p. 71). Such an individual was termed a *team worker* (TW).

Many teams suffer because they are good at starting initiatives but lack the staying qualities to see such activities through. Therefore a person who can perform the role of *completer-finisher* (CF) is a real asset to any team. Characteristically, this person has an eye for detail and a relentless follow-through. They are prone to anxiety, though highly self-controlled, absorbing stress and giving the outward appearance of someone calm and unflappable. They scored through their steady effort, survival qualities and consistency.

Table 5.3 lists these eight useful team roles, summarizing their typical features, positive qualities and allowable weaknesses. It should be emphasized that there are some people with the ability to perform more than one role in a group, but clearly such individuals are even rarer. There are also individuals who fit into no obvious team role and this, it is suggested, is one reason for the lack of success of a team. Such individuals are said to be liabilities rather than assets, and are estimated as being 30 per cent of managers. They are described as having a capacity for spontaneous action, keen wits and a disinclination to consult others. However, one would have thought that there was more than one type of non-team role. Other reasons for lack of team success can be summarized as follows:

1. Low scores on mental ability; absence of at least one person who is clever.
2. The culture of the firm creates a particular type of collective personality; this reduces the team's ability to cope with different types of problem and behave like specialists towards particular sorts of situation.
3. An unfortunate combination of characters in the team may render it ineffectual; this may mean that an otherwise useful person is unlikely to make the valuable contribution to the team that he/she is capable of.
4. Presence of people with no team role.
5. Lack of self-awareness of one's appropriate team role.
6. Tendency to gravitate towards performing jobs one has experience of rather than playing a specific team role.
7. The absence of a corporate team strategy, rather than being locked into a narrow functional or specialist view.
8. Unpredictable team role reversal, i.e. individuals do not, for various reasons, adopt their obvious team roles, so that internal resources are put to sub-optimal effect.

TABLE 5.3 *The characteristics of Belbin's eight team roles*

Type	Symbol	Typical features	Positive qualities	Allowable weaknesses
Company Worker	CW	Conservative, dutiful, predictable	Organizing ability, practical common sense, hard-working, self-disciplined	Lack of flexibility, unresponsiveness to unproven ideas
Chairman	CH	Calm, self-confident controlled	A capacity for treating and welcoming all potential contributors on their merits and without prejudice. A strong sense of objectives	No more than ordinary in terms of intellect or creative ability
Shaper	SH	Highly strung, outgoing, dynamic	Drive and a readiness to challenge inertia, ineffectiveness, complacency or self-deception	Proneness to provocation, irritation and impatience
Plant	PL	Individualistic, serious-minded, unorthodox	Genius, imagination, intellect, knowledge	Up in the clouds, inclined to disregard practical details or protocol
Resource Investigator	RI	Extroverted, enthusiastic, curious, communicative	A capacity for contacting people and exploring anything new. An ability to respond to challenge	Liable to lose interest once the initial fascination has passed
Monitor-Evaluator	ME	Sober, unemotional, prudent	Judgement, discretion, hard-headedness	Lacks inspiration or the ability to motivate others
Team Worker	TW	Socially-orientated, rather mild, sensitive	An ability to respond to people and to situations, and to promote team spirit	Indecisiveness at moments of crisis
Completer-Finisher	CF	Painstaking, orderly, conscientious, anxious	A capacity for follow-through Perfectionism	A tendency to worry about small things. A reluctance to 'let go'

SOURCE R. M. Belbin (1981) *Management Teams* (London: Heinemann Educational Books).

Is it possible, using this research to deduce some principles of effective management team design? Belbin suggests that there are five such interlocking principles:

- Members of a management team can contribute to the achievement of team objectives in one of two ways: performing a functional role, drawing on their specialist or technical knowledge; and performing a valuable team role.
- Obtaining a balance between both functional roles and team-roles; this will depend on the goals and tasks the team faces.
- Members recognize correctly and adjust themselves to the relative strengths within the team in both expertise and ability to engage in specific team roles.
- Personal qualities fit members for some team roles while limiting the likelihood that they will succeed in others.
- A team can deploy its technical resources to best advantage when it has the requisite range of team roles to ensure efficient teamwork.

It is clear that designing a successful management team is an act of creativity in itself and requires considerable expertise and know-how. Essentially, it means collecting sound and reliable information about members of the team to be analysed by experts. However, the designer must also have an eye to the situation of the company. For instance, in a startup situation it may be totally unrealistic for many years to talk about a management team of eight members. The entrepreneur may be the technical specialist whose idea it was that gave rise to the company. While his or her specialist knowledge is important, this expertise does not vest the founder with a team role in Belbin's sense. The danger in this circumstance would be for the expert to become chairperson, although he or she is unlikely to have the appropriate personal qualities for that role. If the entrepreneur has the strength of character and foresight, he or she will delegate the role of chairperson, and select a plant or monitor-evaluator to counterbalance his/her otherwise unrestrained expert power. Finally, in order to reduce the likelihood of disagreement and conflict, a team or company worker would be an appropriate third choice.

OTHER TEAM-BUILDING APPROACHES

It is beyond the scope of this chapter to give a detailed account of the various team-building approaches open to the organization. However, it is useful to categorize such approaches, as has been amply demonstrated by Blake and Mouton (1975). The five interventionist modes they identify are listed below.

The *cathartic* approach is applied to situations characterized by tension, fear and immobilization. The fear may be of the team building exercise itself ('what is happening and how am I supposed to behave?') or the situation which the team of managers find themselves in – as described by Krantz (1985) (see earlier section). 'Catharsis provides the background for building a climate of trust, openness, respect and intimacy which is essential for collaborative effort' (Blake and Mouton, 1975, p. 105).

Catalysis is used to bring changes in team work. It is an intervention which either speeds up an existing change or brings about an entirely new situation. Usually it is carried out by data-gathering and feedback. Dyer's approach is an example of this method. This attempt to get at the 'facts' and present them back to the group in a value-free way contrasts with the intervention known as *confrontation*. Most people are unaware of the value-loaded assumptions they hold about how they and others should behave. These assumptions affect how they operate in teams, and it is the job of the consultant using this method to make such assumptions explicit and understood. This enables team members to become conscious of their rationalizations, justifications and explanations of what is going on. However, the consultant stops short of prescribing how the members should interact.

The *prescription*-oriented approach, on the other hand, does assume that the consultant advises and provides 'answers', guidance and prescriptions for action. The consultant can 'see' what is going on in the group and therefore is not only in the best position to prescribe, but has also been employed to do so. Blake and Mouton (1975) suggest that this type of intervention is most appropriate for handling crisis situations. These crises or unanticipated disasters can leave managers with a sense of powerlessness in how to handle the situation. The consultant who is outside the situation can exercise initiative and direct group members to respond appropriately to the situation. Useful interventions by the consultant can be in terms of agenda setting, scheduling activities and goal formulation. This helps galvanize the team into perceiving what action is *now* needed and what resources are available to them. In taking the lead at such a critical time the consultant gives members a 'breathing space' to recharge, regroup and raise morale.

Finally, there are *theory*-based approaches. There are several theory-based approaches, of which Belbin's approach is but one. The theory there was that in order for any team to operate effectively there needs to be a variety and balance of skills, abilities and characteristics among the membership. Specific constellations of characteristics, abilities and skills vested in any one individual enable him or her to perform a particular identifiable, key team role. People with similar team profiles will compete for the same team role, thus rendering the group less effective. Hence, teams are more successful if they contain different types of people able to perform different, but critical, team roles.

Alternative theory-based approaches which may be more familiar to the reader are those of McGregor (1960) and Blake and Mouton (1964, 1978, 1985). In the former case, management may be operating under an outmoded set of assumptions which best fit a climate of economic survival. They therefore fail to get the best out of their employees by making them feel exploited rather than committed to their work. This may mean teaching entire managements through theory-clarified models that bring *involvement, participation and commitment to the task* to replace traditional ways of pressurizing for results (see Chell, 1985a). Blake and Mouton's Grid approach is slightly different. It is concerned with the theoretical basis of management style and its consequences for planning, controlling, directing and staffing. Managers are said to vary with respect to two dimensions of behaviour: *concern for people* and *concern for production* (see Chapter 6). Once a person's style is identified, it is possible to predict how he or she will deal with the conflict between the two opposing pressures.

Within this fivefold category system, the terms T-group, encounter group or more generally experiential group have not been mentioned. There tends to be considerable confusion over the aims of the T-group (Lakin, 1976); it can either be concerned with raising members' awareness of *group processes*, and as such may be construed as a group development activity, or it can be concerned with individual therapy, increased sensitivity to interpersonal processes which take place in group situations, etc. (Chell, 1985a). In examples of the latter type of experiential group, the T-group or encounter group has no real place in team building, whereas, where the objective is to increase team members' awareness of group processes it may fall into the categories of *catharsis* or *confrontation*. Certainly, if the T-group method is used in a programme of organizational development, then it may be necessary initially to use catharsis in order to overcome the fear that many people have of personal exposure and inability to cope in a T-group situation.

SUMMARY

———— A fundamental consideration for any organization is whether the workgroups and teams within it operate effectively. There are a number of ways of assessing *effectiveness* in this context; it includes smooth interpersonal operations within the group, an ability to have open discussions and disagreements in order to share ideas and learn from each other and an ability to solve problems and arrive at decisions.

———— There are special types of groups, as for example in R & D, whose objectives are those of idea generation and innovation. The problem for the organization is to ask what are the conditions which facilitate sound idea generation and adoption? Organizational structure and culture are two important conditions, as are the roles people play in the project group. Some preliminary analyses of roles are identified, but the main one that emerges from this analysis is that of *integrator*.

———— Groups and teams may not always be operating in the best of economic circumstances, and such conditions may create an atmosphere of fear, blocking fruitful discussion. A further problem for the organization, therefore, is to be able to compose teams of people well able to cope with most eventualities, and where necessary to be able to identify manifest anxiety and defensiveness within a team and to take appropriate steps to dissipate such problems.

———— A useful first step which may be taken is the development of *team organization*. This means giving the team a vision which will unite it; empowering it to enable it to achieve its aims; developing a team culture which will facilitate constructive exploration of issues and the reflection upon past actions and future possibilities. Team effectiveness is thus dependent upon leadership style and an openness which will help avoid escalation in decision-making.

———— The 'effective' team does not simply occur and most organizations need to give thought to the implementation of team development programmes. Ideally, this should be done before problems arise; team development should not occur as a product of crisis management any more than any other activity. A simple, basic team development programme has been suggested by Dyer (1977). This includes the gathering of data from team members by interview, and working through problems identified in this way in group sessions. The later stages of the programme include action planning and implementation.

An alternative approach to team building has been developed by Belbin (1981). The idea was to identify the characteristics of different members which enable them to perform critical team roles. The research which underpinned this approach was carried out over a period of nine years and consisted of systematically planned experiments, in which the composition of the teams was varied so that the ingredients of successful teams could be identified. The ability to say why teams were unsuccessful and how successful teams could be designed for particular purposes were two important outcomes of this research.

A useful way of categorizing approaches to team building has been put forward by Blake and Mouton (1975). There are five approaches: *catharsis* – where the primary purpose is to remove fear, anxieties and tensions in the team which will prevent its effective functioning; *catalysis* – an attempt to change the group situation, for example by collecting and feeding back new data to the group; *confrontation* – where the objective is to expose the value loaded assumptions under which the group is operating; *prescription* – where the consultant sees it as part of his/her job to provide guidance on how the group should act; *theory-based* approaches – which use a theory which is made explicit, tried and tested, to predict how team members and/or the group as a whole will function. Examples of theory-based approaches are McGregor's Theory X and Theory Y, Blake and Mouton's managerial grid and Belbin's management teams.

6 Leadership

INTRODUCTION

The term 'leadership' now is part and parcel of lay vocabulary. Further, its credentials for inclusion in the category of fundamental concepts in organizational behaviour are beyond question. *Leadership* is to organizational behaviour what *attitude* was to social psychology some six years ago (Allport, 1935).

The treatment of the subject of leadership has tended to follow a pattern, commencing with the view that leadership is a quality or personality trait, that is, that leaders are born and not made. The failure of research to identify such a trait led to a change of direction. The focus turned to the identification of leader behaviours, but again no one style was found to be the most effective. One problem was found to be that researchers had not taken into consideration the different contexts and circumstances in which a leader might operate and it became clear that such contexts were influential in determining the effectiveness or otherwise of a particular leadership style. Disillusionment with leadership style approaches gave way to contingency theories, albeit building on the earlier behavioural theories.

It is not the aim of this chapter to review the development of leadership theory from a socio-historical perspective. Such work may be read elsewhere (for example, Bass, 1981; Bryman, 1986; Chell, 1985a; Smith and Peterson, 1988). Rather, it is intended to select some key developments in leadership theory and research and to explore them critically with a view not only to their soundness but also to the practical insights they may give to illumine further the *what* and the *how* of leadership.

For example, the contingency theories are complex and present problems of application and testing. If such approaches are not wholly theoretically sound in the way that a scientific theory must be before it is accepted as valid, should we not be considering dismissing these 'theories' and starting again? A key problem is that, while these theories focus attention on particular issues, they are neither incontrovertible nor substantiated beyond question. They suggest, for instance, that leadership is not a set of personality characteristics *per se*, nor a style of operating which can be learnt, but the ability to respond appropriately to the contingencies of a situation. They raise the issue (but do not resolve it) of whether leader behaviour is constrained by certain personal attributes of the leader such that they can only respond effectively to a limited number of types of situation (Fiedler, 1977), or whether they are sufficiently flexible and able to respond differently and appropriately to a wide variety of situations and circumstances (Vroom and Yetton, 1973). Further, they attempt to make the link between adopting an appropriate leadership style in particular situations (in order to maximize productivity and worker satisfaction) and the concept of motivation (House, 1971).

There are undoubtedly some problems with leadership theories when it comes to application. For instance how generalizable are the 'rules' that they purport to enshrine? Blackler and Shimmin (1984) suggest that the contingency approaches are too mechanistic; they ignore the dynamics and the temporal dimension of any leadership situation. This means that it is critical to understand the detailed exigencies of each manager's situation in order to be able to apply any one of these theories. From the point of view of the average manager, it presents problems of being able to translate and transfer the knowledge learnt from the theory and relate it to the 'back home' work situation.

Perhaps this discussion, in a roundabout way, helps us think about why leadership is important. Leadership, in the practical sense of leading, is important in that by leading effectively, the leader/manager can produce results consonant with the shared goals and aims of the team, workgroup, committee or organization. The theoretical concept of leadership is only important to the manager in so far as it facilitates the achievement of these practical ends. The question thus arises as to whether our theories of leadership are adequate (in the sense of being able to explain all aspects of leadership situations and therefore offer guidance as to how to lead effectively). Certainly the more recent leadership theories have been primarily concerned with leadership effectiveness, though much of the early work was concerned with leader emergence. If we were to lose sight of this earlier work, we might also lose sight of the fact that not all leaders are managers and not all managers are leaders. It would appear that being a leader is only part of the armoury of management skill. It is therefore important to consider what it is about the job of management which enables the incumbent to assume a leadership position; do we have to invoke personality characteristics as part of the explanation of this process? This is just one of the many issues it is intended to raise in this chapter.

The above discussion raises the two issues – *what* leadership is, as opposed to *how* to lead. Management's concern, quite rightly, is in learning how to lead effectively and with that consideration in mind a later section of this chapter considers a model of leadership skill. However, it is not possible or feasible to develop competence or capability of a particular sort in an individual unless there is a concept underlying the training. It was thought important to devote space early on in this chapter to a discussion of what constitutes leadership and to outline some of the approaches which have been taken. The chapter commences with such a discussion, proceeds to an overview of various approaches and is completed by an analysis of leadership skills.

LEADERSHIP AS QUALITY OR PROCESS?

The idea that leadership is a quality or set of qualities which some people are born with and others are not is a myth which is very difficult to dispel. Indeed, the notion has enjoyed something of a revival with increased interest in 'inspirational' and 'charismatic' leadership, coupled with psychohistorical analysis of the biographies of 'great', 'world–class' (usually political) leaders (see, for example, Bass, 1985).

The reasons for this preoccupation with individual personality (and the need to make heroes of individuals) may have to do with our Western cultural heritage (Smith and Peterson, 1988), or the way we attribute leadership qualities to people in higher status or power positions, or possibly a combination of the two. A considerable number of reviews of leadership research have been carried out which have found no substantive evidence to demonstrate that a leader has a distinctive quality or set of qualities which are peculiar to him or her and which are not present in the followership or in others (House and Baetz, 1979; Yetton, 1984). However, if one takes into account the circumstances (for example, the nature of the job to be carried out and the skills and abilities needed to do so), this appears to put a different complexion on the matter. For instance, we saw in the preceding chapter that Belbin was able to describe the personal attributes and mental ability of a person assuming the role of chairperson or shaper and carrying it out effectively. But the point is that while such attributes were highly appropriate for managing that particular job, they were not particularly relevant to performing other tasks. House and Baetz (1979) have suggested that there are three 'invariant characteristics' of all leadership situations. They are *social skills, ability to influence others* and *ability to fulfil task requirements and organizational goals*. The focus has therefore shifted from personality *traits* to skills and abilities (what Mischel, 1968, refers to as *competencies* – see Chapter 1).

The Charismatic Leader

The popular interpretation of the leader with charisma is someone with a personal quality or gift that enables them to impress and influence. For Weber (1947) charisma was just one basis for leader authority. Once charisma is recognized by the followership it is a powerful force, commanding personal devotion and complete obedience. It is what Burns (1978) referred to as 'heroic leadership'. What this particular conception of leadership raises is the issue of 'power' (Burns, 1978; House, 1977). Such an analysis suggests that it is a relational concept and *not* a personality attribute.

> Leadership is an aspect of power. . . . Some define leadership as leaders making followers do what *followers* would not otherwise do, or as leaders making followers do what *leaders* want them to do; I define leadership as leaders inducing followers to act for certain goals that represent the values and the motivations – the wants and needs, the aspirations and expectations – *of both leaders and followers*. And the genius of leadership lies in the manner in which leaders see and act on their own and their followers' values and motivations. (Burns, 1978, pp. 18–19)

The leader–follower *relationship* for Burns is characterized by their interaction, which may be of two types: transactional or transformational. A transactional relationship suggests a relationship based on exchange. Such a relationship is part of a bargaining process and does not extend beyond this; there is no enduring purpose holding the parties together. This contrasts with a transformational relationship in which 'one or more persons may engage with others in such a way that leaders and followers raise one another to higher levels of motivation and morality' (Burns, 1978, p. 20).

Bass (1985) has taken Burns's distinction between transactional and transformational *political* leaders and extended this conceptual framework to organizational behaviour. Both theories incorporate a motivational framework: in the case of Burns it is Maslow's need hierarchy which is invoked, whereas Bass draws on Vroom's expectancy theory. Hence, Bass's *transactional* leader

- recognizes what it is we want to get from our work and tries to see that we get what we want if our performance warrants it;
- exchanges rewards and promises of reward for our effort;
- is responsive to our immediate self-interests if they can be met by our getting the work done (Bass, 1985, p. 11).

Tasks or goals are given, not questioned; subordinates are given confidence to perform the tasks at the required level and for their effort they are rewarded commensurately with their performance.

The *transformational* leader, on the other hand, is inspirational: he or she raises awareness of issues of consequence, the fulfilment of which transcends individual self-interest and is for the group, the organization or society.

This heightening of awareness requires a leader with vision, self-confidence, and inner strength to argue successfully for what he (or she) sees is right or good, not for what is popular or is acceptable according to the established wisdom of the time (Bass, 1985, p. 17).

A key characteristic of transformational leaders is that they motivate people to do more than they originally expected to do. This, according to Bass, is done in any one of three interrelated ways:

- by raising our level of awareness, our level of consciousness about the importance and value of designated outcomes, and ways of reaching them;
- by getting us to transcend our own self-interest for the sake of the team, organization, or larger polity;
- by altering our need level on Maslow's (or Alderfer's) hierarchy or expanding our portfolio of needs and wants (Bass, 1985, p. 20).

This analysis differs from that of Burns (1978) in four ways:

1. it emphasizes the expansion of followers' needs and wants;
2. it recognizes that a transforming leader may not serve society's or the followership's best interests;
3. while Burns saw transactional and transformational leadership at different ends of a spectrum, Bass has put forward the view that leaders may exhibit a variety of patterns of leader behaviour, and it is the proportions which determine how they are viewed;
4. it focuses upon the individual personality of the leader possibly to the extent of losing the emphasis which Burns placed on the leader–follower relationship and the pursuit of jointly held goals.

Bass (1985) developed a questionnaire for the purposes of assessing leader type as judged by subordinates. Factor analysis of the results revealed five factors. They were: charismatic leadership, contingent reward, individualized consideration, management-by-exception and intellectual stimulation. Bass also tested for 'extra effort by subordinates beyond expectations', 'inspirational leadership' and 'active–proactive' versus 'passive–reactive' leadership. The analysis suggested that *transactional* leadership is characterized by the factors of contingent reward and management-by-exception. The *transformational* leader, on the other hand, is characterized by the factors of charisma, individualized consideration and intellectual stimulation. Followers of transformational leaders wish to emulate their leader. They place a great deal of trust and confidence in the vision and values espoused by the leader, and typically develop intense emotional feelings towards him or her.

Bass *et al.* (1987) point out that this model of transforming leadership differs from other conceptualizations of charismatic leadership (for example, that of House 1977). This is in respect of the two additional factors of *individualized* consideration and intellectual stimulation. Transforming leaders pay attention to the individual subordinate, understanding and sharing their concerns and developmental needs. Further, they provide intellectual stimulation by enabling subordinates to think about old problems in new ways, to question and consider alternatives and to solve problems on their own.

For Burns and for Bass the charismatic leader is a model whom the followership emulate. Behaviour of this type of leader is said to cascade outwards to other lower echelons of management (Bass *et al.*, 1987). Tichy and Ulrich (1984) have challenged this view. They suggest that the charismatic/transforming leader presents the followership with a vision which they attempt to implement. Thus, rather than modelling their leader, they exhibit behaviours that support the practical implementation of their leader's vision.

The implications of this analysis are extremely interesting. There are several issues which need to be considered. Many of the behaviours identified by Bass might be construed as skills or competent ways by which the leader–manager may effectively manage his or her followership. A second observation is that this search for the characteristics of the charismatic leader has something in common with the Peters and Waterman approach in *In Search of Excellence*. There is implicitly at least a re-emergence of the 'One Best Way to Manage' syndrome. Thirdly, there is also a very important issue of personal values and of ethics which Bass addresses rather more forcibly than does Burns. The value/belief structure of the leader and the extent to which the followership find it acceptable and are prepared to collude with their leader is particularly apposite, given recent company scandals (for example, the Guinness affair and the more recent collapse of the Robert Maxwell empire).

A fourth consideration raises once more the issue of context: the level at which the leader–manager is operating, i.e. the size of organization and its structure. While Burns was largely thinking about political leaders, Bass was considering leaders of national or even world standing, and Tichy of chief executives of multinational corporations (see Tichy and Devanna, 1986). Further, it is worth reflecting for a moment on the extent to which these models might be in accord with models of entrepreneurial behaviour.

Recent research by the author (Chell *et al.*, 1991) suggests that, within the field of small to medium-sized owner-managed businesses, there are several types of business owner. These they term 'entrepreneurs', 'quasi-entrepreneurs', 'administrators' and 'caretakers'. It may be posited that it is the entrepreneurs and the quasi-entrepreneurs (to a lesser extent) whose style may be characterized as predominantly 'transforming', whereas the caretakers, and to a large extent the administrators, exhibit behaviours not untypical of the transactional type of leader. However, Chell *et al.* (1991) also emphasize that all business owners exhibit a mix of behaviours and that it is the predominance of one set of behaviours over another which provides evidence for the inclusion of a business owner into a particular category.

In conclusion, the issue of the relationship between personality and leadership remains open. Early studies may not have taken sufficient account of context; methodologies have become more sophisticated, as have the tools of analysis. Furthermore, the theoretical perspectives through which questions of this kind are approached have been subjected to considerable critical scrutiny. It is clear that one methodological problem is that of categorization: how these behaviours which are observed in leaders and managers are categorized, what behaviours are included or excluded from the analysis, and how the behavioural set or profile is then labelled. Moreover, we only know *how* people behave *in situations*, so any link between personality and leadership must necessarily be contingent. Associated with *effective performance* is another set of questions. For example, is the personality and hence the behavioural repertoire of the individual leader-manager fixed and immutable, or can people be trained to develop their skills of leadership? The answer to this question is clearly complex, and turns in part on whether a trait or social skills basis is assumed to be fundamental to leadership effectiveness.

LEADERSHIP STYLE

The preceding discussion raises but does not resolve the issue of the distinction between leadership as a personality trait and leadership as a behavioural mode or style. The Bass personality inventory required subordinates to rate the *behaviour* of their superiors and, after factor analysis, an underlying structure of leadership personality was described.

The work which has focused upon leader behaviour, such as that of Bales (1950), has identified two distinct role-related, behavioural characteristics of *emergent* leaders: task orientation and socio-emotional leader behaviour. Bales (1970) subsequently attempted to relate observed behavioural profiles to personality. The sociological studies by Bales' contemporaries tended to confirm these two broad dimensions. However, these studies of newly formed groups and the observation of emergent leaders gave way to another set of influential research, the Ohio State University Studies of leader behaviour.

1 Ohio State Studies

An influential body of work was carried out by Hemphill and his associates at the Ohio State University (Hemphill and Coons, 1957). The interdisciplinary team which carried out this extensive programme of research devised a measuring instrument – the 'leader behaviour description questionnaire' (LBDQ), which comprised 130 items. It was administered to 300 members of aircrews who were required to use it in order to describe the behaviour of their leaders/superiors (Halpin and Winer, 1957). Factor analysis of the results yielded four factors, of which *consideration* and *initiating structure* were revealed to be the most significant.

Consideration reflects the extent to which the leader shows consideration to subordinates. This means that job relations are characterized by mutual trust, respect for subordinates' ideas and regard for their feelings. He or she will show a readiness to explain actions and a willingness to listen to subordinates and allow them to participate in decision-making.

Initiating Structure refers to the extent to which leaders are likely to define and structure their role and that of their subordinates in the search for goal attainment. Typical behaviour includes attempts to organize work, work relationships and goals. The leader characterized as high on initiating structure assigns group members to particular tasks, expects workers to attain and maintain particular standards and emphasizes the need to meet deadlines.

Numerous empirical studies using the LBDQ and a later variant – the LBDQ-X11, devised by Stogdill (1963) – were undertaken. There are many critical reviews of this work and a useful overview can be found in Bryman (1986). When considering the findings of the field research, the fundamental idea that the leadership dimensions of *consideration* and *initiating structure* were *independent* dimensions was not demonstrated. On the contrary, several studies indicated that these dimensions are correlated. Also, attempts to discover the relationship between leadership style and various performance outcomes showed it to be complex. For example, Halpin and Winer (1957) found that *consideration* was positively related to satisfaction, but negatively related to various measures of effectiveness. A study by Fleishman *et al.* (1955) suggested that leaders high on *consideration* were preferred, but that they were not necesarily regarded as being as effective as those leaders who emphasized the structuring of work activities. Yet a study by Halpin (1957) suggested that leaders exhibiting both *consideration* and *initiating structure* were the most effective. It would seem, in retrospect, that an important issue is what outcome measure was being taken. For example, where the outcomes turnover and grievances were considered, Fleishman and Harris (1962) demonstrated a *negative* curvilinear relationship with *consideration* and a *positive* curvilinear relationship with *initiating structure*. As Bryman comments,

> Such findings are crucial, for they imply that at particular sections of the relationship neither consideration nor initiating structure make much difference to observed variation in either of the outcome measures, grievance rates and turnover. (Bryman, 1986, p. 46)

Korman (1966) has carried out an extensive review of the studies which examined the relationship between *consideration* and *initiating structure* and various outcome measures. The review showed wide discrepancies between different studies and raised two issues. Firstly, given that putative leaders were the focus of the analysis, was leadership actually being measured? Secondly, if it was the case that leadership was being measured, is leadership *per se* a key predictor of the outcomes identified?

Several reviewers have noted that the Ohio Studies failed to include situational variables in their analyses and that such factors would have helped explain many of the discrepant findings (see, for example, Kerr *et al.*, 1974). In particular, the path–goal approach has attempted to build upon the Ohio approach by including contextual variables in the analysis (see later section).

A further criticism of the Ohio Studies is the assumed direction of causality. The assumption was made that a particular leadership style would result in or 'cause' particular outcomes. As the studies undertaken were correlational, there was little evidence to substantiate this assumption. On the contrary, it could well be argued that purported 'outcomes' like group performance, satisfaction, climate, etc., are instrumental in determining the nature of the leadership style. Clearly, the direction of causality is crucial for, if leadership style *is* an outcome, it is more likely to be a behavioural reaction to circumstances than an invariant leadership characteristic inherent in the individual.

On the whole, the focus of attention by the Ohio State researchers and other organizational psychologists has been on formally designated leaders, leaving the study of the informal organization and that of informal leadership to the sociologists. This has not helped elucidate the concept of leadership, and may have contributed to a blurring of the distinction between leadership behaviour and management.

There are two further interesting features of the methodology adopted in the Ohio Studies research programme. They concern the group unit of analysis and the data comprised the perceptions of subordinates of their putative leader's behaviour. A potential problem lay in difference of perception between these subordinates and the tendency of researchers to average the responses to produce a group-level description. This method would most certainly mask any important variations in leader behaviour towards individual subordinates. Further, these studies are not based on the observation of actual behaviour, but on ratings made on the basis of recall, etc. Implicit theories of personality and of leadership suggest that people carry around with them unspoken assumptions about the nature of leadership. This raises the question whether questionnaire approaches, like that of the Ohio Studies (and presumably, that of Bass (1985) – see previous section), are based on subordinate depictions of a particular leader or reflect broad, implicit categorizations of leaders (Bryman, 1986).

The Ohio State University studies represent just one extensive research programme with the explicit objective of focusing upon leadership style. Space precludes the possibility of elaboration of other purportedly similar approaches, such as the Michigan Studies. However, a notable feature of such approaches is the emphasis placed upon two dimensions of leader behaviour, variously labelled. For example, 'employee centredness' and 'production centredness' were the labels used by the Michigan Studies researchers. In a later programme of work which appears to have been heavily influenced, at least initially, by the Ohio Studies, Blake and Mouton distinguish between what they term 'concerns' for people and for production. This work led to the development of a normative model which has been extensively used for management training purposes, particularly in an organization development context.

2 The Managerial Grid

The Managerial Grid concept is based on the idea that leadership behaviour is the result of a conflict between two opposing forces within the individual: a *concern for people* and a *concern for production* (Blake and Mouton, 1964). There are degrees to which a leader will exhibit either concern. If these concerns are thought of as dimensions, with nine gradations from 1, a low concern, through to 9, a high concern, then it is possible to depict the variations in leadership style on a two-dimensional grid (see Figure 6.1).

Concern for production may be revealed at an executive level by its policy level decision-making for increased growth, innovativeness or new product development; at a middle management level, in terms of production targets being met, quality being maintained and operations being efficient; and at a foreman level, of keeping to schedule, good timekeeping and standard of workmanship. Concern for people assumes that people are important and is revealed by such behaviours as: demonstrating trust-worthiness and gaining subordinates' respect; being concerned that work-ing conditions are satisfactory; listening to subordinates' complaints and grievances, and offering support, advice and understanding.

Relating these two dimensions of leadership style gives five main *orientations*:

Impoverished management (1, 1) – such a leader does the minimum required to remain within the organization on both production and people dimensions. Typically, he or she shows no initiative, questions little and goes along with what he or she is told, avoids expressing an opinion or taking sides, avoids conflict, lets others take decisions and come to terms with whatever happens, and avoids giving any feedback.

Organization Management (5, 5) – such a leader puts up an adequate performance, balancing the necessity of getting work out with maintaining morale at a satisfactory level. Typically, he or she will 'set a steady pace'; take things more or less at face value, checking only where discrepancies appear; try to meet others half way and find a 'reasonable position' when-ever it is necessary to resolve conflict; attempt to make decisions which others will find acceptable; and give informal or indirect feedback in order to get improvements in performance.

Country Club management (1, 9) – such a leader combines a low con-cern for production with a maximum concern for people; attention is focused upon satisfying relationships which leads to a comfortable, friendly atmosphere and work tempo. Typically, he or she helps and supports others, looks for evidence that suggests all is well, avoids challenging others and will embrace their ideas and opinions, avoids conflict, makes decisions

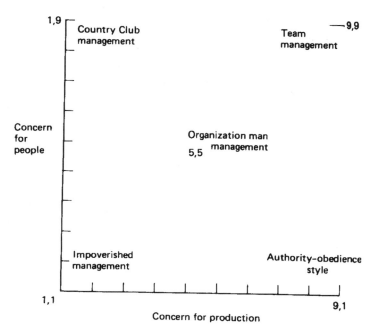

FIGURE 6.1   The managerial grid

SOURCE   R. R. Blake and J. S. Mouton (1964) *The Managerial Grid: Key Orientations for Achieving Production Through People* (Houston: Gulf).

designed to maintain good relations, and offers praise and positive feedback.

Authority–Obedience Style (9, 1) – such a leader combines a high concern for production with a low concern for people. He or she concentrates on maximizing production by exercising power and authority, and achieving control over people by dictating what they should do and how they should do it. Typically he or she will: 'drive him- or herself and others', investigate situations to ensure control and that others are not making mistakes, defend own ideas and opinions, even though it may mean rejecting those of others, deal with conflict by either trying to cut it off or winning own position, make own decisions and be rarely influenced by others, and not be afraid to pinpoint other people's weaknesses and failures.

Team Management (9, 9) – such a leader integrates high production and people concerns by a goal-centred team approach which maximizes commitment and involvement through participation. Typically he or she will exert effort and join in enthusiastically, will listen to other people's ideas and opinions and will be constantly reviewing the soundness of own and other people's positions. He or she believes in expressing concerns and convictions, tries to resolve conflict by seeking out the underlying causes, places high value on making sound decisions and to that end seeks understanding and agreement, and encourages two-way feedback to strengthen operations.

The managerial grid is underpinned by a conceptual framework through which it is possible to depict and describe different types of leader behaviour. In addition to this it is clearly prescriptive; the manager is encouraged to identify his or her own leadership style and is then given guidance as to how it can be modified. This guidance is necessarily of a generalized kind, but the idea is to develop managers with leadership abilities akin to those of the 9, 9 leader. However, the evidence that the grid approach actually works is mixed. There has tended to be a lack of rigour in carrying out evaluations of a number of training programmes which have utilized the managerial grid. A further problem with the approach is that it suggests there is 'one best way to manage'.

3   Binary or Ternary Styles?

Alastair Mant (1983) has suggested that there are two basic leadership styles: *binary* and *ternary*. Mant suggests that a fundamental characteristic of leadership is *how* people attain those positions of power, high office and so on. The binary and ternary styles were intended to represent the structure of thought, not personality per se. In the binary mode, 'the individual is swamped, despite himself, by the interpersonal aspect of relationships. In this mode the main thing is to control, dominate or seduce the Other in the interests of personal survival' (Mant, 1983, p. 4). 'In [the ternary] mode interpersonal power is regulated, some of the time anyway, by some "third corner" – an institution, a purpose or an idea. People who think in this way value the 'third corner', see it as what life is about. Their instinct is to ask not, "Shall I win?" but rather, "What's it for?" ' (Mant, 1983, p. 5).

The binary mode is characterized by the urge to survive 'the rat race' and keep 'on top'; the manipulation of other people as objects in the interest of power; striking deals and adversarial relationships. The binary mode is *transactional*; people who engage in this leadership style are often termed *operators* or *'wheeler-dealers'*. They are often thought of as cunning or clever, but not necessarily intelligent. They make themselves highly visible and create a reputation for themselves which exceeds their output. They are usually ambitious and often single-mindedly so; they are dealers in ambiguity, and may also be mendacious and stupid. Such people arouse strong feelings in others; some may admire them for their skill and cunning, while others may despise or dislike them for what they see as their less desirable qualities. Further it is suggested that people who operate in this way are more likely to attain positions of power than are people who think in a ternary sort of way.

Implicit in Mant's analysis is a value judgement; that the ternary mode is the more desirable, more worthy mode of operating *and*, in the long run, a more effective one. The binary mode is more likely to develop into flawed leadership because of the dependency on striking effective deals, and the susceptibility to mildly, if not blatantly, corrupt practice. In contrast to this, the ternary mode is *transformational* in nature, that is, it is about reform, or changing situations. The ternary mind thinks at a higher level of abstraction about the relationship and the institutional context of that relationship; he or she is therefore less dependent upon the interpersonal nature of the relationship between Self and Other, and is able to invoke other ideas, or institutional aspects outside the relationship in order to regulate it. In this sense, the leader is more detached, able to be firm but fair in his or her dealings with people. Characteristically, he or she is able to see the situation *as a situation* and deal with it.

Implicit in this examination of styles of leadership appears to be a moral (or at least prescriptive) dimension of how the leader *should* or *should not* behave. The binary or ternary patterns of leadership invoke different sets of values.

The ternary mode is not necessarily the more effective leadership style. The choice of styles depends on what length management are prepared to go to in order to achieve the results they want, and whether the costs incurred render the exercise worth it: determination to win may be perceived in quite a different way by employees, the trade unions and outsiders to the situation. In politics, the difference between ternary and binary modes is exemplified by the difference between statesmanship and scoring political points off the Opposition. In education, it is the difference between making deals to further a person's own private ends, but never invoking the values and principles upon which the educational establishment was founded as a regulator of one's actions. In industry, banking or commerce, it is the manipulation of the system to advance a career for the express purpose of mutual support (striking a deal), rather than operating within the best interests of the company or institution.

Mant's interpretation of the two leadership styles is of interest, particularly given the Burns (1978) and the Bass (1985) models (see earlier section). Unlike the latter two theories, Mant places emphasis upon competitiveness at the individual level such that the way the competition is played out shapes the 'transactional' or 'transformational' relationship between the two parties – Self and Other. As is true of the Bass approach, this theory has social-psychological underpinnings. In common with the Burns and the Bass theories, Mant identifies an ethical dimension to leader behaviour which has been absent from much leadership theory hitherto.

The problems with the theory are conceptual and methodological. Firstly, it is at a germinal stage of development, and thus lacks the crisp conceptual clarification necessary to enable a reliable classification of the two types. Secondly, while Mant has supported his arguments by a wealth of anecdotal evidence from the literature, there is no systematic piece of empirical research to give greater credence to his theory. Such research would need to establish criteria for evaluating the effectiveness of the different modes, to examine whether it is indeed true that women tend towards a more ternary mode (as Mant claims), and to establish whether, in general, binary leaders are more likely to 'reach the top'.

CONTINGENCY APPROACHES

The inadequacies and equivocal nature of research on personality traits and behaviour as the basis for the prediction of leader *effectiveness* suggested the need to consider *systematically* the impact of situational factors upon leader and follower behaviour. The general contingency model is such that identifiable situational factors act as moderating or intervening variables in relation to leadership characteristics/style and consequent outcomes usually measured in terms of group performance. There are several different contingency theories of leadership. They each make different assumptions, place differential emphasis upon, for example, personality traits as opposed to leadership style. Yet in common, they assume that it is the leader who initiates action and thereby *acts upon* a group of subordinates. The ideas of interaction, of reciprocal influence, are not explored in the three most influential contingency theories outlined below.

1   The Contingency Model

The contingency model of leadership effectiveness developed by Fiedler (1967, 1977) was the earliest systematic attempt to develop a contingency approach to the study of leadership style. Fiedler distinguished between leaders whose main orientation was towards getting the task done and those whose primary orientation was towards maintaining smooth interpersonal relationships. He suggested further that such orientations were part of an individual's personality and as such exceedingly difficult to change. Thus, there were two options open if one was to optimize management potential: (a) match the leader to the situation which suited his or her style; or (b) change the situation to suit his or her style.

Fundamental to his theory are three different concepts: effectiveness, leadership style and the extent to which the situation provides the leader with control or influence (Fiedler, 1978), previously termed 'situational favourableness' (Fiedler, 1967).

By *effective* leadership, Fielder means that the leader's group performed well, or that it succeeded in comparison with other groups. In other words, leader effectiveness is based on group performance.

In Fiedler's earlier publications (Fiedler, 1967) *leadership style* was referred to as leadership-orientation and encompassed task and relationship orientation. While the same method – the 'least preferred co-worker questionnaire' (LPC) – was used to measure leadership style, the terminology changed significantly to that of measuring the leader's *motivational structure*.

The *LPC* is a simple, bipolar adjective scale. The respondent is required to think of all the persons whom he or she has ever known and then to describe the *one* person with whom it has been most difficult to work. A later version of the LPC questionnaire (Fiedler *et al.*, 1976) consists of eighteen bipolar adjectives (for example, pleasant–unpleasant, supportive–hostile, etc.) which follow a semantic differential format. An individual who describes the LPC in very negative, rejecting terms (a low *LPC* score is less than 57) is considered to be *task-motivated*. A person scoring 63 or above may be considered to be *relationship-motivated* in that they see their LPC in relatively favourable terms. For such a person, 'getting the job done is not everything'; such a leader distinguishes between the fact of their not being able to work together and the possibility that the LPC may be someone with whom they could get along on a personal basis.

A high LPC score does not necessarily imply that a leader will be considerate, nor does a low LPC score imply more structuring behaviour. Rather, leader behaviour is a product of the interaction between the LPC score and the degree to which the situation provides the leader with control and influence.

Thus, fundamental to Fiedler's concept of leadership is that of influence: the extent to which the leader can influence and control group members. This influence or rather the degree of such influence is affected by three situational factors: (a) leader–member relations, (b) task structure and

(c) position power. These factors are measured by means of three subscales. The leader–member relations dimension is the most important: leaders who enjoy the support and loyalty of group members can depend and rely upon them; they are sure that group members will do their best to comply with their wishes and directions. On the other hand, leaders who cannot count on their group are in a difficult position, needing to watch and instruct them far more frequently than might otherwise be necessary.

The leader's control over a group is also determined by the extent to which the task is structured:

> Leaders who have a blueprint or detailed operating instructions are assured of the support of their organization in directing the job. They very rarely get any arguments from subordinates as to the course the group should take. In contrast, when the task is unstructured, as is the case with typical committee assignments or research and development work, the control which leaders can exercise over the task and the group is considerably diluted. (Fiedler *et al.*, 1976, p. 63)

The third dimension which defines situational control is position power. Position power is the degree to which leaders are able to reward and punish, to recommend sanctions, or otherwise to enforce compliance of subordinates. Thus if leaders have the power to give or withold rewards then the more they can constructively use this aspect of their power the more influence they will have.

Dichotomizing these three variables in terms of good-or-poor leader–member relations, unstructured-or-structured tasks, high-or-low position power means that the leader's situational control (or situational favourableness) may be represented on an eight-point continuum (see Table 6.1).

Through his research, Fiedler found that task-motivated leaders were effective in situations which were highly favourable or highly unfavourable, whereas relationship-motivated employees were more effective in situations of moderate favourableness (see Table 6.1). Why should this be so? In a highly favourable situation, a well-liked leader of a bomber crew, for example, is in a position where he has a clear-cut task and the power to enforce his commands. He is therefore an extremely effective leader. In an emergency, he can get things done speedily and efficiently. Whereas, in training sessions, he can still get things done, but be more relaxed and good humoured (thus reinforcing the good subordinate relations), in the full knowledge that the primary goal of task accomplishment is being achieved. In a highly *un*favourable situation, the task-oriented leader is the most effective because, *at least*, he (or she) gets the job done.

TABLE 6.1 *Fiedler's contingency model of leadership effectiveness*

Category	Description of the situation			Example	Effective leadership style
	Leader–member relations	Task structure	Power position		
I	Good	Structured	Strong	Bomber crw	Task-oriented
II	Good	Structured	Weak	Basketball team	Task-oriented
III	Good	Unstructured	Strong	ROTC	Task-oriented
IV	Good	Unstructured	Weak	Board of directors of a cooperative	Relations-oriented
V	Poor	Structured	Strong	Anti-aircraft artillery crew	Relations-oriented
VI	Poor	Structured	Weak	Surveying team	Relations-oriented
VII	Poor	Unstructured	Strong	ROTC	Either
VIII	Poor	Unstructured	Weak	Management teams	Task-oriented

SOURCE   Adapted from F. E. Fiedler (1967) *A Theory of Leadership Effectiveness* (New York: McGraw-Hill), p. 37.

This is because such leaders ignore their lack of popularity. They decide, autocratically, what needs to be done and go ahead and do it whether or not they are carrying the rest of the team with them. (Where their position power is weak, as in category VIII, they may have little choice but to go on alone if necessary.) This is likely to be effective in that some members of the team will be influenced to join in and help their leader because they will see that something is being accomplished, even if they begrudge the way that it is being done. A relationship-motivated leader would be ineffectual in these circumstances essentially because he or she would find the poor member-relations and absence of any other supporting factor stressful. Time and energy would be spent on trying to improve relationships rather than getting the task done. At the end of the day such a leader is unlikely to achieve any of his or her goals. The relationship-motivated leader is most effective where leader–member relations are good, the task unstructured and position power is weak. An example of such a situation is that of leading an R & D team. Here leader–member relations would need to be based on mutual respect. Members of the team would regard themselves as colleagues and there is no sense in which a leader could effectively direct group members as to how they should organize their work and the pace at which they should go. A participative approach which showed consideration and respect for their views and achieved commitment would be effective.

The alternative to matching leader to situation is that of changing the situation to suit the leader (Fiedler *et al.*, 1976). This requires the leader to be able to diagnose the situation accurately, able to measure his or her own leadership-orientation and able to judge what needs to be done in order to change the situation. A leader may be able to change the situation (in the new broom sense), but he or she needs to be very aware of what they are trying to accomplish when *deliberately* doing things differently in order to achieve a particular end. Again, precisely how a situation might be changed is not well documented.

There are several unresolved issues which render Fiedler's theory highly controversial. An important one is what the LPC scale really means: any correspondence with the Ohio concepts of 'consideration' and 'initiating structure', it would seem, are extremely superficial (Bryman, 1986). Other possible explanations including the greater cognitive complexity of high-LPC persons or the existence of a 'motivational hierarchy' have also been found wanting (Larson and Rowland, 1974; Rice and Chemers, 1975). As Bryman points out, a fundamental problem in the interpretation of the LPC scale may be Fiedler's insistence that it measures leadership style. Yet it is used as a measure of personality, not of overt behaviour.

Not surprisingly, the validity of the contingency model has been called into question (Ashour, 1973), although Fiedler claims that there is considerable evidence to validate the theory (Fiedler, 1978). Many of the studies undertaken concentrate on only part of the model, suggesting support for some of the eight octants. However, there are several tests of the complete model (for example, Chemers and Skrzypeck, 1972; Graen *et al.*, 1971; Hosking, 1981; Vecchio, 1977). Even so, Vecchio suggests that his findings clearly disconfirm the theory, and Hosking points out that the correlations in many of the studies undertaken are small and do not reach statistical significance. On the other hand, Mitchell *et al.* (1970) have suggested that because of the wide sampling of behaviours, actors and settings the model has good external validity.

Clearly there is considerable equivocation about this theory. Attempts by Fiedler to apply his ideas using the concept of 'leader match' have been no less controversial. The central idea is that people could, through a process of self-development and the aid of a manual devised by Fiedler (Fiedler and Chemers, 1984), identify their leadership style and learn how to modify their situation, thus enhancing the effectiveness of their particular style. Once again, owing to the controversy surrounding the theoretical underpinnings of the contingency model, many researchers are sceptical about the leader match approach.

Fiedler has introduced a newer version of his theory which he refers to as 'cognitive resources theory' (Fiedler and Garcia, 1987). In this version an attempt is made to measure additionally the leader's intelligence. While some empirical support is evidenced, the criticisms of the old model are not addressed. Smith and Peterson (1988) conclude:

> The attempt to construct a model which clearly differentiates elements of leader and situation must therefore be judged not to have succeeded. Schreisheim and Kerr's (1977) 'obituary' for LPC research appears to have been warranted.

2   Path–Goal Theory

The path–goal theory of leadership effectiveness proposed by House (1971) builds upon the Ohio Studies (see above), the expectancy theory of motivation (see Chapter 3) and the 'path-goal' hypothesis of Georgopoulos (1957). House's stated objective was to reconcile some of the conflicting findings of the Ohio Studies' research. A further idea was to link leadership style to the motivation of subordinates. This link was considered achievable using the expectancy theory of motivation; that is, the leader's job was to ascertain what kinds of rewards subordinates value and which would, consequently, motivate them to perform their job well. Having established such a connection, the leader should (a) be able to reward employees' for their performance, and (b) make clear to them that they will obtain the rewards they desire if they do the job to the required standard. Thus, leaders have a motivational function to perform *vis-à-vis* their subordinates:

> the motivational functions of the leader consist of increasing personal pay-offs to subordinates for work-goal attainment, and making the path to these pay-offs easier to travel by clarifying it, reducing roadblocks and pitfalls, and increasing the opportunities for personal satisfaction *en route*. (House, 1971, p. 324)

People with different leadership styles will be able to offer different kinds of rewards. For example, a leader whose style is primarily one of consideration may offer praise, support, encouragement, security and respect as well as the usual type of *extrinsic* rewards – pay, bonuses, promotion, etc. A leader whose style is primarily one of initiating structure is likely to be much narrower in terms of the range of rewards he or she can offer. However, such a leader is better able to clarify the 'path' the subordinate has to take in order to obtain a reward.

House has developed the theory further into a contingency model. In particular he has looked at the effects of *environmental or situational variables* and *employee characteristics* on the effectiveness of leadership style. House has identified three environmental variables which help determine the leadership style subordinates prefer. They are (a) the nature of the task, (b) the organization's formal authority system and (c) the workgroup.

The *nature of the task* will determine what is an effective leadership style in a number of ways. For example, where a job is *non-routine*, a leader who concentrates first on clarifying what subordinates have to do is likely to be more effective. Where, on the other hand, a job is highly structured and routine, such behaviour by the leader would tend to be counterproductive, a source of irritation.

The *formal authority system* affects subordinates' preferences for different types of leadership style. For example, where a leader has a great deal of upward influence, supportive behaviour towards subordinates will be appreciated and motivating, by making them feel more secure and increasing their respect for their leader. Under such circumstances, subordinates will want to work out, or be told, what they have to do in order to win approval. A leader who can also reduce ambiguity in this respect will have a much more satisfied and contented workgroup.

The *workgroup*, as was explained in Chapter 4, can greatly affect workgroup performance and the style of leadership which is appropriate. In general, it would seem that the greater the interdependence required in the group in order to do the job, and the less developed teamwork norms, the closer the supervision required and the greater the need for path–goal clarification. Where the team lacks cohesion, but basically knows what to do, consideration and understanding by the leader will increase team spirit and lead to more effective performance.

House has also suggested that the *characteristics of the followers* are important in determining the appropriateness of the leader's style. For example, able subordinates who know what they have to do will not respond favourably to a leader who attempts to organize them. In addition, authoritarian subordinates respond differently to a participative style than do non-authoritarian subordinates. Research has demonstrated that authoritarian subordinates only enjoy participation with the leader when the task is non-routine, whereas non-authoritarian subordinates enjoy a participative style irrespective of task structure (Schuler, 1976).

Thus, path–goal theory does attempt some prescriptions about how leaders should behave towards their subordinates in different circumstances. It assumes that the leader is able to modify his or her style to suit the contingencies of the situation. However, there are a number of problems with the theory. The reliance of path–goal theory on the Ohio measures has meant that it tends to share the same problems (Bryman, 1986). Research has tended to be static, stereotyped and narrow in its focus. There has also been a lack of clear unequivocal evidence in support of the theory (Bryman, 1986; Smith and Peterson, 1988). The prediction that interest in this theory will wane appears to be being borne out in the literature.

3   The Rational Decision-making Model

Vroom and Yetton's model for effective management decision-making is a development of the work on problem solving carried out by Norman Maier (Vroom and Yetton, 1973; Maier, 1963, 1970). Basically, it is suggested that a leader has two concerns, the importance of the *quality* of the solution and its *acceptance* by subordinates. Quality solutions are often related to the technical nature of a problem, whether it be with respect to, say, an investment decision, an engineering problem or whatever. If this is the case, the leader/manager may be able to work out the solution or at least know which experts to consult. Other work-related problems may need to be acceptable to the team in order to be effectively implemented, as in the case of introducing new equipment, technological changes which affect job content or new safety regulations. Vroom and Yetton's model was developed to enable the leader/manager to decide when it is appropriate to use a particular leadership style to solve problems of the kind just described. Moreover, the leader was expected to be sufficiently flexible to be able to adapt his or her style to fit the demands of the situation.

The five leadership styles identified were based on different degrees of participation with subordinates. They are: (a) the leader makes the decision on his/her own; (b) the leader asks subordinates individually for information and then makes the decision on his or her own; (c) the leader shares the problem with subordinates individually, obtains their ideas and suggestions, and then makes a decision which may or may not reflect subordinates' influence; (d) the leader shares the problem with subordinates collectively, obtains their ideas and suggestions, and then makes a decision which again may or may not reflect their influence; and (e) the leader shares the problem with the group and they discuss possible alternative solutions until they reach a consensus, which will be the solution that the manager implements.

How can a leader know when to use either of these very different leadership styles? Vroom and Yetton suggest a series of questions which the leader should ask him or herself in order to determine the nature of the problem and the style appropriate to its resolution. For instance: *Is decision quality important? Do I have sufficient information to make a high-quality decision? Is the problem structured? Is acceptance by subordinates critical to the effective implementation?* etc. Depending upon the answer to questions such as these, a suitable style or styles are suggested. When there is more than one option open to the manager, then Vroom and Yetton suggest the following criteria for guidance between the 'feasible set of alternative decision styles':

1. When decisions must be made quickly or time must be saved, managers should choose authoritarian decision styles ('time-efficient' ones).
2. When managers wish to develop their subordinates' knowledge and decision-making skills, the more participative styles ('time investment') should be selected.

The rational decision-making model is thus a set of prescriptions designed to enable managers to decide what leadership style to adopt in order to optimize decision outcomes and performance. The evidence to test this model is sparse, but nevertheless does tend to support its predictions. Key studies, for example, have been carried out by Jago (1978; 1981), Jago and Vroom (1980), Heilmann *et al.* (1984), Field (1982) and Margerison and Glube (1979).

What the model offers is guidance as to when it is appropriate to engage different levels of participation in decision-making from autocratic to openly participative. Vroom (1984) has revised the model in order to attempt to reflect more closely the reality of decision situations. The number and nature of questions which a manager should ask him or herself in order to define the situation has been extended. For example, *how much prior information and ability do subordinates have? Is there a time constraint upon problem solution? How important is subordinate development? and How valuable is time in this situation?*

It has been suggested that the model is too complex for the busy manager to use in practice. However, the actual principles which underpin the model are very few and they are ones which will present little difficulty to most managers in assimilating. Moreover, the model appears to reflect the reality of most management situations in that all managers will want to consult over some issues and will believe it not unreasonable to take a decision on their own in some circumstances. However, some researchers go further and point out that this reflects a 'pro-management bias' (Smith and Peterson, 1988):

a manager working within the guidelines of the model would presumably need to explain to subordinates that it was not within the interests of the organization that they should participate in all decisions. (Smith and Peterson, 1988, p. 26)

It is nevertheless an empirical question as to whether subordinates from all sectors of industry and commerce would expect or prefer to participate in all decisions and how responsibility for those decisions might be dealt with. Pursuit of this line of inquiry opens up a number of avenues for further research.

The rational decision-making model indicates different styles of leadership and the need for flexibility and responsiveness to defined situational contingencies. By the same token this model is about how these situations should best be handled. Thus, a practical implication of the model is that for a manager to be really *effective* it is necessary for him or her to develop the following skills:

● Ability to diagnose situations accurately on the lines that the question prompts indicate.

- Ability to handle subordinates in face-to-face, consultative and participative situations.
- Ability to deliver, and be seen to deliver by subordinates, once a decision is reached and action is taken.

LEADERSHIP RECONSIDERED

Leadership research has followed particular paradigms – the trait, the behavioural, the contingency approaches – and yet each of these approaches has yielded few insights and considerable criticism. These approaches have one thing in common: they all adhere to the positivist, empiricist tradition (Dachler, 1988). The positivist tradition is based on a set of four key assumptions (Burrell and Morgan, 1979); they concern:

1. the basic ontological question of whether the 'reality' to be investigated is external to the individual;
2. the nature of knowledge: whether it is hard, real, tangible and 'knowable' in that sense, or more subjective, spiritual, based on experience and insight;
3. the view of human nature as either deterministic (that is conditioned by external circumstances) or voluntaristic (in which human beings are both creators of, and controllers of, their environment);
4. the way in which one investigates the social world. Thus, it is possible, on the one hand, to identify methodologies employed by social scientists which treat the social world as if it were the natural world, as being hard, real and external to the individual. The alternative methodologies place emphasis upon the interpretative processes involved in developing an understanding of human nature and the position of individuals in relation to their environment.

The approaches investigating leadership which have held centre stage have assumed the positivist stance, objectifying reality and assuming causal connections between variables. Progress for these social scientists is the support of hypotheses with data systematically collected in order to measure key variables, and the identification of new relationships between variables so that further elaboration of the theory can take place.

The alternative put forward by Dachler (1988) is the social construction paradigm (cf. Hampson's social constructivist approach to personality outlined in Chapter 1). There is no one objective reality awaiting discovery but multiple realities:

The issue is not that one constructed reality will ultimately prove to be the 'correct' or objective one, that exists apart from our values and preconceptions. The issue is to understand the way different leadership realities are constructed. (Dachler, 1988, p. 266)

Progress towards gaining insights into the leadership process by adopting this anti-positivist, nominalist approach, is made by understanding the socio-political processes, the value base and the culture of the leadership context. Thus different constructions may emerge and contribute to our understanding of a social order. Some of these social constructions will disappear more quickly than others 'as the patterns and substance of relationships in society or in some collectivity change' (Dachler, 1988, p. 266).

Understanding leadership does not progress to an ultimate and objective truth. Understanding leadership . . . is a continuous and unpredictable pattern of emerging constructions of realities. Through the emerging patterns of new reality constructions, the complexity of the social situations can be interpreted, reinterpreted, and found meaningful within given contexts. Alternatively, such complexity can be found useless or meaningless for the interpretations of a constructed social order. (Dachler, 1988, p. 266)

There are two crucial implications of Dachler's position: one is the ethical consideration of how social and organizational psychologists/ behaviourists transmit knowledge of their findings, and the other is how the questioning of the assumptions underlying a particular leadership theory casts doubt upon the practical ramifications of that research, for example, in terms of leadership skills training. The former issue emphasizes the considerable responsibility the social researcher has in transmitting the insights gained from their research. The latter issue – that of leadership skills training – will be dealt with in more detail in the ensuing section.

LEADERSHIP SKILLS

Hosking and Morley (1988) criticize previous approaches to social skills analysis on the grounds that none gives a systematic account of the concept of skill which would serve to integrate relations between leadership and organization.

Hosking and Morley have put forward a general model of the process of leadership where leaders are engaged in complex decision-making in organizations. In their general model leaders are defined as *those people who are both perceived, and expected, to make consistent, influential contributions to the process of complex decision-making.* The core process of complex decision-making includes such activities as information search, interpretation, influence and choice. The structuring of these processes is through *the knowledge base, networking,* and *problem identification.*

There are different kinds of knowledge: skilled leadership depends upon skilled perception and ultimately the management of meaning. In effect leaders 'promote persuasive scripts that help others to interpret their actions, and events, in relation to the "core values" of their social order, (Hosking and Morley, 1988, p. 97). Skilled leaders make sense of events and activities which may lead to change in the status quo – the well-understood social order. These changes may be perceived as threats or opportunities; they may throw up dilemmas to be resolved. The skilled leader, they suggest, is the individual who can facilitate decision-making by removing ambiguity, clarifying issues and setting the pace at which decisions are made and the resultant negotiated social order re-established.

The ability to 'network' is a crucial leadership skill. Most decision situations are characterized by 'mixed evidence'. Leaders play a critical role in moving around and gathering information and intelligence concerning the multiple perspectives on a particular issue of concern. Leaders thus not only influence others in this process, but participate in the sociopolitical process of ultimately placing a particular interpretation on those events.

A skilled leader has three types of problem to resolve: problem identification, development and selection. A leader must be able to identify *the* problem – that is, know what is going on. He or she must be able to generate alternative solutions and be a dominant influence in the 'selection' of one or other solution.

It is clear that all three facets – knowledge bases, networking and the handling of core problems – are interrelated. Further, they are interrelated in relation to the dominant values and interests of a group. Skilful leaders make choices in respect of the handling of information, the resolution of problems and the networking process in order to protect those dominant values and interests.

The advantage of the Hosking–Morley model of leadership skills is that it is a general model which is intended to be applicable to those individuals assuming leadership behaviours as described, whatever their position or level within an organization or other social context. Thus leadership behaviours are seen to be analytically and actually distinct from managerial behaviour and do not derive from a person's ascribed status. The model does not, of course, describe the micro-detail of effective leader behaviour in specified contexts. These would need to be developed in the course of implementation of the model for particular training purposes. Wright and Taylor (1984), for example, put forward detailed advice on specific leadership issues, such as problem diagnosis, the interpretation, and handling, of information and the adoption of a particular style of handling subordinates skilfully. Drummond (1991a) outlines for managers the practicalities of complex decision-making, pointing up many of the social and political difficulties of doing this effectively. What these practical guides do is describe the leadership process as one of organizing; in so far as the Hosking–Morley model also indicates the centrality of this concept to the process of leadership, the connection between leadership and organization as a social psychological process is made.

SUMMARY

——————— Leadership research is fundamental to organizational behaviour. Theoretical developments have advanced from the notion of leadership as a quality of trait, a behavioural style or a variable mode determined by an identifiable set of contingencies.

——————— Although little evidence has been adduced to support the view that leadership is primarily about the personality of individuals, there has been a revival of interest in the idea of charismatic leadership. In this regard the contrast has been made between so-called 'transactional' and 'transformational' leaders.

——————— An alternative avenue of research pursued the idea that leadership is based upon a set of behavioural characteristics which shape a leader's *style*. An influential body of work based at the Ohio State University distinguished between two styles – 'consideration' and 'initiating structure'. This work has been heavily criticized.

——————— Much of the research on leadership has dichotomized the behaviour style of the leader. The work of Blake and Mouton distinguished between two leader orientations – 'concern for people' and 'concern for production'. The idea was to develop managers with a high concern for, and capability to handle, both aspects.

——————— Mant has suggested that there are two leadership styles which are based on the individual's mode of thinking about (and consequently handling), situations. The *binary* style is characterized by power relationships – making deals and 'keeping on top'.

The *ternary* style is based on an ability to think beyond the self-interested concerns of the parties involved; to invoke principles outside the relationship in order to regulate it. These ideas are interesting, not least because they bring to the fore the socio-political dimension of leader behaviour, and raise questions about the value-basis and ethical aspects of leader behaviour. However, as yet these ideas are largely untested.

—————— The leadership style approaches all emphasize a behavioural mode of operating which the individual can develop. However, their drawback is that they adhere fundamentally to the principle that there is 'one best way' to achieve leadership effectiveness. The contingency models, in contrast, suggest that it all depends upon the situation that the leader finds him or herself in as to whether one behavioural mode is more effective than another.

—————— Each contingency model has particular features. Fiedler has suggested that the contrasting styles of task- and relationship-orientation of a leader are based upon fundamental aspects of personality. As such it is sugggested that it may be easier to manipulate the situation than to attempt to change the individual.

—————— The 'path–goal' approach of House builds upon the Ohio Studies research and expectancy theory of motivation. The job of leading entails ascertaining what kinds of rewards subordinates value and would motivate them to perform their job well. The leader should be able to reward employees for their performance and make clear that they will obtain those rewards if they perform the job to the required standard. The precise style the leader adopts in handling subordinates will depend on various contingencies including the nature of the task, the formal authority system and the characteristics of the workgroup.

—————— The 'rational decision-making' model of Vroom and Yetton suggests that a leader should vary his or her style from autocratic to participative, depending upon the nature of the problem to be solved, the degree of information at his or her disposal, the sources of that information, whether a quality solution is required and/or whether acceptance by subordinates is critical. Reviews of this model are relatively favourable, although it has been criticized on the grounds of its complexity and pro-management bias. It has clear implications for leader behaviour in terms of the need for flexibility and responsiveness and the development of key interpersonal and diagnostic skills.

A degree of disillusionment with prior theoretical approaches to leadership heralded the need to take stock and reappraise the very assumptions underpinning those approaches. An alternative to positivism has been put forward by Dachler in the form of a social construction paradigm. This places emphasis on gaining an understanding of the social context and the different social constructions of leadership which emerge in these contexts and which give insights into the social order that regulates behaviour.

Hosking and Morley have put forward a general model of the leadership process, which, they argue, can be developed to form the basis of a systematic approach to leadership skills training. Leaders, they argue, are engaged in complex decision-making and as such they need to be able to handle information, network and identify the nature of the problems confronting them. A leader also needs to be able to manage the meaning of the information at his or her disposal and so exert influence over others. Skilled leaders can, moreover, engage the core values of the group and so re-establish social order.

7   What are Organizations?

An organization is the rational coordination of the activities of a number of people for the achievement of some common explicit purpose or goal, through division of labour and function, and through a hierarchy of authority and responsibility. (Schein, 1980, p. 15)

An organization is a collection of interacting and interdependent individuals who work toward common goals and whose relationships are determined according to a certain structure. (Duncan, 1981)

An organization is a relatively enduring social system which is purposive and hierarchical. (Mansfield, 1984)

What do these definitions have in common and what do they tell us about the modern concept of an organization?

First of all, they suggest that organizations are shaped by the activities of people whose behaviours are geared towards the achievement of a goal or goals; these may or may not be shared in common (see the later section on contingency theory). Secondly, implicit or explicit in the concept of organization is the idea of *structure or ordered activity*: activities are coordinated, there may be a division of labour, and relationships are shaped into a hierarchy according to people's authority and their responsibilities. However, as Mansfield points out, organizations are not people; they are a theoretical abstraction. While senior management may be largely responsible for shaping organizational goals, organizational goals are conceptually distinct from those of any single individual manager's goals.

Indeed, it is not unusual for there to be a large measure of disagreement as to what the organization's goals actually are! This leads to a further refinement of the concept of goals, formally defined goals or *charter* goals; and *operational* goals (Perrow, 1961). Charter goals tend to be written in very general terms, laying down the objects of the institution but not how these should be arrived at or achieved, while operational goals are the goals set by members of the organization with the intention of achieving what they perceive to be the organization's goals. Thus, for example, the formal charter of a charitable trust may be couched in such general terms as, for instance, that it is established to alleviate the problems of the sick and needy. It is then up to the trustees to determine how it should act in order to best fulfil the spirit and intent behind this charter (see Table 7.1). Table 7.1 summarizes the nature of organizational goals on five dimensions. In a large, complex organization the levels may consist of several tiers between organization and workgroup. Secondly, the degree of formality tends to vary according to hierarchical level; divisions, departments or sections tend to have formal functions to perform, whereas the workgroup tends to be sufficiently small to fulfil employees' social needs. Moreover, it is at this level that the broadly based organizational objectives are operationalized, that is, translated into specific tasks which can be performed. Individual managers and operatives have their own formally specified task functions to perform – though, in addition, they may well have their own personal or non-formal goals to which they aspire. In essence, it is the function of line management to translate and interpret higher order goals into a series of tasks whose efficient performance will result in the fulfilment of those goals.

There are many different kinds of organization within the industrial, commercial, banking, educational and medical spheres. While the objective of a firm in a particular industry may be to produce widgets efficiently, that of a traditional university is to pursue and disseminate knowledge. This begs the question *how* such diverse objects may be operationalized at lower management and grass roots levels – how standards are to be applied and maintained; how performance is to be measured (if indeed it can be); and the extent to which the organization is responsive to its environment.

Furthermore, as has already been indicated, organizations are differentiated into levels or hierarchy. The precise number of such levels will vary, some organizations being described as being relatively 'flat' and others relatively 'tall'. A 'tall' organization is said to have *high vertical differentiation*, whereas 'flat' organizations are said to have *low vertical differentiation*. This aspect of structure, however, carries with it yet a further implication – that of the command of authority and responsibility. In general terms, the 'higher' a person's position in the hierarchy, the greater his or her authority to act and command others and the greater his or her responsibility for those actions and their consequences. Paradoxically, greater seniority does not necessarily equate with more power (Pettigrew, 1973). Management can occur only with the consent of the workforce, as is frequently demonstrated by the countervailing forces of the trades unions.

Organizations may also be said to be differentiated *horizontally*. The extent of this is indicative of the extensiveness of task specialization across the organization. The fact of differentiation poses a problem of *integration*. *Vertical* integration concerns coordination and control within the hierarchy.

TABLE 7.1 *Characteristics of organizational goals at different hierarchical levels*

Hierarchical level	Degree formality	Generality/ specificity	Time span	Goals
Organization	Formal	General (charter)	Timeless/ Long-term	To produce those goods and/or services for which the undertaking was established; to make a sound return on investments; to maintain standards of excellence in performance, etc.
Division	Formal	General	Timeless Long-term	To optimise the performance of the division; to maintain its autonomous decentralized position within organizational decision-making process
Department/ section	Formal	General/specific/ operational	Medium-term	To produce widgets efficiently and cheaply
Workgroup	Formal Informal	General/specific/ operational	Medium- / short-term	To maximise productivity and performance; to fulfil members' social needs; to maintain morale and worker satisfaction
Individual	Formal Non-formal Personal	General/specific/ operational	Short- / medium-term	To run a 'tight ship'; to be one of the lads; to maximise one's earnings etc.

How this is exercised is apparent in communication flows, leadership and management style, expressions of power and authority. *Horizontal* integration concerns coordination and control between functions and departments. This raises the issue of how the potential conflicts and frictions between such subgroupings are managed.

Thus, from a behavioural perspective, organizations may be thought of as patterned activities which are coordinated and integrated. These activities tend to form a cycle; they endure for a particular length of time and then tend to be repeated. This constancy of behaviour makes organizations recognizable for what they are and what they are aiming to achieve (Blackler and Shimmin, 1984). Occasionally, changes in this pattern occur, and the study of organizations is to understand the reasons why, and the processes by which, such changes arose. Further, these recognizable patterns of behaviour are associated with particular tasks or functions, that is, in terms of 'roles' which must be fulfilled in order to achieve the organization's goals. How the performance of these tasks is done will vary, depending upon the skills and abilities of the role incumbent. Indeed, the extent to which the performance of the task requires the performance of routine behaviours will also vary. Even senior managers with non-routine jobs may develop various rituals in order to add some structure and some semblance of routine to their day. Further, organizations must be understood in relation to what it is they are there to do – the work they are there to perform:

effective organization is a function of the work to be done and the resources and techniques available to do it. Thus changes in methods of production bring about changes in the number of work roles, in the distribution of work between roles and in their relationship one to another. Failure to make explicit acknowledgement of this relationship between work and organization gives rise to non-valid assumptions, for example, that optimum organization is a function of the personalities involved, that it is a matter connected with the personal style and arbitrary decision of the chief executive, that there are choices between centralized and decentralized types of organization, etc. (Brown, 1960, p. 42)

Finally, if we distinguish between the organization theorist's perspective on organizations and that of the psychologist, we will see that the psychologist does not usually view the organization in terms of formal, rational, planned activities to achieve specific objectives (Blackler and Shimmin, 1984). Rather, psychologists are concerned with (a) the implications of organizational structure for behaviour within organizations, (b) the nature of informal activity within organizations and its relation to formal requirements, (c) how people's needs are satisfied within organizations, (d) how decisions are arrived at and actions executed and (e) the effects of work and organization upon the individual.

ORGANIZATIONAL STRUCTURES

There are three basic concepts which enable one to describe organizational structure. They are (a) the organizational chart, (b) the role occupied or position within the structure and (c) the division of labour (or specialization). Most people are familiar with the idea of an organizational chart. It depicts in a formal way the functional relationships within the organization on a horizontal and vertical plane. A schematic diagram of such a chart is given in Figure 7.1. The vertical dimension depicts the chain of command – the authority or superior-subordinate relations. The horizontal dimension depicts the functional divisions, for example, sales, production, R & D departments, etc. This is the formal or *manifest* situation (Brown, 1960). In practice, the interactions between role occupants may not work out quite like this.

The term *role* is descriptive of the part to be played within the organization in order to fulfil a particular set of task requirements (associated with the role) or a particular function. Roles describe specific forms of behaviour associated with given tasks; they develop originally from task requirements. In their pure or organizational form, roles are standardized patterns of behaviour required of all persons playing a part in a given functional relationship, regardless of personal wishes or interpersonal obligations irrelevant to the functional relationship (Katz and Kahn, 1966, p. 37).

Problems arise when people fail to have a clear conception of what their role is or entails, and when other people's expectations of them are different from their own (Kahn *et al.*, 1964). The implications of this role ambiguity or lack of clear role definition are (a) inappropriate behaviours and actions will be wrongly associated with the role; (b) decisions may be taken by the wrong people; and (c) conflict both within and between role occupants may arise. Typical manifestations of these problems may be that someone fails to carry out a particular task or procedure, that someone may give orders to another occupying a role of equivalent status or that someone may take it upon themselves to take a decision without consulting their 'boss'.

Brown (1960) has a useful set of concepts for analysing such situations. They are:

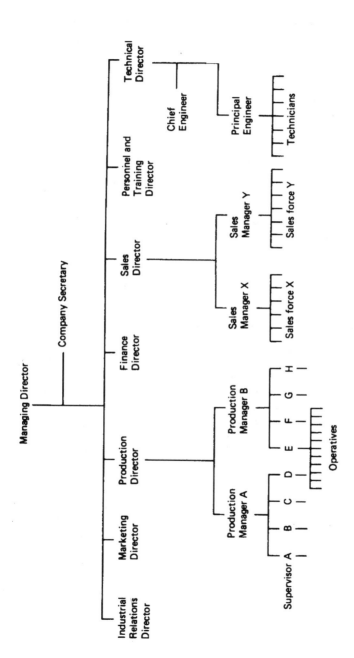

FIGURE 7.1 *A schematic diagram of a partial organization chart*

- *Manifest* – the situation as formally described and displayed.
- *Assumed* – the situation as it is assumed to be by the individual concerned.
- *Extant* – the situation as revealed by systematic exploration and analysis.
- *Requisite* – the situation as it would have to be to accord with the real properties of the field in which it exists.

As Brown elaborates, Manager A has in his office an organizational chart, depicted on which are three subordinates, B1, B2 and B3. This is the *manifest* organization. It is *assumed* that these three subordinates are of equal status and receive no instructions from any other role than that of A. Investigation reveals, however, that B1, who is very much the senior of B2, has the habit of giving instructions to B2. Thus the *extant* or actual situation differs from the assumed one. A investigates further and realizes that some of the problems that she has had in the past have arisen from the fact that B1 has been giving instructions to B2. It is therefore necessary in future to ensure that B1 does not give instructions to B2. This is the *requisite* organization.

Division of labour arises as a result of the increasing number of operations that have to be performed. Even a small business start up situation may need the help of a partner to do the paperwork or the parttime services of an accountant to sort out the financing of the business venture. As the firm grows there is an increasing need for functional specialization, as it is termed. The reasons for this are fairly obvious: (a) the amount of work entailed in performing each function exceeds that of one individual's capacities and (b) increased specialization results in greater efficiency. Such a characteristic, Weber argued, is typical of a *bureaucracy*.

THE NATURE OF BUREAUCRACY

1   Classical Theory

Classical theorists, in particular Weber (1947), suggested that bureaucracies have the following characteristics:

- *Specialization* or division of labour.
- A hierarchy of *command* or *authority*.
- Written *rules* and *regulations*.
- The *rational application* of rules and procedures.

What do these characteristics of 'rational organization' imply? First of all, people have 'spheres of competence' such that

> not only must each participant know his job and have the means to carry it out, which means first of all the ability to command others, but he also must know the limits of his job, rights and power so as not to overstep the boundaries between his role and those of others and thus undermine the whole structure. (Etzioni, 1964, p. 53)

Further, the justification for written rules is tied up with Weber's concept of the efficient organization:

> Rules save effort by obviating the need for deriving a new solution for every problem and case; that facilitates standardization and equality in treatment of many cases. (Etzioni, 1964, p. 53)

It is irrational, if not dysfunctional, to treat each individual client as a unique case. How is it, though, that the so-called rules and norms associated with each office are perpetuated even in the light of a change of personnel? Weber's answer is that it occurs through specialist, technical training. This means that the mark of the efficient bureaucrat is his or her technical skill and knowledge. From this derives the legitimacy of his/her authority.

There are two other features of bureaucracy which Weber identified. These are:

- The need to separate the administrative heads from ownership of production.
- The need to record acts, decisions, rules, etc., systematically, in writing.

In the first case, the complete segregation of ownership from control is in direct contrast to an alternative organizational structure, the small business owner-manager. In the latter case, the exercise of management may be typified by the idiosyncrasies, eccentricities and whims of the owner-manager. Such a system Weber perceived to be irrational and individualistic which, due to its reliance on single individuals creates difficulties of succession and possible discontinuity. The second feature is often viewed as being a less essential characteristic of bureaucracies in so far as it generates 'red tape' and implies an irrationality of its own.

Tied up with Weber's concept of bureaucracy is the idea of the legitimacy of authority necessary for its smooth functioning. The types of authority which he identifies are *traditional, rational–legal, charismatic* and *expertness*. An example of a traditional source of authority is that of inheritance; a high-ranking position in an organization may be passed down along family lines and accepted by subordinates as 'right' or legitimate, even though the particular family member may have no obvious competence or expertise to perform the job.

The basis of rational–legal authority is that of consent to a common set of laws or rules and the procedures for arriving at such laws. This consensual process also means that 'rationality' would be maximized in the sense of attempting to derive laws that 'made sense', were in the interests of the majority, protected human rights, and provided a system of rulership based on demonstrated competence (Schein, 1980).

Both the traditional and rational–legal types of authority suggest a clear chain of succession, on the one hand through inheritance and on the other through the due processes and procedures of law. Charismatic authority, however, is quite different to this. Here the basis of authority resides in the personal qualities of the leader (see Chapter 6). This magnetism which emanates from him or her may create a sense or aura of mystique. Followers or subordinates thus act with unquestioning allegiance and loyalty. Finding a replacement for such a leader presents enormous problems and may result in the organization's subsequent instability.

The final type of authority is that of pure rational authority or expertness. Here authority is vested in someone who has the required skill or expertise to perform a particular job, as in the case of a medical doctor. As such skills are not generally to be found in the population at large we are dependent on such experts to exercise their skills. However, in order to be sure that someone really is an expert in a particular field we have a rational-legal set of procedures for selecting and testing that individual's competence.

2   Rationality

The idea of 'the impersonal application of a system of rules' suggests that rationality is a key feature of the bureaucratic form. But what does this mean? There are some fundamental questions to be asked which enable us to crystallize the key issues.

A key issue concerns the nature of rationality. It has been suggested that rationality is about applying rules impartially, disinterestedly, systematically and objectively. This begs the question: Is it veridical to suggest that *irrationality* is about the partial, subjective, inconsistent application of rules which serve factional interests? An example may help clarify the problem. In the National Health Service in the UK there has been considerable debate about the best way to deliver health care, the use and the prioritization of resources. Clearly in situations where there are no established sets of rules and guidelines consensually arrived at and agreed, a process of debate is needed to establish what 'the rules' are. Thus, in complex situations, it is too simplistic to suggest a strict dichotomy between rationality and irrationality.

A further related issue to consider is the value base which underpins a set of rules. Rules are based on principles rather than personal whims and, in that sense, can be said to be objective and justifiable. From such rules a set of procedures can be established which, at one level, enable personnel to do their job efficiently and, at another level, enable organizational goals to be attained. Such goals are valued. Therefore it is the values and beliefs which underpin the rules for enabling goal attainment which provide the justification for a particular course of action.

A primary role of the leadership of an organization is thus to determine the goals and the choice of means by which those goals may be reached. This aspect needs to be considered in relation to the basis of the leader's power and authority (see next section).

Where the ends or objectives of an organization change it is likely that so too will the rules. However, a prior question is to consider the extent to which the belief system (about the way the organization has operated) can be sustained. For instance, where the politico-economic system external to an institution is the impetus for a fundamental review of goals and means of achieving those goals, further questions may be raised:

1. To what extent can the administrative system effectively question the ends posed by the politico-economic (i.e. external) system?
2. Is the role of the administration merely to work out the most efficient way of achieving those given ends?
3. To what extent may the authority be tempered as a consequence, in part, of the specialization and expert knowledge within the system? Thus where valued ends change there may arise a *countervailing force* which effectively slows down the rate of change.

Indeed, the logic of this analysis leads to yet a further set of questions: First of all, for whom is the organization rational – who benefits? It is possible to speculate about possible beneficiaries, for example, management, employees in non-executive positions, customers, society, etc. What are the interests of these widely differing groups? Where do possible conflicts of interest lie? Furthermore, at what juncture do the interests of efficiency undermine the wider aims of the institution and thus conflict with the values underpinning the system? (Clegg, 1990).

Carnall (1990) argues that there is no simple dichotomy between the rational and the irrational. Change exposes the nature of rationality in organizations. For example, when faced with short-term changed circumstances, people will reflect upon the causes and the consequences of the change and develop responses and decisions based upon reason. What people regard as *reasonable* is based upon their knowledge and experience. So-called 'rationality' emerges through the processes of thought, emotion, action and decision-making. Thus these sources of 'rationality' lead men and women to construct different arguments about, and draw different conclusions in respect of, the changes which affect them.

Environmental stability provides security and little impetus to change the rules – the rational–legal basis of the institution. But bureaucracies are no more closed systems than any other organizational types. Exposure to changing circumstances leads to a change in knowledge and beliefs and a questioning of the values implicit in the system of rules. The real issues, Carnall argues are: (a) the ability to recognize the real nature of these changes; (b) managing and dealing with those externally imposed changes by the development of new rules and procedures for dealing with them; and (c) gaining the acceptance of the new ends by key personnel.

3   Compliance

Undoubtedly, one of the key issues in organizational behaviour is understanding the nature of people's involvement and commitment. Why do personnel accept and comply with the system of rules within their organization? What is the basis of their motivation? Etzioni suggested that there are three basic motives:

- *Love* – internalization of norms and values.
- *Money* – remuneration, greed.
- *Fear* – coercion.

These motives give rise to different kinds of power and also different kinds of involvement.

Table 7.2 shows that there are three compliance structures which are congruent with the type of organization: where the basis of power and control in an organization is *normative* then involvement tends to be *moral*; coercive power results in *alienative* involvement; and *remunerative* power produces *calculative* involvement. A difficulty for this theory is that there appear to be so few 'pure' types. People who enter the social services may

TABLE 7.2 *'Pure' types of involvement, commitment and power in organizations*

Kind of power	Kind of involvement		
	Moral	*Alienative*	*Calculative*
Normative	Novitiate WRVS 1		
Coercive		Inmates of a prison 2	
Remunerative			Waged employee 3

do so from a sense of moral involvement (wishing to help others, etc.). However, it would appear that only charitable work would qualify as a pure example of this type. It is also arguable that the basis of involvement and commitment has changed in some organizations, for example academic institutions. Finally, this analysis also changes the focus from *what* a person does in their job to *why*: that is, the nature of their involvement has implications for the nature of their motivation, whether it be intrinsic or otherwise.

4 Power

Management, it has been argued, is a political activity (Pfeffer, 1981; Stephenson, 1985) and it is the exercise of power which is fundamental to the process of management. The concept of 'power' has been argued to be an attribute of certain individuals – those who have an overriding need and desire to exercise it (McClelland, 1961). On the other hand, it has been argued that power is vested in situations. Thus, through one's position it is possible to increase one's power base by various forms of symbolism and so on (cf. Drummond, 1991b). 'Power' is also said to be a relational concept. Power when exercised concerns a dependent relationship between A (person or group in a position of authority) and B (person or group requiring something of A). In other words, A has power over B in so far as A has resources that B wants. *Dependence* is therefore seen as being critical to the power relation (Emerson, 1962; Pfeffer, 1981).

Power may be the 'power over others'. This implies dominance, hierarchy and control. It also raises a question concerning the *legitimate* basis of such power. A senior manager, by virtue of his or her position, holds legitimate sway over subordinates. In contrast, a person holding potentially damaging information about another, may be able to exercise considerable power over them. Blackmail or unprincipled use of information is a non-legitimate use of power.

'Power to do' is the kind of power most managers seek (Drummond, 1991b). French and Raven (1959) suggested that there are five bases of power. A person can feel 'empowered' through the backing of his/her group and/or a 'significant other' such as the boss. Such *referent* power is energizing and may be reinforced by *rewards* – another source of power – or blocked by countervailing organizational forces, for example, individuals using *their* position power, or counter-arguments derived from their *expert* knowledge. Further, people may be able to exert considerable influence by virtue of their personalities – their charisma and hence their personal power (see also discussion of charisma in Chapter 6).

Coercion, punishment and the witholding of rewards are generally regarded as non-legitimate sources of power, though there are subtle differences between them. To coerce another (for example, at gunpoint) to carry out an action against their will is an abuse of power. To punish someone is a negative way of exercising control. On the one hand, it may be used to take a person firmly in hand and show them 'who is boss', as in the cases of detention, meting out 'lines' or requiring the offender to carry out a difficult or not particularly pleasant task. A potential problem with this legitimate exercise of power is the resentment that it may engender and the resistance to future control. On the other hand, where the punishment is perceived to be punitive and result in suffering a question arises about the legitimacy of this form of control. To withold rewards is a widespread means of control: parents do it in order to control their children. In organizational terms, the legitimacy of such action will depend upon the reasons and thus the basis for the decision to withold a reward.

Power underlies organizational politics. It is concerned largely with group relations and not, simply, about the power vested in a particular individual. Power, in this sense, finds expression in relationships where one party has the means, and is willing to use them, to get another party to act in a manner which is contrary to that party's interests. This form of power tends to lead to resistance and conflict and to two-party intergroup relations and rivalry (see Chell, 1985a).

To exercise power is to influence others; it is the ability to affect attitudes, decisions and, on occasions, overt behaviour. The impact of the exercise of power may be judged by:

- its *weight* – the 'amount' of effect it has on other people;
- the *domain* – the range of persons and groups affected;
- its *scope* – the range of issues covered by the use of power in a given situation (Stephenson, 1985).

Organizational analysis involves the identification of loci of power – whether they be centred on individuals, groups or organizational structures. Power tends to crystallize around a few key organizational issues:

- The distribution of *scarce resources* (e.g. cash, equipment, expertise, promotions, rewards, information, etc.)
- The system of *formal authority* (power may be enhanced by centralization, dominant coalitions, choice of technology and the manipulation of what is thought to be legitimate)
- *Access to information* (e.g. this may be controlled by a person's position – the 'gatekeeper', how the information is interpreted and presented, timing of the release of particularly sensitive information, control of access through exclusivity, committee membership, etc.)
- Organizational environment characterized by *uncertainty*. (A key issue is how such uncertainty is managed. Some people can cope better than others with ambiguity and can use this to their advantage to create situations of dependency. Uncertainty can be engineered through, for example, a monopoly of knowledge and the use of jargon; by means of mystification rather than clarification.)
- *Leadership style* and attempts to bolster one's personal prestige (on the charismatic leader, see Chapter 6).
- The *stakeholders* in the organization have a vested interest in pursuing policies which enhance their power position. (A key issue for the purpose of organizational diagnosis is the identification of key players and interest groups and how their interests may be served in order to be able to predict the likely consequences of present actions and decisions.)

5 Bureaucratic Organization Revisited

Clegg (1990) identified fifteen key dimensions of Weber's bureaucratic organization and examined the organizational consequences of the manipulation or change of one or more of these dimensions for the rest. For example, in the case of *reliability* and *predictability*, Clegg asks: what is the impact of executive pressure towards greater reliability and predictability on the actions of organizational members? The answer is a tendency towards greater *formalization* and *standardization* with members becoming strict rule followers in order to ensure the legitimacy of their action. The *cost of such a move*, it is suggested, is considerable *rigidity*. Furthermore, where there are new, externally imposed challenges, organizational responses will be increasingly inappropriate.

One way to produce a more responsive organization is through increased *delegation*, that is, slackening the tendencies towards *centralization, hierarchy* and *status discrimination*. There are a number of associated costs. These include: (a) the time involved in communication and consultation; (b) the tendency towards increased *specialization* and '*credentialization*'; (c) the probability of a bifurcation of interests as subordinates with delegated authority create their own agendas and goals to which they show an increasing commitment in contrast to their waning commitment to organizational goals; (d) consequently, a greater effort is needed to legitimize organizational goals which have executive approval and to 'delegitimize' delegate actions.

Treating these dimensions of a bureaucratic organization as variables has enabled Clegg to demonstrate that such a structure is not 'an iron cage'; its nature can be varied and there are consequences which flow from this. Furthermore, it is also possible to examine the structure for *internal consistency*. Let us posit the following example. Organizational goals are referred to as 'ends'. Different aspects of organizational structure will enable the achievement (or otherwise) of those ends:

Means

specialization	(complexity)
centralization	(hierarchy)
formalization	(formality)
stratification	(status differentiation)

Ends

adaptiveness	(flexibility)
production	(productivity)
efficiency	(competitiveness)
job satisfaction	(motivation)

Thus, the key question is: If you vary the means what impact will it have on the ends? For example, if you increase *stratification*, that is the number of horizontal layers between the top and the bottom of the organization, does this increase or decrease job satisfaction? Likewise, if you engineer greater *formalization* then you are likely to have higher efficiency at the cost of lower adaptiveness and so on.

From this analysis it also follows that the nature of the external environment will also have an effect upon the appropriateness of organizational structure. A *stable* environment ensures greater predictability of events and as such a *mechanistic* or bureaucratic structure is effective (see also, Burns and Stalker, 1961). A *turbulent* environment is highly unpredictable and so an *organic* structure is needed and a total relaxation of those dimensions which constitute the bureaucratic organization.

Finally, Clegg (1990) argues that although an essential aspect of the Weberian organization is governance by a system of rules, those rules must be interpreted and enacted upon by organizational members. Thus, although the 'objective' structure of the rules may remain the same, what those rules might mean depends on the context of their enactment. The fundamental issues are: who usually initiates the rules (that is, where in the organization is the locus of power?), whose values legitimate the rules and whose values are violated by the rules being breached or enforced? Thus, changes in the external environment or changes in the personnel (especially at senior levels) may transform the nature of the rules, and change the tendencies, and the type, of bureaucracy.

In conclusion, it would seem that the ideal type of the classical (Weberian) model of bureaucracy is not an inevitable structure, imprisoning its members in an increasingly complex system of rules. Nor is it invariably the most efficient or effective organizational structure. The modern approach of Clegg to understanding organizations has demonstrated the variation that can be achieved. Furthermore, the exposure of organizations (such as the NHS, institutions of higher education, etc.) to externally imposed change exemplify the issues raised above concerning the appropriateness of structure, internal consistency and external adaptiveness, the chief beneficiaries of change, the ability to sustain commitment and maintain morale and the ways in which 'the rules' might be modified and changed.

In the next section we review an alternative approach to organization structure – the 'open systems' approach.

THE OPEN-SYSTEMS APPROACH

The psychologist's criticism of Weber's theory of bureaucracy is that it fails to account for human needs (Silverman, 1970). The Weberian model was far too mechanistic; people were something of an irrelevance – dispensable. It was the system of rules and procedures that should endure. On the whole, this seemed to be an inadequate account of organizations in general. An alternative conception was to think of them not as mechanisms but as biological organisms: not only was the organism a system, but it had other attributes, such as in-built self-regulatory mechanisms, ability to adapt to changing environments, etc. which could be readily likened to the functioning of an organism. As organizations interact with their environment, the idea of the organization as an *open* system took on greater credence. The organization's exchange relationship with its environment arises as a consequence of the following cycle of activities: there is an input from the environment, and transformation processes which result in an output back to the environment. In manufacturing firms, for example, this cycle is perpetuated because the inputs – raw materials – are transformed into goods which are sold, so that the revenue produced enables more raw materials to be purchased and the cycle repeated. The idea behind this model is thus exceedingly simple. In practice, the reality is more complex. Rice's study of the calico mills at Ahmedabad demonstrated the need to think of the total organization as a collectivity of sub-systems (Rice, 1970). These subsystems may correspond to particular departments, as, for example in textiles, Production may be sub-divided into preparation, spinning, weaving, bleaching and finishing. At each stage of the process materials are imported, processed and then passed on to the next stage in the process (Rice, 1970, p. 41 *et passim*). However, this production or *operating system* must be distinguished from the *management system*; not only must each subsystem have its own management system, but there must be a management system which is external to the operating system which controls and services the whole. The management system at this level is said to operate on the boundaries of the organization controlling the relationship of the production system to the organization's environment.

How does this systems concept explain organizational hierarchy? Where, in a large organization, such levels of operation are apparent, the division is termed the first-order operating system, departments are second-order operating systems, sections are third-order operating systems, and primary workgroups are undifferentiated fourth-order primary production systems (Rice, 1970).

A further aspect of the open-system concept is that of entropy (Katz and Kahn, 1966); that is, the system must be capable of perpetuating itself. This means that features such as interaction, interrelatedness and interdependence occur between subsystems within the total system, and that there must be a feedback mechanism from the final exported product to the beginning of the cycle, as, for example, where the sale of goods produced enables the purchase of raw materials, etc.

SOCIO-TECHNICAL SYSTEMS

The socio-technical systems concept is a special case or development of the open-systems concept. Assuming the open-systems framework, the socio-technical systems theorists differentiate between the technical and managerial aspects of the system and those aspects which are social and psychological. The terminology has been developed further to encompass what happens within a system. Thus each system or subsystem has a *primary task*. In the case of a weaving shed, it is the weaving of cloth.

> Import into a weaving shed is yarn on *beams* and *bobbins*. Conversion is the manufacture of *grey* cloth. Export is the delivery of the grey cloth to a cloth department, external to the weaving shed, where it is inspected, measured, and made up into lots for subsequent processing. (Rice, 1970, p. 52, my emphasis)

In order to complete the primary task successfully, various operations must be carried out. Clearly, the extent to which these are performed by persons depends on the degree of automation of the machinery. In the case of the automated weaving loom, there were 14 identifiable occupational roles, including weavers, smash-hands, battery fillers, gaters, cloth carriers, jobbers and assistant jobbers, oiler, feeler-motion fitter, humidification fitter, bobbin carrier, sweeper, top supervisor and shift supervisor. Despite the interdependence of all these tasks, Rice found that there was no internally stable workgroup, and that the lines of authority (who could tell whom what to do) were far from clear. In this way, the organization of the operating (i.e. technical) system could be shown to have implications for the social relations of the workers and for their psychological state (whether or not they were happy, for example). This study mirrored in many ways the findings of the Trist and Bamforth investigation of the longwall system of coal-getting (Trist and Bamforth, 1951). More specifically, from Rice's study it was clear that the 29 workers were more of an aggregate than a group; there was task confusion (particularly between shifts), confusion over authority relations and responsibilities, and uncertainty over role and territorial boundaries. There was disappointment over performance and no one saw the completion of a task. Under such circumstances, it is hardly surprising that two important consequences were inefficiency and the problem of maintaining morale. There was, in this organization, a desperate need for change (Rice, 1970). In essence, Rice's solution was two-pronged: to make the supervisory system more effective and to reorganize the workgroup so that it had a stable internal group structure. Such issues as these – of organizational change – will be taken up and explored more fully in Chapter 8.

WORK ORGANIZATION AND THE ROLE OF THE PSYCHOLOGIST

There are several implications of the socio-technical systems approach spearheaded by researchers at the Tavistock Institute of Human Relations:

● The social and psychological aspects of work organization are as important as the technical and managerial.
● A system of work organization which causes the fragmentation of tasks leads to job dissatisfaction and a lack of cohesion in the workgroup.
● Autonomous workgroups given responsibility for 'whole tasks' would ensure worker involvement, self-management and self-discipline on the job.

Ideas such as these challenged the established way of thinking about work organization. Indeed, this new paradigm questioned the idea of employees being extensions of machines; saw them as resources to be developed; played down the need for external controls and emphasized the need for internal self-regulation and control; substituted a participative leadership style for an autocratic one; and saw collaboration, commitment and innovation as being central to workgroup effectiveness (Trist, 1981). Some of the criticisms of this new approach were that it placed too great an emphasis on intrinsic factors as satisfiers to the neglect almost of extrinsic factors. Secondly, critics queried the extent to which it presented a real challenge to the 'managerial prerogative'; in other words, was it merely a 'cosmetic' exercise? Further, it was suggested that if people have a low regard for what they produce then work organization is unlikely to increase their job satisfaction or enable them to get greater fulfilment through work (Blackler and Shimmin, 1984).

An intervention measure of redesigning jobs in order to create semi-autonomous workgroups has wider implications for the organization in terms of employee training, selection practices, payment and bonus systems, promotion and reward systems, and other workgroups. But how successful are semi-autonomous workgroups? One of the most frequently cited examples is that of the Kalmar truck assembly plant of Volvo. In the early days of this experiment (1974–6), using a static assembly method, a high performance was realized and considerable savings in man-hours were made. However, management apparently did not like the idea of leisure on the job as a reward for meeting daily production quotas. Indeed, as the economic recession bit in the late 1970s, relationships between management and trade unions soured and a climate of distrust prevailed. There was little protest from the trade unions at the demise of the experiment. This raises some of the wider issues regarding work reorganization using job redesign methods. For example, at a series of conferences at Aston University, England, delegates have put forward an alternative, critical perspective to 'conventional wisdom' on job redesign. Some have argued that, since Taylorism (see Chapter 8), the interventions of psychologists to humanize the workplace and increase the quality of working life of the workforce have been fundamentally misguided (Knights *et al.*, 1985). Far from the psychologist playing a 'neutral' role within the organization, he or she has increasingly been forced to 'develop techniques that appeal to and accommodate the more immediate interests of management' (Knights *et al.*, 1985, p. 3). Job redesign for these authors is the 'outcome of political, economic and social forces that intersect within the organization' (Knights *et al.*, 1985, p. 10). It is indisputable that such factors play a significant role within any organization, indeed the Kalmar plant was just such an example of the interplay of political and economic forces, which caused the ultimate demise of the progressive system of work organization at that plant. However, as Child (1985) argues, while managerial strategies are formulated in order to achieve organizational objectives, there may be considerable room for manoeuvre between those intentions embodied in the particular strategy and the processes of implementation. Furthermore, the factors that impinge upon senior managerial thinking, when it is deciding which strategic option to adopt, include culture and tradition, organizational and task-related factors and market conditions. Whether one is talking about a capitalist or 'state collectivist' (socialist) mega-system, both involve hierarchy and a managerial function. In other words, what is in management's and the organization's interests is not necessarily outwith the interests of the labour force. At the bottom line, the survival of the company is of interest to all those dependent upon it for employment, while growth and profitability increase job security. A problem arises when, in order to survive, an organization has to compete in world markets on the price and quality of its goods. A not uncommon strategy is that of reducing the labour bill by increasing automation and deskilling. There is, however, no inevitability about *how* this should be achieved, and in this sense there may be a role for the expert (psychologist). By making themselves more aware of the issues, the alternatives open to management and the strategic implications of a decision, psychologists may be able to influence the nature of work organization. Such an intervention would need to reflect realism, understanding and an acknowledgement of a pluralism of interests.

On the more general question of how work organization should be achieved, Blackler and Shimmin (1984) argue that job redesign is not an end in itself; rather there is a need for more creative, localized solutions to be developed. Networks of people, including managers, workers and trade unionists, who have useful experience which can be brought to bear on the job redesign issues should be brought together: job redesign knowledge should not be the property of outside experts.

There is also a need for a *multi-level* approach to organizational reform:

> The economic, political, legal and technological dimensions of organizational activities and environments are such that psychologists working in organizations should not restrict their attention to personal and interpersonal issues only. They need to consider and explore the consequences of technological change, organizational hierarchies, ownership and control, and of relevant government policy and legislation in relation to psychological health and well-being. (Blackler and Shimmin, 1984, p. 121)

Moreover, psychologists should develop a *sensitivity to the prevailing concerns of others*. This means defining the nature of problems according to the perspectives of those groups of actors within the situation, not according to the psychologist's own pet theoretical position. It also means *listening* to trade unionists as well as managerial points of view and incorporating these considerations into a work redesign intervention. In the case of the introduction of new technology,

> Psychologists have an important . . . role to play . . . in helping to ensure that the new technologies are used in sensible ways, to encourage greater decentralization and employee responsibility rather than facilitating more efficient centralized control. (Blackler and Shimmin, 1984, p. 123)

Finally, Blackler and Shimmin suggest that 'progress in improving the quality of work experience should be evaluated *less in terms of the achievement of specific objectives and more in terms of the development of self-managing processes*' (p. 123, emphasis as in the original). This means placing less emphasis on how many jobs have been restructured and more on ways of evaluating the development of employees' skills of self-management and the value they place on their involvement in the job restructuring project.

CONTINGENCY THEORY

Contingency theory has arisen from the realization that organizational effectiveness is a function not simply of organizational structure *per se* but of changes in the environment. The environment may be '*stable*' or '*turbulent*'. Where the environment is stable and predictable then a bureaucratic or *mechanistic* structure works quite efficiently. However, where the environment is *turbulent* then organizational structures should be such as to allow flexibility of response to meet changing demands, needs and markets. This may mean changes in the roles of personnel, tasks to be performed and, more generally, behaviour.

Child (1984) suggests that this should be termed '*task* contingency theory' in order to distinguish it from '*political* contingency theory'. The primary purpose of the task contingency approach is precisely that organizational tasks be performed most effectively in order that organizational objectives be fulfilled.

The organization of the work and of the people contributing to it must be designed with existing contingencies in mind. Environment, diversity, size, technology and type of personnel are the categories of contingency most often identified. The task contingency approach seeks to identify those organizational designs which will be efficient for given contextual situations. (Child, 1984, pp. 217–18)

The *political* contingency perspective suggests that the choice of organizational design and arrangement is not simply a function of efficiencies which may accrue but, rather, of what is acceptable to various power groups and/or management of the organization. The distributions of such power may vary from time to time, but different groups may manoeuvre themselves into a position to influence or resist policies on organizational design.

The limitations of the task contingency approach concern:

1. Determining a causal relation between the contingencies, organizational structure and performance.
2. The effect of non-organizational variables.

Taking these points in the order in which they have been presented, there is no unequivocal research evidence to substantiate the suggested causal relationship. One of the drawbacks of much of the research in this area is that there are few multivariate analyses to demonstrate the effect of multiple contingencies on structure and performance. Indeed, multiple contingencies cause further problems for analysis because, in practice, they may require intra-organizational structural variations which may result in internal conflicts, tensions, and poor communications. Finally, task contingency theory assumes a rational view that 'the sole purpose of organizational design is to achieve efficiency' (Child, 1984, p. 229). This view has been called into question; the effects of non-organizational variables may hold more sway in certain circumstances. These include not only the preferences of groups and/or managers but also the effects of market conditions and political institutions.

Table 7.3 compares and contrasts the three major structural arrangements discussed in this chapter on the key themes of adaptability, organizational *goals, authority, resolution of disputes* and *integrative effort.*

SUMMARY

————— Organizations are purposive social systems with hierarchically ordered goals. Organizations are differentiated both vertically (owing to a hierarchy of command and authority) and horizontally (owing to increased specialization and functional differentiation). A key problem therefore is the integration of this diversity. Behaviourally, they may be thought of as patterned, cyclical activities which are coordinated and integrated and which enable them to be recognized for what they are and are aimimg to achieve.

————— It is not always clear how organizational goals are to be operationalized at lower levels; how standards are to be applied and maintained; how performance is to be measured (if at all); and the extent to which the organization is responsive to its environment.

————— Organizational theorists suggest that organizations comprise rational, planned activities, the aims of which are to achieve organizational goals and objectives. In contrast, psychologists are concerned with (a) the implications of organizational structure on behaviour within organizations, (b) the nature of informal activity within organizations and its relation to formal requirements, (c) how people's needs are satisfied within organizations, (d) how decisions are arrived at and executed and (e) the effects of work and organization on individuals.

————— Formally organizational positions and functional relationships may be depicted by the organizational chart. 'Role' is descrip-

TABLE 7.3 *A comparison between three major structural arrangements in organizations*

Key issues	Bureaucracies	Socio-technical systems	Political contingencies
Organizational adaptability	stable and predictable environment; rule, role and authority systems limit flexibility and adaptability	sensitive to environmental change as it affects the task system; responsive to change and needs of internal social competition externalized	adapts to internal power differences and differential perceptions of what external threat for change means competition intra-organizational
Organizational goals	purpose clearly stated and consistently pursued	purpose subject to modification, but then consistently pursued; ability of groups to learn higher than in bureaucracy	purpose politicized primacy of task goals questioned
Bases of leaders' authority	position power rewards and punishment	participative leadership; task and representative functions	complex network of authority based on participation, expertise, power play, commitment and social skills
Methods for resolving disputes	rules, hierarchical/ legitimate authority	problem-solving; negotiation; integrative effort	open confrontation more frequent; political manoeuvring; win–lose situations; depends upon strength of political factions
Integrative effort	individuals are assigned to differentiated tasks and their efforts pooled	individuals are assigned to group tasks; efforts of different groups pooled	factionalization makes integration of effort difficult specialization and support for own group's efforts; desire to see own group in primary position

SOURCES   F. Blackler and Shimmin (1984) *Applying Psychology in Organizations* (London and New York: Methuen); J. Child (1984) *Organization: A Guide to Problems and Practice* (London: Harper & Row).

tive of the part to be played within an organization in order to fulfil a set of task requirements or particular function. Problems may occur when people misperceive what the role is or entails. A distinction may be made between the role as *manifest, assumed, extant* and *requisite* (Brown, 1960).

Bureaucracies are typified by functional specialization, hierarchy of command, written rules and procedures and the rational application of those rules. The authority system within a bureaucracy may be described as *rational–legal*. Other bases of authority within organizations are *legitimate/ non-legitimate, traditional, charismatic* and *rational*. Each has implications for the power relations within an organization.

Rationality is considered to mean 'the impersonal application of a system of rules'. A logically prior question, however, is: How are the rules arrived at? It is suggested that this is achieved by a process of debate by interested parties. This process exposes the value-base of 'the system' and the fact that it is a dominant group whose position, objectives and formulation of procedures and rules find broad acceptance.

Externally imposed change may impact an organization by, among other things, effecting a review of goals and objectives, the means by which these goals may be attained and the rules and procedures adopted for achieving them. Such an analysis raises a further issue, that is, for *whom* is the organization rational, and who are the chief beneficiaries? The management implications of such changes are: (a) recognition of the nature of the changes, (b) developing new procedures for dealing with them and (c) gaining acceptance by key personnel.

Etzioni asked the question, why is it that personnel comply with 'the rules'? He suggested that there are three basic motives: (a) *normative*, which stems from the internalization of norms and values at the heart of an institution and results in a *moral* involvement, (b) *money, which is at the basis of an employment contract – the selling of one's labour, etc. – and results in a* calculative involvement and (c) *fear*, through which people are coerced into compliance and which results in an alienative *involvement*.

There are many definitions of the concept of power. A basic distinction concerns 'power over others' and 'power to do' (Drummond, 1991b). French and Raven (1959) suggested that there are five sources of power in organizations, which they termed: legitimate, referent, reward, coercion and expert power. Power underlies organizational politics and involves intergroup relations. It tends to be manifested over a number of key issues, for example distribution of scarce resources, the system of formal authority, access to information, the management of uncertainty, leadership style and the interests of stakeholders.

— Clegg (1990) identified 15 dimensions of a bureaucracy and examined the consequences of the manipulation of one or more of these dimensions on the rest. He was able to demonstrate that such a structure is not an 'iron cage': it can be varied and there are predictable consequences of this.

— Open systems may be contrasted with the bureaucratic model. They are characterized by an open exchange with the environment and an inbuilt self-regulatory system. Open systems take in materials, transform them and export an output. They also have a feedback mechanism which permits self-regulation.

— The socio-technical systems approach led to experimentation with new forms of work organization, one of which being the semi-autonomous workgroup. This arose, in part, as a reaction to the fragmentation of jobs, consequent deskilling, alienation of labour, boredom and dissatisfaction. It suggested that workgroups be responsible for 'whole tasks', that they regulate their own work and that participative leadership be practised. The predicted outcome was greater job satisfaction, which it was thought would maintain (if not result in increased) productivity. Several noteworthy experiments with semi-autonomous workgroups were tried, but could not be sustained through an economic recession.

— Several criticisms of the psychologists' interventionist role have been made which suggested collusion with managerial interests. Such a criticism is difficult to evaluate, given (a) that there are likely to be a multiplicity of interests within any one organizational level, and (b) that the implementation of a managerial strategy does leave room for the accommodation of different interests through negotiation and bargaining. However, it alerts the organizational psychologist to the need to be constantly aware of different interests and the wider economic and political consequences of particular interventions.

— Contingency theory of organizations suggests that effectiveness depends upon their responsiveness to various factors. *Task* contingency theory assumes the fulfilment of organizational objectives to be primary, so that organizations need to be structured to respond to changing demands, needs and markets. *Political* contingency theory suggests that organizational design should not have as its primary goal task fulfilment and increased efficiencies, but rather should be responsive to what is acceptable to various power groups and/or management of the organization.

8   Developing Organizations

Organizations, as was made apparent in the preceding chapter, must be seen within a wider context – that is, an economic and political environment. A stable environment will tend to make for a stable internal structure, the development of routine ways of handling problems, systems of control and so on. Little change or development as such may be evident in such organizations. On the other hand, where economic conditions change frequently, and there is a general lack of certainty about the environment, an organization tends to adapt various systems, becoming more flexible in its responsiveness to externally imposed change.

Where the impetus for change is in some circumstances forced upon an organization, for example, as in the case of the 1973 oil crisis, or the current world-wide recession, this has tended to precipitate particular forms of reaction: organizations faced with such dire circumstances have attempted to become 'leaner and fitter' by shedding labour, rationalizing their activities and becoming more competitive in the market place. In some organizations, the impetus for change comes from within. In the case of highly innovative organizations, such as small, 'high tech' firms, the success of the product and the entrepreneurial behaviour of the founder has led to many high growth businesses. How do such firms sustain their success and how, if at all, do they manage the changes necessary to maintain growth and development?

In essence, therefore, organizations develop or decline as a natural consequence of their ability to meet market and externally-imposed demands, to be flexible in their practices and adaptable in their behaviour. But how can an organization's management team consciously and deliberately sustain its development even in a hostile environment? Put yet another way, is there a role for organization development – the subject which draws from all the behavioural sciences for intervention techniques with which to facilitate the improvement and renewal of an organization? In this chapter we will do two things: (a) consider the problems of successfully changing and developing companies and (b) examine the role of organization development as a possible source of expertise for facilitating change.

SUCCESSFULLY DEVELOPING COMPANIES

In the early 1980s, particular efforts were made to identify the characteristics of many successful companies (Peters and Waterman, 1982; Abernathy *et al.*, 1983). The approach taken took the form of the development of a catalogue of characteristics for the benefit of other companies whose senior management might choose to draw the lessons and model their own company on these exemplars of *excellence* (Child, 1984). Child has referred to this as 'the search for universals'. He has identified three organizational attributes which were linked with superior economic performance:

- An emphasis on methods to communicate key values and objectives and to ensure that action is directed towards these.
- The delegation of identifiable areas of responsibility to relatively small units, including workgroups.
- The use of a lean, simple structure of management which is intended to avoid the rigidities of bureaucracy, the complexities of matrix, and the overheads of both.

In addition to the above, he suggests, there is:

> the role of intense informal communications both for infusing this commitment (to action) through the organization and for bringing together collective contributions where these are required in planning action. This is integration through direct contact: a visible and accessible management (for example, Hewlett-Packard's 'management by wandering around'), and the use of small, short-lived task forces. (Child, 1984, pp. 213–14)

An alternative 'recipe' or set of universals is that exemplified by the Japanese. Here the key is economy in manning and supervision, with flexibility in deployment and innovation characterized by constant attention to ways of improving performance. The adoption of a 'total quality' approach to management and the use of *quality circles* are methods by which these characteristics are maintained (see Chapter 9).

Rosabeth Kanter (1984) has sought to identify those characteristics which typify low- and high-innovative companies. They include:

- The development of organizational environments that *stimulate* people to act and give them power to do so.
- The design and implementation of *progressive* human resource practices.
- An *integrative* (as opposed to *segmentalist*) approach to problem-solving.

These dimensions are quite compatible with a task contingency model (see Chapter 7), where external environment is a major variable. Indeed, Kanter's thesis has developed from a knowledge of the tough and changing environment of the 1970s. What she has identified are dimensions of effective management practice which enable the manager to get the best out of his or her subordinates, and where creativity, development and implementation are seen to be important dimensions of performance, success and growth.

Table 8.1 shows a list of seven organizational dimensions and compares a generalized high-innovating company with a low-innovating one. In all these respects these companies contrast markedly.

The problem would appear to be that many of the older, traditional industries have a preponderence of companies 'locked into' structures and practices which have long ceased to be effective in bringing about growth. This suggests that changes in these areas are long overdue. This can occur only with a recognition by senior management of the nature of the organization's problems and the need for change, the identification of areas where change is appropriate and desirable, the development of policies and practices for bringing about those changes, and an awareness of, and ability to overcome, resistance to change.

TABLE 8.1   *General characteristics of high- and low-innovating companies*

	High-innovating companies	Low-innovating companies
Economic climate	up	down
Organizational structure	matrix/decentralized	centralized
Information flow	free	constricted
Communication emphasis	horizontal	vertical
Culture	clear; individual initiative, participative, good treatment of people	idiosyncratic; security, maintenance, protectionism
Current emotional climate	pride in the company team feeling	low trust, high uncertainty, confusion
Rewards	abundant	scarce

SOURCE   R. M. Kanter (1984) *The Change Masters* (London: Unwin).

TACKLING THE PROBLEMS OF CHANGE

1 Awareness

Inability to compete and to produce what the market wants have been the major impetuses for change. Growing awareness of new technological advances in an industry, and the competitive edge that this has given those companies that have invested and brought themselves up to date on methods of working, has been a further impetus. Awareness, however, is insufficient in itself; for any individual company it still leaves open the questions of (a) whether they should change, (b) if so, what to change and (c) how to set about doing it.

2 Identification of Problem Areas

Problems associated with change range from the very general to the very specific. Lawrence and Lorsch (1969) have identified three very general problem areas. These are:

1. The organization–environment interface.
2. The group-to-group interface.
3. The individual–organization interface.

By *organization–environment interface* they mean *planned transactions*, that is, the idea of a

> deliberate strategy which the management of an organization adopts for conducting these external transactions in a way that promises to generate a surplus of resources for the organization. The key development problem . . . is not initial strategy formulation . . . but also continuing evaluation of the constant changes in the organization's environment and the effect of these changes on the quality of the transactions (Lawrence and Lorsch, 1969, pp. 4–5).

The second problem these authors identified is that of integrating groups which have arisen from the process of division of labour and have developed their own task characteristics, technical language, structure and organizational processes. This is, in part, a problem of communications that have arisen from structural differentiation and it requires the development of purposive strategies for handling integration.

The third developmental issue is identified as being the 'shifting psychological contract' between the employee and the organization. This comprises such issues as (a) the commitment to organizational goals, (b) the sense of autonomy and free expression versus dependence and conformity, (c) the optimal use or squandering of human resources and (d) policies to 'anticipate and provide for talents necessary to implement new strategies attuned to environmental change' (Lawrence and Lorsch, 1969, p. 7).

Apart from these very general problem areas, management will want eventually to be more specific in the identification of the problem area facing their organization and possible ways of tackling it. Woodcock and Francis (1981) have developed an *Organizational Priorities Survey*, which differentiates between eight sources of organizational change problems and then lists appropriate techniques for handling them (see Table 8.2).

TABLE 8.2   *Eight sources of organizational change problems*

Blockage	Focus of OD intervention
1. Unclear aims	Management by objectives; corporate planning processes; communication strategies; systematic problem solving.
2. Unassertive leadership	Assertion training; gestalt groups; leadership theory and skills; team manager role analysis.
3. Ineffective management	Systems analysis; decision-making; audits; organisation and methods studies; open systems planning; cybernetic modelling.
4. Negative climate	Survey feedback; systematic diagnosis; value clarification; motivation programmes; transactional analysis.
5. Inappropriate structure	Socio-technical analysis; contingency theory; bureaucratic models; 'small is beautiful' research.
6. Unbalanced power relationships	Conflict management; negotiation skills; social class models; confrontation theory; third party consultation.
7. Undeveloped individuals	Job analysis; training plans; personal goal planning 'unblocked boss' approach; action learning; counselling; personal growth experiences.
8. Ineffective teamwork	Team diagnosis; structured experiences; open systems planning; teambuilding; interpersonal skill training.

SOURCE   M. Woodcock and D. Francis (1981) *Organizational Development Through Teambuilding* (Aldershot: Gower) pp. 6–7.

3   Development of Policies and Practices

There are several necessary conditions for the development of policies and practices. These have been identified by Brooks (1980) as:

- Recognition that change is possible and that choices exist in the form of alternative courses of action.
- Areas of potential conflict must be identified and handled; antecedent problems analysed.
- Commitment from top management to the idea of change, and commitment by major parties to collaboration and to the people involved.
- The need for skills of effective participative decision-making.
- The development of support systems and networks through the use of working parties or steering groups for sustaining commitment.
- The surrender of power and control over resources.
- Respect for resistance to change, allowing time for attitude change to occur.

4   A Strategy for Organizational Change

A strategy is a pattern of objectives and purposes or goals which includes major policies and plans for achievement. It is an overall, multidimensional plan for action and achievement which also describes the style of operation and implementation tied to the organization in question. The strategy is designed so as to enable the change initiator and the recipient of change to cope more effectively with, and adapt better to, the competing and conflicting pressures, demands and expectations that they impose on one another in the process of negotiating the degree and extent of change (Brooks, 1980, p. 211).

The strategy identifies and takes account of the stages of development in the process of change in terms of the concerns of people involved and their effective resolution. This process is one of negotiation and *not* imposition! The strategy can be viewed on three levels: (a) primary concerns in the stages of organizational change, (b) the identification and awareness of unresolved concerns and (c) resolution of the concerns.

According to Brooks (1980) there are four primary concerns:

- Gaining the acceptance and identity of individuals and groups with the change objectives.

- Giving feedback of, and involvement with, the change initiatives.
- Goal integration.
- Control and influence over organizational change.

These aspects of the process need careful and expert handling. Each will create problems which need to be managed. For example, before acceptance is complete, people will express dissatisfaction and raise other problems; there may be conflicts of interest; there will be doubts and fears over the prospects after the change. On the matter of feedback, employees, shop stewards or others, may raise concerns about the extent to which their interests are represented when decisions are taken; they may question the authority of those handling the change, the credibility and reliability of the sources of information, and also the assumptions, attitudes, values and beliefs underlying the change initiative, etc. Goal integration involves an examination of present ways of working and of customs and practices, looking at the new priorities and the aspirations and objectives of the people involved. Finally, in order that management can gain and maintain control over the change process they must both achieve commitment, involvement and support and also examine the impact of the change on people's roles, responsibilities and accountability. A major part of this strategy involves management and subordinate examining and evaluating how these unresolved concerns can be dealt with by means of data gathering, problem analysis and managerial decision-making. Table 8.3 summarizes how management may attempt to resolve these concerns.

5   Overcoming Resistance to Change

People who fear for the future, whose established ways of working are threatened, and who feel helpless as they witness disruption and the imposition of change, are likely to do all they can to resist change. Their behaviour may appear irrational, but from their perspective it is not; there is no necessary reason why they should accept the managerial stance. To appreciate this is to understand what Brooks referred to as *respect* for resistance to change. The question then becomes one of how management can gain the acceptance of the workforce for the proposed change and how they can overcome this resistance. A fundamental part of the answer lies in the ability to change attitudes (Chell, 1985a). An illustration may help elucidate the problem and its resolution.

TABLE 8.3   *Management issues and means of resolution*

The issues	Means of resolution
1. Gaining acceptance dealing with people	Participative decision-making
2. Assessing the capability of the system to change	Social audit; technical and business audit
3. Giving feedback	Establish terms of reference Clarify aims in relation to company policy Develop programme of communications
4. Goal integration	Develop superordinate goals Agree key issues Decide priorities Establish operating norms and practices
5. Control and Influence	Secure agreement Establish ways of handling concerns *jointly* Action planning Build commitment, encourage initiative and joint problem-solving

The Proposed Change

Pitprop Engineering Plc proposes to introduce new technologically advanced equipment into the company. However, it discovers that the attitudes of its employees to this move are far from accepting of the proposed change. Senior management holds a series of meetings in which they discuss the strategy to be adopted and what can be done to change attitudes of the workforce from unfavourable to favourable.

Social Audit

The first thing they do is to carry out a social audit. This tells them that their employees feel threatened by the new technology; they fear that the consequences for them will inevitably be redundancies at worst, or, at best, greatly degraded work. The reality as far as management is concerned is that far from creating redundancies it would make the company more competitive in getting out tenders more quickly. It should produce more firm orders and therefore *secure* people's jobs.

Strategy for Change

The company is located on two sites – plant A and plant B. Plant B has a history of industrial unrest and management is particularly concerned about hardening attitudes there. It decides on two approaches to the problem: at plant A they will invite an outside consultant to give a lecture about the merits of installing the new technology. The idea is that installation will then take place at this plant and be a showpiece to assure the workforce at plant B, who will then, suitably impressed, acquiesce to the proposed changes. Meantime, at plant B they instigated a series of group discussions regarding the installation of the up to date equipment.

At plant A the lecture method seemed to have variable success. For instance, when they invited a consultant from a large firm in the Southeast, it appeared that the workforce were initially impressed by his smoothness, but there still remained an air of scepticism and distrust. They next called in a consultant from a local firm. This consultant seemed to hold more sway with his audience. He put the arguments clearly, succinctly and logically. He was an older man, highly experienced and authoritative. The employees did seem to believe him; the only trouble was that after a few days their memory of the talk seemed to fade, and the old anxieties rose to the fore.

There were a number of anticipated problems at plant B. There the trades union was particularly strong and management felt it had an even greater problem on its hands to convince the workforce that the new technology was not a threat. They decided that they would have to talk to their employees, but it would be too time-consuming to talk to each person individually. They therefore organized small discussion groups. The group discussions were structured in the following ways:

1. The issues were presented to each group in terms of the need for the firm to become more competitive and win more orders. The argument was put that the firm might eventually have to contract if it did not attempt to modernize. The fact of the company's decline was indisputable; each person knew the state of the order book.
2. The issue was considered by the group. They were asked to discuss the action required and any objections they might have and to consider their feelings towards the proposals.
3. The group manager who was conducting the meetings listened to the objections as they were raised *without* disapproval.
4. Discussion was *encouraged* so that as many of the hitherto unresolved concerns were brought out into the open.

5. All questions requesting further information were answered.
6. When the discussion had reached a natural close, the group leader asked the members to make a decision about whether or not they would carry out the desired action.
7. Those members in agreement with the proposed course of action (to introduce the new technology) were asked to show.

The company found that this method of *active participation* was far more effective in bringing about a change in employees' attitudes. It seemed that they were suddenly far more involved in the issues, seeing the positive aspects of the change and the benefits that could accrue to them. They went away from the meeting still discussing the matter. The leadership style of the manager was such that he had enabled people to put their points of view; and in the final analysis there was the desired commitment from the workforce to the change.

Conclusions

PITPROP Engineering feels that it will always use the group discussion method in order to get the commitment of the workforce behind any future change. Even if the outcome of the change had been redundancies that is, an adverse situation, it believes that the arguments would eventually have been accepted.

PITPROP Engineering illustrates the following points:

- The advantages of using participative techniques for changing attitudes rather than the static lecture method.
- The salient features of the communications process, comprising (a) the characteristics of the presenter or group leader, (b) the 'medium of the message' or how it is put across (in this case in a non-threatening way), (c) the content of the message and (d) the characteristics of the audience.

ORGANIZATION DEVELOPMENT

Organization development is a *long-range* effort to improve an organization's *problem-solving and renewal* processes, particularly through a more effective and *collaborative* management of organization *culture* –

with special emphasis on the culture of formal work *teams* – with the assistance of a *change agent*, or catalyst, and the use of the theory and technology of *applied behavioural science*, including *action research*. (French and Bell, 1978, p. 14, my emphasis)

Organization development (OD) is about the more effective use and management of human resources in an enterprise. The development of techniques and abilities to achieve such an end takes time; hence, OD is a *long-range effort*. It is about the identification of human relations problems and of *refreshing* management practices for dealing with them. It is about the *collaboration* between management and subordinates and therefore implies a *participative approach*. In so far as it deals with people's feelings, their attitudes, the way people in the organization treat each other and the norms they develop, it is implicitly about the organization's culture. A primary focus of OD is that of the workgroup and a well-developed technique that of team building (Child, 1984; French and Bell, 1978; Woodcock, 1979; Woodcock and Francis, 1981; see also Chapter 4 of this volume). Development and change is a *planned* process and needs to be handled by someone with experience and status. Usually, this is someone external to the organization; the role of the *change-agent* is non-directive and facilitative. The idea is that he or she enables management to identify problems and develop, with guidance, solutions to them. Finally, OD translates and draws upon the behavioural sciences and develops, from such knowledge, applicable programmes of action.

1 Strategies for Change

Chin and Benne (1976) have described three types of strategies for changing. They are:

- Empirical–rational strategies.
- Normative–re-educative strategies.
- Power-coercive strategies.

Empirical–rational strategies assume that people are rational and motivated by self-interest. They will therefore only change if and when they come to realize that the change is advantageous to them. The normative–re-educative strategies assume that norms underpin behaviour and that change will only occur when the old norms disappear and are supplanted by new and appropriate norms. The third strategy – power–coercion – assumes that change will occur only through the compliance of those with less power to the desires of those with more power. OD is essentially normative–re-educative in that it assumes that knowledge and information is an insufficient condition for bringing about change. Norms are part of the fabric of social interaction; they are imbued with people's beliefs, feelings, attitudes and values (Bennis, 1969). People will only become committed to change once their normative orientations to old ways and patterns of behaviour are relinquished and new ones put in their place (see also Chell, 1985a, chapter 4; Fishbein and Ajzen, 1975).

2   Action Research

Action research assumes the gathering of data as evidence of the extant situation. These data are fed back to key players in that situation. This process is likely to result in a revision of the perceptions of the situation and thereby begin to bring about change. Thus, fundamental to understanding action research is understanding the status of the data themselves. As French and Bell (1978) put it:

> Many OD interventions are designed either to generate or to plan actions based on data. A key value inculcated in organization members is a belief in the validity, desirability and usefulness of *data about the system itself*, specifically, data about the system's culture and processes. (French and Bell, 1978, p. 79)

This means:

- The value of data is emphasized; members are encouraged to collect, work with and utilize data for problem-solving.
- In OD the data are about human and social processes, not technical, marketing or financial data.
- The data are used by the people who generate them and are not the property of top management.
- Data which contradict accepted views or whatever are regarded as important because they point up differences in attitudes, perspectives and motivations.
- Evaluation of data shifts from an emotive 'good' or 'bad' to a consideration of their consequences or functionality.
- Data are used not to punish people but to aid them in problem-solving.

● The use of data in OD is akin to their use in the scientific method in so far as decisions are made on the basis of empirical facts rather than power, position, tradition, persuasion or other factors.

● The data arise from the stated needs and problems of organization members, and in this way enable greater anticipation and awareness of, and responsiveness to, such needs.

The role of the change agent in all this is to facilitate such a process; to help people to generate valid information; to create conditions under which free and informed choices can be made around the data; and to enable members to feel a commitment to the decisions reached (Argyris, 1970). People may become so familiar with particular ways of going about their business and thinking about problems that they cease to realize that choices have already been made and that there are other options, other alternatives. One type of data which may be generated is that of increasing self-awareness. For example, a not untypical reaction to the use of participative techniques by frustrated managers is that they have tried them and as far as they are concerned they do not work. This may be explained by a distinction made by Argyris (1976) between *espoused* theories and theories *in use*. An espoused theory is what people say they believe and a theory in use is what appears to guide their actual behaviour. Thus, a manager may espouse the idea of participative management. His or her behaviour may still be dictatorial and non-collaborative. The upshot will be that the manager, being unaware of his or her style or the need to modify his or her style of leadership, concludes that participative management does not work. Greater self-awareness might lead to other conclusions.

How does action research fit into all this? French and Bell (1978) define action research as:

the process of systematically collecting research data about an ongoing system relative to some objective, goal, or need of that system; feeding these data back into the system; taking actions by altering selected variables within the system based both on the data and on hypotheses; and evaluating the results of actions by collecting more data. (French and Bell, 1978, p. 88)

The procedure is rather like taking a series of snapshots. After each photograph has been taken it is shown to the people in the picture for their comments, and in the light of this a modification is made before the next picture is taken. In other words, data are collected, they are fed back to those people who generated the data, and discussion takes place as the data are worked through, with the outcome that action is taken. This can happen several times so that there is in effect a *cycle of interactions.*

An alternative way of defining *action research* is as

the application of the scientific method of fact finding and experimentation to practical problems requiring actual solutions and involving the
collaboration and cooperation of scientists, practitioners and laymen.
The desired outcomes of the action research approach are solutions to
the immediate problems and a contribution to scientific knowledge and
theory. (French and Bell, 1978, p. 90)

The scientific method comprises four stages: (a) the identification of a problem, (b) the formulation of hypotheses about possible causes, (c) data collection and (d) the falsification of particular hypotheses. From the deductions which have been made and which have caused the rejection of certain hypotheses and not others, it may be possible to set up particular situations in order to test the remaining hypotheses further. Further data are then collected leading to a narrowing of the possible causes. Certainty is never attainable, only a level of probability that a particular explanation is the correct one.

Similarly, in action research a problem and possible causes are identified. This suggests that some remedial action should be taken. Data are collected on people's perspectives of what the problem is and how it might be solved. Several possibilities emerge. In order to decide on appropriate action, the possible actions generated may be prioritized and worked through systematically. They should be tested systematically and evaluated for their effects through data collection.

Non-positivists have argued that it is not possible to collect valid data which depict organizationally based phenomena by means of the 'scientific method' (see, for example, Burrell and Morgan, 1979; Dachler, 1988 and chapter 6 of this volume). The non-positivist argues for the need to get close to situations, that taking an 'objective' stance is not possible, and that a holistic approach to understanding phenomena is the only approach which will yield insights and a depth of understanding. The 'variable' approach, in contrast, isolates artificially aspects of a situation deemed to be important by the researcher, *qua* external observer. As such it does not account for complex interactions which result in 'patterns' without identifiable causes. Nor does it allow for the assumptions being made implicitly by the 'objective' observer (the researcher) or the legitimacy of multiple perspectives on the situation.

This alternative perspective, at the very least, reminds us of the complexities of organizational phenomena and that trying to plummet their depths is by no means an easy task. In attempting to research organizational culture – an organizational phenomenon which raises similar methodological issues – it has been argued that the 'holistic' approach lacks 'analytical bite' (Pettigrew, 1979), though researches which counter this view may be identified (Chell *et al.*, 1991). Sackmann (1991) takes a middle course and puts forward a set of generic concepts which, while identified primarily for the purposes of depicting the nature of organizational culture, may serve to analyse different kinds of organizational data. They are:

● Dictionary knowledge	descriptive categories	'what is'
● Directory knowledge	causal-analytic attributions	'how things are done'
● Recipe knowledge	causal-normative attributions	'should do' 'ought to'
● Axiomatic knowledge	basic reasons	'why certain things happen'

These different types of organizational knowledge inform individuals' beliefs and actions. *Dictionary* knowledge describes a slice of organizational reality. *Directory* knowledge comprises expectations about cause–effect relations in respect of operations and concerns perceived actions and their respective outcomes. *Recipe* knowledge, on the other hand, concerns cause–effect relations of *hypothetical* events. Recipe knowledge is recommendatory; it comprises recommendations of how things *ought* to be done and in effect prescriptions for action – *recipes for survival and success. Axiomatic* knowledge is about ultimate explanations and basic reasons as to why certain events happen. These four types of knowledge comprise the organizational member's cognitive map. They enable us to elucidate the different kinds of data which inform organizational members' actions and beliefs. However, they enable a description of the extant and the assumed situation; OD is about change and development of individuals and groups. We now need to consider the next stage in the process – that of the OD intervention.

3   OD Interventions

OD interventions are *sets of structured activities* in which selected organizational units (target groups or individuals) engage with a task or a sequence of tasks where the task goals are related directly or indirectly to organizational improvement. Interventions constitute the action thrust of organization development; they 'make things happen' and are 'what's happening'. (French and Bell, 1978, p. 102)

OD interventions have been classified in various ways. This may be done in the form of a three-way table or cube, the three dimensions of which constitute the *type* of intervention, the *focus* of the intervention and the nature of the *problems diagnosed* (see Figure 8.1). Diagnostic activities comprise any available method for data collection, whereas survey–feedback includes, additionally, action plans based on the collected data.

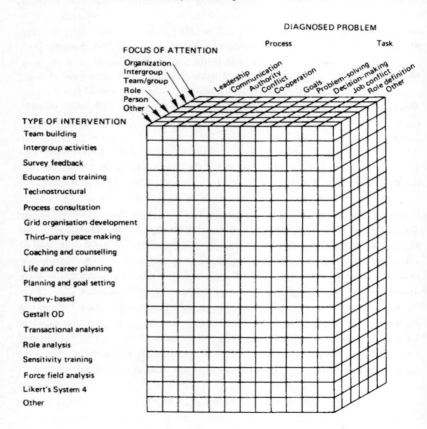

FIGURE 8.1   *The OD cube: a typology of intervention*

Adaptation of R. A. Schmuck and M. B. Miles (eds) (1971) *Organization Development in Schools* (San Diego, CA: University Associates) p. 8.

Team-building activities are used to enhance the effectiveness of teams, while *intergroup* activities are designed to focus upon and improve the operations of interdependent groups. *Education and training* activities may be directed at individuals or groups and may focus on any issue relevant to the party concerned. *Technostructural* activities comprise interventions which are aimed at improving the effectiveness of changes in task, organizational structure and technology. *Grid organization development* has been described in Chapter 4 of this volume. *Process consultation* is a method by which a client learns how to diagnose and handle process issues which occur within his or her own organizational environment (e.g. communications, problem solving and leadership issues). *Third-party peacemaking* is the mediation of an experienced consultant (the third party) between two parties in conflict; this conflict is usually interpersonal. *Coaching and counselling* are used to enable an individual to become more effective behaviourally and in terms of goal achievement, while *life and career planning* activities focus on the personal objectives of individuals. *Theory-based* interventions include Lawrence and Lorsch's contingency theory, while other types of intervention include sensitivity training and transactional analysis (TA).

4 Process Consultation

A broad aim of process consultation (P-C) is that of helping a manager diagnose accurately organizational problems and to develop action programmes to deal with them. In process consultation, the diagnosis is carried out *jointly*, that is, between the client and consultant. A more specific aim of P-C is to improve organizational processes. These may range from work flow, interpersonal relations, communications, intergroup relations and so on. Schein (1969) identifies the potential target areas as (a) any aspect of the communications process, (b) the functional roles of group members, (c) the processes of group problem-solving and decision-making, (d) the establishment of group norms and development, (e) leadership style and the exercise of authority and (f) intergroup processes.

P-C is a set of activities on the part of the consultant which help the client to perceive, understand, and act upon process events which occur in the client's environment. (Schein, 1969, p. 9)

The process consultant is therefore trying to give the client an *insight* into the processes by which the organization operates, to identify problem areas and develop effective ways of tackling them.

The first stage of P-C is the *initial contact with the client organization.* Establishing a relationship with the client is an important part of the process; the critical issue is that of assessing whether or not the consultancy is likely to be successful. This assessment is made on the basis of initial impressions and concerns the degree of openness of the client and his/her ability to examine organizational processes critically.

The next stage comprises setting up an *exploratory meeting.* This will be attended by the contact client and a purposefully selected group of other organizational members. The criteria for selection are (a) status and influence, (b) understanding of behavioural science and process consultancy and (c) ability to identify the problem(s). At this stage it is essential to avoid the inclusion of hostile individuals. Through discussion the process consultant will be able to determine what the problem is, and assess whether he or she can be of help and whether the problem is of interest. If so, then future action plans can be formulated.

Schein (1969; 1980) makes a distinction between the formal contractual relationship between client and consultant and the *psychological contract.* In the first case, there is a need to establish the amount of time needed to do the job, the services to be performed and the rate of pay. The psychological contract, on the other hand, concerns the expectations which consultant and client have of each other:

> The client may expect me to give him personal evaluations of the people in his organization; he may expect me to tell him how to deal with 'problem people' in his organization; he may expect me to give 'expert' opinions on how he should handle management problems . . . and so on. . . . On my side, I have to be clear as I can be in what I expect of the organization and of myself in my role as consultant. For example, I expect a willingness to diagnose and explore issues . . . to take some time to find out what is going on . . . to be supported in my suggestions as to *how* to gather data; I expect organization members to be committed to the project, and not to be dragging their feet or persisting in a veiled resistance. (Schein, 1969, p. 85)

The consultant in such preliminary meetings moves towards establishing the following objectives:

1. To expose any misconceptions.
2. To conceive of the whole organization as the client.
3. To establish the need for trust.

4. To shape the client's expectations of the consultant, for example that his function is *not* as 'expert'.

In addition, he must get his client used to the idea that the consultant is there to listen and may appear relatively inactive. He must make clear decisions about his own role, for example, to avoid discussion or involvement in interpersonal processes unless requested to do otherwise and to avoid getting drawn into discussions of the content of what the group is talking about.

The third stage of the process is the selection of the setting and method of working. What is observed when should be worked out with the client; this means that the activity is highly focused. Schein suggests the place to start is the 'top' of the organization, because this is where greatest impact and influence for change can be achieved. Naturally, the setting should be one where it is relatively easy to observe interpersonal and group processes and should be of 'real' work, with members performing their natural role and function. The method of carrying out the consultancy work should be as congruent as possible with the values of P-C. Data-gathering goes on all the time, but everything the consultant does, every question he asks, must be regarded as an intervention. Therefore he must think through all that he does in terms of its probable impact upon the organization. As for purposeful methods of gathering data, the use of the questionnaire survey technique is rejected on the grounds that it is too impersonal; it tends to distance the consultant from the clients. The interview is the main tool, the preliminary ones being most important as they indicate to the consultant who and what to observe. The content of the consultant's questions should be relevant and not obscure. Indeed, such questions may be a powerful educative tool in themselves, giving the client a fresh way of viewing the organization, the workgroup and his/her network of relationships within it.

Although it is difficult to distinguish between data-gathering and interventions in that the two are intimately interwoven, it is possible to suggest a broad classification scheme of interventions (Schein, 1969). This comprises: *agenda-setting*, where, for example, the group may focus attention on process issues or rearranging the agenda; *feedback*, which may be either to the group or to individuals, must be done with sensitivity to the feelings of the recipient; *coaching or counselling*, which is a natural consequence of the feedback process whereby a manager discovers an inappropriate behaviour and wants advice as to how he or she may change it; *structural suggestions*, which are rare in that the consultant is not usually in a position to suggest how work should be carried out – indeed his role is one of enabling clients to solve their own problems, not to solve them for them.

The final stages of the P-C are those of evaluation and disengagement. This concerns the problem of assessing whether the consultation has been successful, which raises all the problems of what constitutes success in this instance, and by whose lights. Whatever conclusions are arrived at, success can only be measured in relative terms and a measure of the client's satisfaction is the ability to disengage gradually rather than that an abrupt termination of the contract occur!

5   Conflict Management: Third-party Interventions

Attempting to bring about changes in an organization can result not only in resistance, but also in conflict. Where such issues constitute a need for change in work practices, for instance, the trades union may be involved and the issue be resolved by means of negotiation. However, there are areas of conflict which may be of an interpersonal nature and may be resolved by the expert intervention of a third party, who may be internal or external to the organization. This is not to suggest that such conflict is bad or destructive, rather that it needs to be handled.

Walton (1969) has developed a model of interpersonal conflict (see Figure 8.2). He describes conflict as *cyclical*; an event may *trigger* opposition between two parties who then engage in 'conflict-relevant behaviours'; various issues emerge as being pertinent to the conflict; the conflict temporarily subsides, but is not necessarily resolved. The cycle repeats itself, although the issues may, typically, undergo change. This is noticeably so where the conflict is initially *emotional*, that is, has arisen from anger or distrust of the other party, and an issue is seized upon in order that the conflict be seen as *substantive*. Barriers to resolving conflict may be *internal* to the individuals due to their feelings, attitudes and values, or *external*, for example as a result of group pressures or norms. There may also be some *physical* barriers to conflict resolution, arising from such constraints as role position, time available, location factors, etc. However, conflict management is not simply about conflict resolution *per se*. It is about understanding and being able to weigh up the costs compared with the gains; the consequences of recurrent conflict; developing an appreciation of the issues involved, identifying desired outcomes and developing a strategy for achieving those outcomes.

There are several methods for dealing with conflict; they are *avoidance*, *constraint* and the use of *improved coping methods*, and *confrontation*. Interpersonal peacemaking, according to Walton, involves the adoption of the well-managed confrontation. If applied, this method should result in

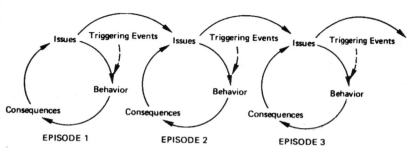

FIGURE 8.2   *A cyclical model of interpersonal conflict*

SOURCE   R. E. Walton (1969) *Interpersonal Peacemaking: Confrontations and Third Party Consultation* (Reading, Mass.: Addision-Wesley) p. 72.

greater understanding of the issues involved, greater authenticity and enhanced personal integrity. There are, however, certain conditions which will increase the likelihood of the confrontation being successful. These are:

● Ensuring that both parties have incentives to resolve the dispute.
● Establishing power equality between the two parties.
● Synchronizing efforts between the two parties to confront each other, that is, getting the timing right.
● Allowing adequate time for the *differentiation phase* – airing of views and differences of opinion – before moving into the *integration phase* – the discovery of common ground, etc.
● Creating conditions which favour openness.
● Increasing mutual understanding through effective communication.
● Maintaining the stress and tension in the situation at a moderate level.

In order for the third party or consultant to be effective, it is advisable that he/she should carry out preliminary interviews with the two parties separately and give careful thought to the nature of the setting for the first confrontation; it should take place on neutral ground. The degree of formality of the setting should be considered, as should the time allocated for the first meeting. And, finally, a judgement should be made about the composition of the group: would it be useful, productive or whatever, to invite people in addition to the two protagonists?

What part may the third-party consultant play to regulate and steer the confrontation towards a positive conclusion? He or she can referee the interaction to ensure the two parties have 'equal air time';˙determine the agenda for discussion; summarize and restate the issue; give feedback and make observations about what is going on as it is happening; encourage diagnosis by the two parties; prescribe what should appropriately be discussed at different points in the confrontation; and handle dialogue which blocks further discussion. The consultant must also be able to plan for future dialogue in subsequent meetings.

6   The Continued Relevance of OD

In many ways, the practices of OD could not be more relevant in the current economic climate where externally imposed change from economic pressure and global competitiveness suggests the need for managed organizational responsiveness. Further, keeping up to date in terms of new technological advances needs flexibility, adaptability and responsiveness to change. Where attitudes are locked into the old ways of doing things, where employees feel threatened by the thought of change, where different perspectives on solutions to problems are inevitable, and where there is a need to optimize the allocation of resources: all such problems need to be dealt with effectively. When stripped down, these problems are human problems with which the various techniques, and interventions of OD are tailored to deal. Passmore (1978), comparing socio-technical systems, job redesign and survey feedback interventions, suggested that even in a capital-intensive setting the survey feedback approach was of value. It not only enabled management to understand employees' feelings about an issue, but also was the basis of building trust between management and workforce. The problem of using the socio-technical approach without survey–feedback is that it does not dispel the suspicions of the workforce, who may see it as yet another management 'gimmick'. Combining the two methods is a balanced and potentially more effective approach to organizational change (Passmore, 1978).

Such interventions cannot be divorced from the wider organizational context – technological push and its implications for changes in job content, factory layout and workflow. This takes us beyond the original conception of OD as defined by French and Bell (1978) and outlined in an earlier section of this chapter, to a consideration of the impact of work redesign and the ability of management to introduce new technology and ways of working, with people as the primary object of concern. Guest (1984) has pointed out that OD itself has changed in recent years and has tried to accommodate such issues as work redesign (Hackman and Oldham, 1980).

Despite such a shift, the effectiveness of OD interventions has come increasingly into question in recent years (Jones and Pfeiffer, 1977; Legge, 1984). Guest (1984) takes a more optimistic view, while Cox and Cooper (1984) sit on the fence, suggesting that 'evaluation of other types of intervention is almost impossible; in the case of OD . . . there is no way of knowing what would have happened without the psychologist' (p. 164). One problem is that the culture of the organization affects the process of evaluation of OD. The reason for this is that in attempting a systematic assessment, it is only possible to do so by adopting criteria which one party deems relevant. A related objection to the OD approach is that of *corporatism*, assuming that its efforts are directed towards the achievement of organizational objectives (see the brief discussion of this point in Chapter 7). Indeed, Littler (1985) goes further and suggests that 'in the USA job redesign has been pioneered by *some* consultants as a way of undermining, or avoiding trade unions'. This issue may be more poignant if one is considering the role of *internal* rather than *external* consultants. The external consultant is hired to help an organization diagnose and resolve a constellation of problems which may be bound up with attempts to bring about change. The internal consultant, however, may be in a different position:

> Internal consultants have a vested interest in change. This is how they legitimate their presence. Many client groups have a vested interest in relative stability. They have quotas to reach, deadlines to meet and empires to protect. There is no reason to expect them to readily accept changes which are against their interests. That is why the relationship between internal consultants and clients is a problem one. (Pettigrew, 1976, p. 205)

This and other problems associated with the role of managers as internal consultants or change agents are discussed by Blackler and Brown (1980). Their reassessment of a major intervention at Shell not only comments on the ineffectualness of those managers as change agents, but also on the intervention strategy *per se*. The way forward for the implementation and evaluation of change interventions is possibly one of (a) clarifying the objectives of the change programme, (b) examining the different values and perspectives of the parties involved, (c) looking for contradictions in positions and the effect these are likely to have on post change evaluations, (d) establishing what are the priorities in organizational change effects and (e) adopting an evaluation approach which is directed towards examining the target effects, while bearing in mind the roles played by different 'stakeholders' in the evaluation study (Legge, 1984). The dilemma which remains is that there is still a choice which has to be made. The options, according to Legge, are those of making a professional judgement which is accepted by the client or offering technical services which are utilized at the behest of the client. She recommends the latter approach. Either step must be taken against a prior decision to relinquish the role of applied behavioural science researcher.

In sum, there are values and political considerations of attempting to bring about change. However, these should not be regarded as crippling, that is, leading only to inaction. Rather, they should lead to a heightened awareness by management of various organizational complexities which can inhibit the change process. For the change agent, and more particularly the evaluator of the change, this process presents choices. The options are clear: (a) to evaluate the change by the different criteria of the parties involved including those of the change agent, but not necessarily to the satisfaction of any one party, or (b) to design an evaluation around the requirements of those with power to bring about change. While the latter option would seem to be compatible with the dictum 'he who pays the piper calls the tune', there is a greater likelihood of the change being implemented and the results of the evaluation utilized. This still leaves open the possibility that if the client's values are too widely discrepant from those of the consultant, such that an unsuccessful intervention is foreseen, then the consultant can decline to take the job on (Schein, 1969). These are just some of the considerations in the development of an effective strategy for bringing change about.

SUMMARY

———— The stimulus for organizational change can come from external or internal forces. Those companies identified as having a superior performance, financially and economically, also seem to have developed, and draw upon, their human resources effectively.

———— Awareness of the need to change has to be followed through by an identification of the problem areas: at the organization-environment interface, and the levels of the group and the individuals. In addition, the organization must develop a detailed plan for bringing about development and change. This should be accompanied by a well-thought-out strategy for effective implementation. Such a strategy, it is suggested, should be characterized by the clarification of the company's aims and the involvement of subordinates, the identification and resolution of people's concerns, joint decision-making on priorities and ability to secure agreement.

A major problem is people's natural tendency to resist change. The example of Pitprop Engineering Plc illustrates two methods by which management might attempt to change the attitudes of its workforce to the introduction of new technology. The 'lecture' method was less effective than the 'group discussion' method. Such discussion enabled employees to air their views and express their feelings, and was handled in such a way that they were not made to feel inhibited. The groups were thus able to arrive at a lasting agreement.

Organization development is about the more effective use and management of human resources in an enterprise. A long-term view and participative approach are adopted. The change process is planned and usually implemented by a change agent.

The strategy for change is assumed to be a normative–re-educative one: that is, change will occur only when the norms which underpin behaviour are supplanted by new and more appropriate ones.

Effective and lasting change can occur only if people's beliefs and attitudes are based on valid data. These data are about human and social processes and are used to facilitate problem-solving, conflict resolution and decision-making. Action research is a method by which data can be collected about the social system.

Non-positivists criticize action research in so far as it assumes the validity of the 'scientific method'. They criticize the assumptions of the scientific method pointing out that it is not possible to be objective or to isolate variables. A holistic approach is advocated.

Sackman has put forward a model for analysing organizational culture. This enables the depiction of different types of organizational knowledge. It is potentially a powerful tool for gaining insights into the knowledge and understanding which inform organizational members' actions and beliefs.

OD interventions are sets of structured activities whereby groups or individuals engage in tasks whose goals are organizational improvement. Two well-known interventions are process consultation and third-party interventions. The aim of process consultation is to enable a manager to diagnose organizational problems and develop plans to deal with them. The methods used are usually interview and observation and the main focus is usually the group. An agenda will be set and the consultant will observe the group process, giving feedback where it is thought appropriate; some counselling may also be given to those participants whose behaviour is in some way unacceptable.

Resistance to change may result in interpersonal conflict. The use of a third party or consultant is one way of effectively managing the conflict. The consultant interviews the parties before bringing them together to confront the issue. The consultant's role is that of referee and regulator of the interaction. He or she may give feedback and make observations, and may also encourage the two parties to diagnose what is going on. It may take several such confrontations before the issue is finally resolved.

Organization development techniques which address themselves to the problems of attitude change, conflict and the need for organizations to be flexible, adaptable and innovative are highly relevant in today's economic climate. One lingering question is how effective is OD? Criticisms include corporatism and the use of internal consultants. Serious attempts to evaluate change programmes must (a) clarify its objectives, (b) examine different perspectives and values of the parties concerned, (c) look for contradictions in positions and their possible effects on post change evaluations, (d) establish what are the priorities in organizational change effects and (e) adopt an evaluation approach which is directed at the target effects.

9 Controlling and Managing Organizations

INTRODUCTION

Anyone who is managing others must in some sense feel that the situation is under control; it is *how* this state of affairs is achieved which is at the crux of managerial success. *To control* is to 'dominate, command; hold in check . . .' (Fowler and Fowler, 1964). It is to have influence over others in such a way as to be able to hold their behaviour and actions *in check* (Tannenbaum, 1962). A person may dominate by means of *coercion* (for example, holding a pistol to someone's head). This method of control is frequently used by terrorists and criminals, and increasingly by the police. Physical punishment as a means of controlling offending school children has, until recently, been used with restraint in schools. But coercion, i.e. the use of force, is not a common method for managing people in industry. The use of *authority* is a more normal practice. Authority arises from the hierarchical command structure. It gives seniority to some and subordinates others. It establishes a 'pecking order', clarifies a person's work identity through their position within the hierarchy. It also legitimates their position. The armed forces rely upon this method of control, as does industry to a large extent, but the need to establish and maintain authority and discipline is by no means the whole story. Other aspects of control have to do with concepts like *consent* and *involvement*. In other words, there has to be a will to do what is required of one or the work will not get done. Further, the argument goes, if a person is *involved* in the job, that is committed, they are more likely to be highly motivated to do the job to the best of their ability and produce an output of good quality. The problem for management is that one cannot force people to consent, nor can one make people feel involved. It is a *real* problem, because the natural style of some people is to want to *tell* others what they should do, whereas management is so much easier when people realize what needs to be done and *want* to do it.

In a sense, the whole of this book has been about managerial control, and so it is hoped that this chapter will pull together much of what has gone before. First, some of the approaches to organizational and managerial control will be examined; these include scientific management, technology-led and end-user approaches, participation, quality circles and the total quality management approach. Finally, the chapter will be concluded with

211

a discussion of some control issues which are part of the effective management of human resources for optimizing performance.

SCIENTIFIC MANAGEMENT

Frederick Winslow Taylor was the so-called father of scientific management. This approach is associated in the minds of many with the degradation of work, the deskilling of jobs, boredom and exploitation. Taylor's intention was to increase the efficiency and productivity of labour by methodically and systematically working out the best way of doing a job, and thus eradicating wasteful movement and effort. Once the most efficient way of doing a job was found, it was then timed to see how long it would take to complete and this work (conceived of by the Gilbreths) led to the method of time and motion study.

Taylorism may be thought of as a managerial ideology or a system of work organization (Klein, 1976; Littler, 1982). As a managerial ideology, it has largely been discredited (Fox, 1974; Rose, 1975), yet as a system of job design practices it still persists. It affects work design, the structure of control and the employment relationship. Taylor's concept of the worker was that of a lazy individual too stupid to work out the best way of doing a job for him/herself. It was therefore management's role to decide what work should be carried out and how it should be done. The basic idea was to 'decompose' jobs into their simplest constituent parts. This resulted in the following set of design criteria:

- Maximum fragmentation of tasks.
- Minimization of skill requirements (employees being limited to carrying out a single task).
- Minimization of operator learning/training time.
- Reduction of material handling.
- Specialization of work by limiting the variety of tasks done.
- Increased repetitiveness of job content.
- The divorce of planning from doing.
- The divorce of 'direct' and 'indirect' labour, all preparation and servicing tasks being removed to be performed separately by unskilled and cheaper workers.
- Increased substitutability of employees.

These principles help to reduce the costs of production and, combined with the establishment of standard times for every task, could be linked to an incentive payment system. Taylor's ultimate idea was that of establishing a separate planning department. Even without this, with the planning process entirely in management's hands, this represents a shift of an order of magnitude nearer to total managerial control. The study of jobs involved (a) gathering information, usually through observation, about how a job was done, (b) selecting the right person for the job, (c) training in the new scientific method and (d) eliciting cooperation between management and worker. The application of scientific management also meant discovering which were the right tools for the job. For example, in Taylor's study of shovelling pig-iron, he discovered that the tonnage shovelled is optimized if the length of the handle is shortened and the load that the shovel will take is twenty-one and a half pounds (Taylor, 1947). The incentive to change working methods was that of offering an increase in pay of, according to Taylor, about 60 per cent. If an employee kept falling short of the target he would be disciplined or fired. In some cases the incentive (apart from the increase in pay) was competition with another workgroup, as in the case of Gilbreth's bricklayers and the reinforced-concrete workers! Cooperation was seen to be possible through this new method of handling workers: that is, Taylor appeared to see it in terms of their personal development; they would be trained to be skilful pig-iron shovellers, bricklayers or whatever.

Many of the problems and therefore criticisms of scientific management were apparent even in Taylor's day. There was an implicit assumption of unitarism (Fox, 1966), i.e. that workers and management alike were (or should be) pulling together towards a shared organizational goal. It is management's prerogative to set the standard for performance on that job, by scientifically measuring what performance can be achieved. Employees must trust management to arrive at a performance standard that is fair and achievable and to offer an equitable incentive. However, implicit in Taylorism is a cynical view of employees as people who are *solely* motivated by money (hence, Taylor's ideas are associated with an economic model of human nature, see Schein, 1980). While money is one important source of motivation at work because it enables people to fulfil many of their off-the-job needs, numerous research studies have shown that it cannot obviate the problems of alienation, boredom, industrial sabotage and so on (Roethlisberger and Dickson, 1939; McGregor, 1960; Rose, 1975). On the other side of the coin, Taylorism has been thought of as exploitative (Brown, 1954), a means of increasing output for the benefit of the owners.

Littler (1982, 1985) has discussed some of the implications of Taylorism for job design, managerial control over task performance and the employment relationship. As was pointed out above, Taylorism is associated with job fragmentation and deskilling and divorcing mental from physical work. The idea is to reduce a skilled job into its component parts and to ensure that each worker carries out one component of the job, specializing but at the same time becoming less skilled. This has implications for cost control, given that the labour of a semi-skilled or unskilled worker is cheaper than that of a skilled employee.

The practice of Taylorism is limited to industries where there are mass markets and hence a need for mass production and throughput. It is also constrained by the nature of the technology, certain tasks being fundamental until a change in technology occurs. The implications for managerial control are in the need to coordinate this extensive division of labour; these costs may be high. Furthermore, during an upswing in the economic cycle, the price of worker compliance will be increased. A further problem for management occurs if competition in the market place for the sale of their goods is not regulated solely or even primarily by price. Where reliability, quality and design assume greater importance, this implies a need for worker cooperation and commitment. But it is precisely those qualities which are not cultivated by a Taylorite managerialism. Thus managerial control of the quality of output is severely undermined. A final but by no means trivial criticism of Taylorism is the implicit ideology of the employee as an extension of the machine. This issue is pursued in more detail in a later section of this chapter.

PARTICIPATION

Participation has been viewed by some as a managerial tactic for achieving organizational outcomes such as increased productivity without any commensurate gains for the workforce. In other words, it has been perceived as a managerial tool of manipulation rather than as a genuine attempt to involve employees in their work or to devolve power down the organization. Worker participation in management (WPM) takes two distinctly different forms: *direct* and *indirect* participation. Direct participation means involvement in the nature of the job, its content, how it is done, etc., while indirect forms of participation imply some form of system of representation which enables the views of the shopfloor being put to management.

Two models of participation have been put forward (Heller, 1976), but neither is sufficiently comprehensive or adequate. They are the human relations model and the human resources model. The human relations model assumes that participation (presumably direct or indirect) leads to increased worker satisfaction and morale, which in turn leads to lowered resistance and increased compliance. The very idea of worker compliance suggests that control is still firmly in the hands of management, and it is easy to see how a cynical view could develop of participation within a particular concern. The human resources model emphasizes the reserves of untapped resources, skills and know-how inherent in the workforce. In order to release this resource, management must consult, discuss and encourage participation so that the organization can benefit by making sounder decisions on all matters of which the workers can be expected to have knowledge and experience. Thus participation in this case would lead to improved decision-making and control, which in turn would result in increased subordinate satisfaction and morale. Not only that, but the improved satisfaction and morale would feedback in a cyclical way, thus having a secondary effect in improving decision-making and control. Both models can be criticized for their implicit unitarism and because they do not consider any need for increased *worker* control or power as an explicit consequence of genuine participation. Nor do they, as Heller points out, take into account the sorts of contingencies which will affect the degree and extent of participation over different issues at different points in time.

Locke and Schweiger (1979) have critically examined the effectiveness of participation using the criteria of increased satisfaction and productivity (see Chell, 1985a). They make the point that there is no evidence to suggest that participation results in increased productivity, although there is evidence that it results, on the whole, in increased satisfaction. Strauss (1982) makes the additional point that evaluating the effectiveness of participation on those criteria alone is too restrictive; he suggests two additional criteria – increased power and control. Assessing the extent of employee power and control is facilitated by considering the following critical dimensions: organizational level, degree of control, issues and ownership. Organizational level determines whether direct or indirect methods of participation are appropriate. Involvement at the job level may make work more meaningful and satisfying, but it will give employees no say over wider organizational issues which affect them. At the other extreme employee involvement at board level can be achieved only through a representative system (Brannen *et al.*, 1976; Bullock, 1976; Chell, 1983). The effectiveness of either approach depends ultimately upon the extent to which employees *can* influence decision-making (Strauss, 1982). The issues which are discussed interrelate with organizational level, while ownership may or may not include control. For example, when the coal industry in the UK was nationalized it did not increase the mineworkers' influence or control. In Yugoslavia, self-management has not resolved the relationship between bottom-up participation and top-down management; workers still view managers as all-powerful, even though managers regard themselves as being hamstrung by red tape (Rus, 1970; Strauss, 1982).

Experiments with worker participation at board level have highlighted the critical importance of knowledge and expertise as a power equalizer (Chell and Cox, 1979; Mulder, 1971; Strauss, 1982). However, where the production technology is complex, this increases the reliance on experts and may increase the knowledge gap between the technical expert and the worker representative. Indeed, on the critical issues, such as an investment decision which implies technological change, affecting job content and numbers employed, the representative either takes an adversarial position or is accused by the shopfloor of having 'sold out' to management. Unless there are equal numbers of worker representatives, they cannot control the decision outcome. They can act only as a communications channel to the shopfloor, keeping them informed of what is going on, and attempt to influence critical decisions as they arise by putting forward a well-researched, alternative case. This would increase the options open to management, but would necessitate that the worker representative/director have a backup team to enable him or her to make out a case and that he or she have countervailing expertise.

The degree of control exercised is not simply a function of expertise, but also of motivation to participate. Shopfloor workers, in general, prefer to discuss issues which affect them directly, and have less interest in, or enthusiasm for, organizational policy. Involvement at job level is motivating for several reasons: (a) it creates a sense of belonging, and as such reduces worker alienation; (b) it draws on the workers' knowledge of the job and enhances their self-respect; (c) it increases their feelings of well-being; (d) it increases their sense of autonomy and responsibility for outcomes, such as a job well done; and (e) through feedback, gives them knowledge of results. High internal work motivation (Hackman and Oldham, 1980) may be a necessary but not sufficient condition for satisfaction with the job and the employing organization. In addition, the relationship between satisfaction and performance or productivity is tenuous to say the least (Locke and Schweiger, 1979; Wall and Lischeron, 1977). A further condition, therefore, would appear to be receipt of equitable rewards (Adams, 1965; Porter and Lawler, 1968). However, such a condition is by no means easy to achieve in the first place nor to sustain (Opsahl and Dunnette, 1966; Vroom, 1964).

A fundamental fact of organizational life is economic control of one sort or another; its relationship to organizational effectiveness, productivity, distribution of power and influence and worker satisfaction. Here the contrast may be made between capitalism, where economic, financial and managerial control rest with the employer and shareholders of a company, and the Yugoslavian self-management system together with isolated experiments such as Mondragon. A middle alternative is that of issuing shares to employees. In the latter case, it would seem that the *psychological* impact of shared ownership is reduced *if* perceived influence over management decisions is low and is duly exacerbated where there is a lack of trust in management (Chell, 1980).

In sum, if participation is to work:

● Participants should *want* to participate.
● They should have knowledge and skills to participate effectively, including both social/organizational skills and content/technical skills.
● Both management and workers should view participation as legitimate.
● Efforts made to participate should be rewarded by influence over decision-making and the receipt of extrinsic satisfiers equitably distributed, which may be symbolic of the success of the participatory scheme (see the later section on quality control circles).
● There should be a psychological sense of owning – owning the worker participation scheme, if not ownership in the company.
● The role of the worker representatives should be clarified; their incumbents should be able to deal with role conflict, and communicate with, educate and listen to their constituents.
● The participation scheme should be so managed that it achieves an early success.
● Formal (*de jure*) rules legislating for participation should be employed; these will increase the employees' sense of influence and involvement.

THE TECHNOLOGICAL IMPERATIVE VERSUS THE END-USER APPROACHES

How management chooses to exercise control is exemplified when decisions are made to implement technological change. Blackler and Brown (1985, 1986) have developed a useful conceptual framework to demonstrate the different forms this control may take. An outline of these contrasting models which they refer to as the *task-and-technology-* and *organization-and-end-user-* centred approaches is presented in Table 9.1. The contrast is between management, whose priority is that of increasing the efficiency of operatives through the introduction of new technology, by engaging

TABLE 9.1 *Technology- versus end-user-centred approaches to organizational work design*

Model 1 Task and technology-centred approach	*Model 2 Organization and end-user-centred approach*
Phase 1 Initial review	
(a) Operating conditions (b) People are a costly resource, to be reduced if possible (c) Key actors: top and senior managers	(a) Operating conditions (b) People are a costly resource to be more fully utilized (c) Key actors: initially from any part of organization, then top management
Phase 2 Exploration and prior justification	
(a) Tightly prescribed planning objectives (b) Central coordination and control (c) Expert driven (d) 'Most modern' syndrome (e) Key actors: managerial project team including technical and financial experts	(a) General policy formulation (b) Decentralization, staff involvement (c) Concern for end users (d) System development potential rather than machine capability (e) Key actors: a diverse and representative group, or a consulting project group, or a management plus shadow group Trades union involvement

Model 1 Task and technology-centred approach	Model 2 Organization and end-user-centred approach
Phase 3 Design of the system	
(a) Machines over people	(a) People to use machines
(b) Task fragmentation	(b) Job enrichment, teams
(c) 'Clean design'	(c) Operators' maintenance needs
(d) 'Final design'	(d) Incremental and educative design approach
(e) Key actors: design engineers and technical consultant	(e) Key actors: design engineers, technical consultants, behavioural advisors within consultative procedure
Phase 4 Implementation	
(a) Machine capability	(a) User support
(b) Only minor modifications expected	(b) Pilot projects used where possible
(c) 'Once off' skill training	(c) Continuing staff and organization development
(d) Responsibility to line management	(d) Continuing reviews of operation
(e) Key actors: as Phase 3, also line managers and end users	(e) Key actors: as Phase 3, also line managers and end users
Trades union negotiations on conditions	Trades union negotiations on conditions, training, etc.

SOURCE Based on F. Blackler (1986) 'Information Technology and Competitiveness: Signposts from Organizational Psychology', paper presented at the British Psychological Society, January 1986.

engineers/technical consultants to design such a system and implicitly to redesign their jobs, and an organization which involves its workforce at an early stage in discussions over technological change and job redesign. In the technology-centred approach, it is only at the final stage, that of implementation, that the operatives, supervisors and trade unions are brought in. In other words, those people most affected by the change in their work are the ones who have *least* say in what might constitute the job. This is scientific management in yet another guise: jobs are deskilled through technological advancement (as in the clothing industry), and it is assumed that operators are too stupid to be able to contribute anything of value to the planning process. Furthermore, as a management practice it is short-sighted in that it ignores the psychology of the situation, that is of involving employees, because a workforce that has had a genuine say is more likely to be committed to the change provided they have had a *real* influence over it and will duly be a great deal more satisfied.

Consonant with the idea of introducing new technology is that of strategic considerations. There are two schools of thought of what constitutes the notion of *managerial strategy*. They are (a) those who view strategic thinking as a rational process and (b) those who view it as an iterative and rather more fluid process (Child, 1985; Pettigrew *et al.*, 1986). (Mention should perhaps be made of a third view, which suggests that strategic thinking is no more and no less than the 'science of muddling through' (Lindblom, 1959).) The rationale for the introduction of new technology is likely, in general terms, to be that of improving the competitive position of the firm. The goals towards which this strategic initiative is directed are: (a) to reduce unit costs, (b) to increase flexibility of the production system, (c) to improve quality and (d) to enhance control. Each of these objectives has clear implications for the design of jobs and for the labour process, such as the reduction/elimination of labour costs, the spread of contracting, the dissolution of traditional job or skill demarcations, and the degradation of jobs through deskilling (Child, 1985). However, the point which Blackler and Brown (1985, 1986) are making in contrasting the two models of management is their implicit view of the value of the human resources of the organization. On the one hand, there is the task-and-technology-centred managerialism which views people as a *costly* resource to be reduced if possible, and, on the other hand, an organization-and-end-user-centred approach which views people as a costly resource to be more fully utilized. This and the three subsequent stages – justification, design and implementation – involve the issue of *whether people really matter*, that is, are to be involved or ignored in the decision process.

QUALITY CONTROL CIRCLES

So far the discussion has focused upon the theme of involving people, that is, employees, in the process of change. The extent to which management and employees exert control over these processes has been the nub of the issue. It is clear, however, that the assumption has been one of a managerial prerogative to initiate change, with employees being involved (or not as the case may be) at subsequent stages. A problem with such an approach is that employees can easily become cynical and disillusioned, believing that ultimately things are still being done *to* them and that they have no *real* say or influence.

During the 1980s, the notion of a quality control circle (QCC) was introduced into Western management practice. A fundamental idea was that the QCC would allow workgroups to identify and tackle problems within their immediate work environment. By this means they are able to develop a degree of self-control. The QCC draws on the expertise of the workforce and, it is said, increases their sense of responsibility while making savings. Three benefits could thus be readily identified: increased employee involvement, enhanced business effectiveness and an opportunity to change company culture (Hill, 1991).

The quality circle concept originated in Japan (Hutchins, 1985), although Dale and Barlow (1984) attribute its origins to the Americans. Its central tenet of *quality* concerns competition: the ability of a firm to produce the best, cheaply and at low cost, and thus to give customer satisfaction. This goal of increased quality can be achieved by increases in productivity (that is, by producing more for the same effort) or, by reducing waste and/or other production costs (such as machine breakdowns, energy costs, labour disputes and low motivation).

A quality circle is:

A small group of between three and twelve people who do the same or similar work, voluntarily meeting together regularly for about an hour per week in paid time, usually under the leadership of their own supervisor, and trained to identify, analyse, and solve some of the problems in their work, presenting solutions to management, and where possible, implementing the solutions themselves. (Hutchins, 1985, p. 1)

In what ways do quality circles differ from other participative groups? A crucial ingredient is that of self-control within the group. Under Taylorism, employees were expected to *do their job*, while management controlled, planned, checked and took action where improvements were thought necessary. The craftsman, by contrast, controls the whole cycle of planning, doing, checking and taking action. However, s/he does this as an individual, producing high-quality, high-cost products. The advantages of *both* systems can be gained by vesting control in the group so that it is 'responsible for the achievement of its own levels of performance within the framework of corporate goals and targets' (Hutchins, 1985, p. 27). Circles are not simply problem-solving groups.

The QCC does not attain self-control immediately; its development goes through four distinct stages, culminating in self-control. These are: the initial phase; monitoring and problem solving; and innovation phases. Initially the workgroup needs to be trained to identify, analyse and solve some of the more pressing problems in its work area. QCCs commence with brainstorming in order that the group can identify as many problems as possible. These problems are then categorized under the following heads: (a) non-circle-controllable, (b) partially circle-controllable and (c) totally circle-controllable. It is important that any problem which is outside their sphere of control should be eliminated. The problem (effect) may be associated with multiple causes; it is therefore important that the group decide which are the most significant causal factors, and usually this is done by collecting evidence (data). Systematically, they will identify such probable causes under the following heads: (a) *manpower* – the people doing the work; (b) *machines* – equipment or tooling used to do the work; (c) *methods* – specifications or job instructions; and (d) *materials* supplied or required to do the work. A second brainstorming session is then set into motion in order to generate as many ideas as possible as to likely causes in each category. The next stage is evaluation of the suggestions. Only those ideas which are thought to be major causes will be circled on the diagram or list. The QCC next has the task of ordering the causal factors so identified. The presentation to management is extremely important, not least because it is the culmination of the group's work, but also because if done well and accepted by management it gives the circle and non-circle employees a sense of its worth. Initial training must be given to group members in order to ensure they are able to present their case well. Management will then decide whether to accept the circle's recommendation. If it only partially accepts or rejects, management must give clear reasons why.

The success of QCCs is bound up with management's attitudes and style: a Theory X style is not conducive to the implementation of QC, although it is compatible with Taylorism and scientific management (Brown, 1954; Hutchins, 1985; McGregor, 1960; Schein, 1980). A Theory Y style, which is more open and participative, is a condition which is more likely to facilitate the operations of QCCs. Two additional conditions which management must get right are (a) environmental factors, which means ensuring that there are no hindrances to group operations and that resources are available to facilitate the work of the group, and (b) motivational factors, ensuring that the QCCs are encouraged and properly supported in their efforts.

According to path–goal theory, the circle's members should feel that (a) the circle leader or supervisor facilitates problem selection and resolution by drawing upon the skills and abilities, and understanding the limitations, of the group, guiding it through difficulties, steering it towards task achievement; (b) management cooperates with the circle to remove any obstacles which would otherwise prevent successful task completion; (c) circle members can expect that their efforts will reasonably result in successful task completion (that is, identifying the problem and being able to recommend what should be done about it); (d) their performance will be instrumental in leading to multiple outcomes which are rewarding, such as that their efforts and performance are valued by management. The essential point is that it is management's responsibility to create a climate conducive to the successful operation of QCCs, so that gradually they become part of the culture of the organization.

The rewards promised by the introduction of quality control circles was impressive:

● Work itself would become more interesting through greater involvement. Many other problems would 'just disappear' through less carelessness on the part of workpeople.
● General productivity would increase through higher morale.
● There would be lower absenteeism because of greater job interest.
● There would be fewer grievances.
● There would be a greater team spirit.

The potentiality of an effective QCC for the achievement of savings for the company are clear. However, there is a view which is promulgated that to pay circle members a financial reward would (a) be against the whole philosophy of the quality circle and (b) cause considerable problems (Dale and Barlow, 1984; Hutchins, 1985):

The object of circles . . . is to create an organization where all are made to feel that their organization is better for their being there, and that their contribution is recognized. The aim is to develop a sense of corporate loyalty and corporate identity among all employees. This cannot be achieved by treating one group of people differently from another, and no one else is paid directly for solving problems. (Hutchins, 1985, p. 197)

The problems which would result include those of (a) the need to develop a policy regarding whom to pay (for example, should one pay non-circle members who have given help?), (b) the size of the savings (for example, these may be compared with the budget of another department), (c) 'getting a return' is likely to bias the judgement of circle members as to the kinds of problems they should be looking at, and (d) payment will take one into the area of formal negotiations, where the circle's activities are likely to be used as a negotiation counter. In contrast to this, it is argued that the rewards which *should* accrue to circle members are *intrinsic*: for example, *recognition by management* of work well done. The ultimate reward, it has been suggested, is to allow members to decide how the savings should be spent. This represents just one view promulgated by QCC advocates. However, it is worth examining the issue of pay in relation to quality more closely. It has been found to be extremely problematic. In a recent paper, Drummond and Chell (1991) pose the question, should organizations pay for quality? Within the context of the QC, actual payment, it has been argued, would destroy the intrinsic motivation which the QC is attempting to foster. Fundamentally, however, the quality movement seeks to involve employees in the management process without consonant rewards. Moreover, the outcomes of the QCC have not been integrated into an appraisal system, and consequently there is no formal recognition of QCC member achievement, either collectively or individually. Further, other forms of recognition – praise, for example – have not materialized. In the absence of senior management's commitment, the employee relations problems become those of taking for granted the goodwill and initiative shown by circle members and a cynical commitment by management to circle philosophy and ideals.

Other criticisms of quality control circles are now evident (Lawler and Mohrman, 1985; Hill, 1991). Several fundamental difficulties have emerged with the introduction of QCCs in the West. One is that of introducing a management technique which is reputed to have been successful in one culture to another culture where traditionally and historically emphasis has been placed on individual rather than collective achievement. A second difficulty is that of introducing QCs in a vacuum rather than in the context of a total system of quality improvement (Ishikawa, 1985). A third problem is one of structure, that is of effectively operating a dual structure with insufficient integration to enable effective operation of circles. The fourth difficulty has proved to be the lack of commitment of senior management (Hill, 1991). Many of the detailed operational problems of introducing QCCs stem from the fact that these more fundamental issues have been neither recognized nor addressed. These include:

- A concern with production and not administration – the problem is defined as that of product quality.
- A problem of establishing frank and open communications on relevant issues.
- A difficulty in engaging the commitment of 'elite' groups, who have no wish to share information, skills and technical knowledge, and who would see this as a reduction in the mystique associated with their job and a consequent reduction in their power.
- How the QCC is introduced into the organization.
- Resolving any contradiction between the work of the QCC and production imperatives.
- QCCs are not part of the normal chain of command, this may create uncertainty for everyone.
- The cultural issue in that in some contexts for the 'blue collar' employee to seek personal investment and involvement in work goes against the grain and may be viewed cynically by the employee as (yet another form of) management manipulation.
- The fact that QCCs may be seen as an additional burden, because there are no rewards to managers either for running QCCs.
- To really engage the workgroup, a 'winning of hearts and minds' type of commitment is needed. This requires a special sort of leadership skill (see Chapter 6) – a charismatic appeal and a transforming approach. This kind of characteristic is unlikely to be sufficiently widely distributed in the population.
- A fundamental requirement is to have both confidence in the workforce and the ability to switch to a collective consensual approach – thus effecting such a change is a major step for a large proportion of Western-style managers.

TOTAL QUALITY MANAGEMENT

The cultural issues, combined with the internal perception of QCs as isolated groups not well integrated into the organizational and managerial structure, were, along with the many difficulties discussed above, fundamental reasons for their eventual demise. 'Total quality management' (TQM), on the other hand, not only addresses the issues of quality within an organization but is a totally embracing philosophy of management which is intended to imbue all aspects of organizational and managerial behaviour.

The TQM movement has its origins in Japan (Deming, 1982). In the late 1970s and throughout the 1980s there was a growing momentum to introduce TQM in the West – in the USA and the UK. The message of the TQM movement concerns the decline of Western industrial society, its lack of competitiveness and its inability to fulfil customer needs. It is about the raising of standards of work relations and it addresses issues concerning the quality of *processes* which enable the delivery of a quality product or service to a customer. It is about not simply product quality but also the 'continuous improvement' of both product and process. TQM is far more than a management tool; it is a philosophy of management which some have likened to a religion, and the different forms in which it manifests itself are led by 'prophets' or 'gurus' (DTI, 1990).

One such 'guru' -- Dr W. Edwards Deming – adopts a rigorous and systematic approach to quality, an approach which has its roots in statistical process control (SPC). An essential element in Deming's theory is that of *variation*. Variation may originate in either 'special' or 'common' causes, which is another way of saying uncontrolled and controlled causes. Understanding these causes leads to 'profound knowledge'; that is, to deep understanding based upon systematic observation. It is the job of management to identify correctly the most important sources of variation, to reduce or eliminate them such that *quality* can be improved (BDA, 1989).

Deming's teachings comprise a philosophy of management at the heart of which are ethical principles and a 'code of practice'. These principles are encapsulated in the adoption of the 'Joiner Triangle', the need for a *system* of profound knowledge and the guidance implicit in Deming's 'Fourteen Points'.

The pinnacle of the 'joiner triangle' is 'obsession with quality', which manifests itself ultimately in 'delighting the customer'. Improvements in quality not only make a company more competitive, but ultimately enable them to create more jobs. The obsession with quality or 'continuous improvement' is achieved by means of total teamwork and a 'scientific approach' which embraces SPC. As already stated, understanding the causes of variation leads to profound knowledge, but – suggests Deming – there is a need for *a system* of profound knowledge. Put simply, the aim of the system is that 'everybody wins': gains accrue to everyone from shareholders to the community over the long term. This ethical position is associated with the need to optimize the system. Further elements of the system include some knowledge of the theory of variation, a theory of knowledge and a knowledge of psychology (see Neave, 1990).

Deming (1982) put forward 'Fourteen Points' for the transformation of American industry. These points require considerable interpretation and thinking through before they are capable of implementation within a particular organization. They comprise a set of prescriptions:

1. To create constancy of purpose toward improvement of product or service.
2. To adopt the new philosophy.
3. To cease dependence on inspection to achieve quality.
4. To move towards a single supplier relationship.
5. To constantly improve system for increased quality and productivity and to decrease costs.
6. To institute on-the-job training.
7. To institute leadership.
8. To drive out fear.
9. To break down barriers between departments.
10. To eliminate slogans, exhortations and targets asking the workforce to achieve 'zero defects' and/or new levels of productivity.
11. To eliminate work standards and management by objectives (MBO).
12. To remove barriers to a pride in workmanship.
13. To institute a vigorous programme of education and self-improvement.
14. To involve all employees in the process of transformation.

A number of these prescriptions are counterintuitive, or at least run counter to 'received wisdom'. Accepted practice in most industries would, for example, recommend that a company does not adopt a single source of supply, but in the TQM system envisaged by Deming this dependent relationship is not a problem but an advantage. Philosophies such as Deming's are not intended to be 'quick fixes'; they require a change of management style and organizational culture, and a commitment from the top. Deming cites Japan's own transformation of economic performance since the mid-1940s as evidence of the success of his philosophy of management. Many major companies in the West are now in the process of adopting the Deming approach to TQM, and there exists both an American and a British Deming Association.

CONTROL OF PERFORMANCE – ANOTHER LOOK

The approaches outlined in this chapter illustrate the contrasting assumptions made by management about their workforce and therefore the very different ways in which they can have influence and control over them. The crux of the control issue concerns the extent to which management feels it is necessary to exert direct control over subordinates' task-related behaviour, or whether they believe some other means of achieving the desired levels of performance is possible. At the bottom line, control commences with the selection and recruitment of appropriately qualified people for the job at hand; in order to do the job, they must have the necessary abilities and skills (or be capable of being trained to the requisite level) *and* be motivated. However, while these conditions are necessary, they are not sufficient for effective task performance. The employee must know *what* has to be done, *how* it has to be done, and how *well* it has to be done (Kerr and Slocum, 1981). In terms of an employee's willingness to do the job, a controlling variable is the extent to which his or her behaviour is subject to internal or external sources of influence. Most work-related behaviour is affected by a combination of internal and external controls; that is, by intrinsic motivators which create self-control and a system of rewards and punishments which provide incentives to perform well, while discouraging dysfunctional behaviour. The precise combination of internal and external controls for effective performance depends upon:

- Organizational constraints such as culture, climate, structure, technology, etc.
- The relationship between leader and subordinate, in terms of the compatibility of their personalities, expectations and degree of consent
- Leader behaviour/style, such as task structuring versus consideration participative styles.
- The characteristics of the employee, for instance, degree of independence, attitude to authority, professionalism, job knowledge, etc.
- The nature of the task, i.e. whether it is routine, automated, skilled varied, with or without inbuilt flexibility.

Organizational structure, such as Burns and Stalker's mechanistic versus organic typology (see Chapter 7), has clear implications for the exercise of control. Formal leadership functions, such as role clarification, goal setting initiation of structure, feedback and the administration of rewards and punishments, are all present in a mechanistically organized establishment which operates in a stable environment and is not subject to constant change. In contrast to this, *substitutes for leadership* (Kerr, 1977; Kerr and Jermier, 1978) – such as the professional orientation of staff, responsiveness to the workgroup, the use of OD and training programmes to increase employee task responsiveness – are more typical of the nature of control in organic structures. Such factors maximize the adaptability of the organ ization to the need for change.

The relationship between leader and subordinate is affected by the compatibility of their personalities, their expectations of each other, their abilities, and so on. Control is a reciprocal phenomenon (except where coercion is involved), so that the subordinate should not be thought of as merely complying with the wishes of his or her boss, but rather consenting to the relationship. A problem can occur when a manager misperceives a subordinate's flexible and cooperative behaviour for submissive compliance rather than consent: that is, the manager may not appreciate the fact that the subordinate recognizes that there is a particular job of work to be done and that it falls within his/her remit to do it.

A vast number of theories have been developed to explain leader behaviour, to identify the critical features of effective leader behaviour and the conditions under which they are likely to be successful. The nature of the task – whether it is routine or non-routine, or indeed ambiguous – affects whether the manager's role is more effective if his/her behaviour is largely controlling, in the sense of giving instructions, organizing and guiding the behaviour of others, or essentially supportive and hence considerate of subordinates' feelings and well-being (House, 1971). Under other circumstances, such as introducing a change in work practices, it may be necessary to involve subordinates in the decision-making process. Some managers perceive this as being threatening to their status, power and their prerogative – the right to manage. Such are not necessary consequences of participation if the process is handled correctly. Indeed, some authors go as far as to suggest that participation increases the total amount of *organizational* control (Tannenbaum, 1962). The effective adoption of TQM would seem to substantiate this point. Furthermore, if acceptance of a decision by subordinates is critical then participation *should* increase such control (Maier, 1963, 1970; Vroom and Yetton, 1973).

Subordinates, for their part, are critical to the control process. If they think that they are unfairly treated by management or are bored by routine, repetitive, mindless jobs, they may indulge in industrial sabotage, and absenteeism, labour turnover and grievances are likely to be high. Care must be taken in the design of jobs, the organization of work and the way such employees are treated in order to minimize dysfunctional behaviour. Even where the job is inherently interesting, employees may not respond positively to their boss. This may be due to their allegiance to professional standards, which they do not see him/her as representing, or simply the lack of any necessity for prominent leadership where an employee or group of employees are following professional standards or routine procedures (Kerr and Slocum, 1981).

Finally, the nature of the task significantly affects the control exercised by management and worker. Where a job requires craftsmanship, the worker may exercise considerable control (as was the case in the printing industry in the UK). With increased automation, tasks lose their skills content and employees, apparently, their control. As the job becomes more routine, employees resent close supervision. A job may be so repetitive as to require almost automatic responses on the part of an employee, and in this sense it may become a substitute for leadership: the worker is in effect controlled by the technology, not the supervisor or boss. Where jobs are routine and boring, employees will often exercise their ingenuity to build in what variation they can and thus exert some degree of control. In some cases the meaninglessness of their work may result in instances of industrial sabotage as alienated workers have responded aggressively to their perceived powerlessness. However, as Klein points out, employees are quite capable of accommodating to deskilled and routinized work:

> Precisely because the methods of 'scientific' management are not as scientific as all that, loopholes exist which have enabled workers to regain a considerable measure of control over their own work situation. Individual piecework is a good example: in many industries it is popular, not only because of the possibility of high earnings, but also because it makes people to some extent responsible for their earnings, frees them from close personal supervision, and gives them a feeling of independence. In addition, the process of deciding the time for a job is itself susceptible to manipulation, and the battle of wits with time study has the function of adding stimulus to an otherwise dull work situation. There may also be considerable opportunities to optimize one's personal resources of time and energy in the way that output is recorded. The pieceworker who works very hard on Thursdays, saves the pieces overnight, and feeds them in on Fridays so as not to be too tired for the weekend is, after all, being entirely rational. (Klein, 1976, pp. 17–18)

CONCLUDING REMARKS

The 'old philosophy' of Taylorism and scientific management has not stood the test of time; it works best in an expansionist economy, but because workers were treated as dispensable extensions to the machinery they operated, it resulted in poor industrial relations and an adversarial attitude towards management. Attempts at participation in decision-making and WPM were often treated with scepticism by the workforce in many UK companies. It was merely a sop which made no or little difference to their working lives, their jobs or their attitudes. The steady erosion and decline of manufacturing industry in the UK over the past decade has caused industrialists, academics and politicians alike to attempt to identify the problems and their possible resolution. It is insufficient to say that industry should become more competitive; it is fundamental to ask how it might become so. The danger lies with the new growth companies, investing in new technology, and seeing that as *the* solution. Rather, *the* solution, as I have tried to show in this chapter, lies with management and their ability to create an organization culture which treats employees with respect, enables them to enjoy work and want to work, and makes them proud of the organization that employs them. Such a change in attitudes is not easy to cultivate or demonstrate.

The adoption of TQM is one method whereby management may be able to demonstrate and sustain such a change. This approach reduces the 'us and them' negative stereotypes and changes win–lose adversarial situations into those in which all participants can 'win'. In addition, it does not adversely affect the so-called *managerial prerogative* – the right to manage, while paradoxically it also increases employees' control and influence within the organization. In extending trust to employees and giving them scope to function effectively, management may enhance its ability to manage, having fewer industrial relations problems to deal with and more support from a greatly satisfied workforce; it can spend more time in detailed long-term planning. In these ways the company will become more competitive.

SUMMARY

——————— To control is to have influence over others in such a way as to be able to hold their behaviour and actions *in check*. Control may be exercised by means of coercion, authority or by consent. Personal involvement is one way of ensuring *commitment*.

——————— One approach to exercising control over the workforce is that of *scientific management*, developed by F. W. Taylor at the turn of the twentieth century. Tasks are reduced to their simplest constituent parts; workers specialize and need little skill; their jobs are repetitive and boring; and planning becomes part of management's task. Standard times are worked out for each task and these are linked to an incentive payment system.

——————— Worker participation in management (WPM) has often been viewed with suspicion or cynicism. The human relations model encourages compliance on the part of the employee, while the human resources model develops the idea of the workforce as an untapped reserve of skill and know-how. Neither model attempts to shift control towards the workforce and both assume a unitary perspective.

———— The question of the *effectiveness* of WPM has been well researched. WPM depends on equality of knowledge and expertise. WPM may be successful at *job level*, where shopfloor workers may, in addition, be more highly motivated to participate, but relatively unsuccessful at organizational/policy levels, where worker representatives may lack the expertise (and the numbers) to be significantly influential. Other conditions include the perceived legitimacy of WPM by both sides, the need to achieve an early success and the equitable distribution of rewards, role clarification of workers' representatives and the use of formal rules legislating for participation. Outcomes for employees should be an increased *psychological* sense of ownership, influence and involvement in decision-making.

———— The rationale for increased automation may be increases in efficiency and competitiveness of the organization. Management's approach may be summarily that of *task-and-technology-* or *end-user*-centred. The critical issue is where employees are involved in the design process and whether they really do matter to management.

———— Quality control circles (QCCs) comprise *a small group* of people who do the same or similar work, voluntarily meeting together regularly for about an hour per week in paid time, usually under the leadership of their own supervisor, and trained to identify, analyse, and solve some of the problems in their work, presenting solutions to management, and where possible, implementing the solutions themselves.

———— It is important that management be cooperative and supportive in order to make the QCCs a success. Outcomes of this success include a reduction in 'people problems', increased productivity and morale, lower absenteeism, fewer grievances and a greater team spirit. QCCs reach the peak of their success when they achieve self-control and are trusted by management to decide how the savings made should be spent.

———— To be effective QCCs should be part of a total quality approach to management (TQM). There are several 'gurus' of the TQM movement – one of the originators and most well known is Deming. TQM is a *philosophy* of management which aims to achieve quality in both product and process through continuous improvement in methods of working. Its basis is a rigorous and systematic approach to quality through statistical process control and a code of practice.

The balance between managerial and worker control over performance depends upon (a) the worker's ability to do the job and (b) his or her motivation. In addition, the extent of internal and external control of performance is affected by (i) organizational constraints, such as structure, culture, technology, etc., (ii) the relationship between the leader and subordinate in terms of the compatibility of their personalities, expectations and degree of consent, (iii) leader behaviour/style – task structuring versus consideration/participative style, (iv) the characteristics of the employee in terms of the degree of independence, attitude, job knowledge, professionalism and (v) the nature of the task, whether it is routine, automated, varied or structured.

Bibliography

Abernathy, W. J., Clark, K. B. and Kantrow, A. M. (1983) *Industrial Renaissance Producing a Competitive Future for America* (New York: Basic Books).

Adams, J. S. (1965) 'Inequity in social exchange' in L. Berkowitz (ed.) *Advances in Experimental Social Psychology*, vol. 2 (New York: Academic Press) pp 267–300.

Adams, J. D., Hayes, J. and Hopson, B. (1976) *Transition: Understanding and Managing Personal Change* (London: Martin Robertson).

Alderfer, C. P. (1969) 'An empirical test of a new theory of human needs', *Organizational Behavior and Human Performance*, 4, 142–75.

———— (1972) *Existence, Relatedness, and Growth: Human Needs in Organizational Settings* (New York: Free Press).

Allport, G. W. (1935) 'Attitudes', in C. Murchison (ed.) *A Handbook of Social Psychology* (Worcester, Massachusetts: Clark University Press) pp. 798–844.

Anderson, N. H. (1976) 'Equity judgements as information integration', *Journal of Personality and Social Psychology*, 33, 291–99.

Argyle, M. (1976) 'Personality and social behaviour', in R. Harré (ed.) *Personality* (Oxford: Blackwell).

———— and Little, B. R. (1972) 'Do personality traits apply to social behaviour?', *Journal for the Theory of Social Behaviour*, 2, 1–35.

Argyris, C. (1957) *Personality and Organization* (New York: Harper & Row).

———— (1970) *Intervention Theory and Method: A Behavioral Science View* (Reading, Mass.: Addison-Wesley).

———— (1971) *Management and Organization Development: The Path From XA to YB* (New York: McGraw-Hill).

———— (1976) 'Theories of action that inhibit learning', *American Psychologist*, 31, 638–54.

Asch, S. E. (1951) 'Effects of group pressure upon the modification and distortion of judgements', in H. Guetskow (ed.) *Groups, Leadership and Men* (Pittsburgh: Carnegie Press).

———— (1956) 'Studies of independence and conformity: A minority of one against a unanimous majority', *Psychological Monographs*, 70, 6.

Ashour, A. S. (1973) 'The contingency model of leadership effectiveness: an evaluation', *Organizational Behaviour and Human Performance*, 9, 339–55.

Atkinson, J. W. (1964) *An Introduction to Motivation* (New York: Van Nostrand)

———— and Birch, D. (1979) *Introduction to Motivation* (Princeton, New Jersey: Van Nostrand).

Bales, R. F. (1950) 'A set of categories for the analysis of small group interaction', *American Sociological Review*, 15, 257–263.

———— (1970) *Personality and Interpersonal Behaviour* (New York: Holt, Rinehart & Winston).

Bandura, A. (1969) *Principles of Behavior Modification* (New York: Holt, Rinehart & Winston).

———— (1977) *Social Learning Theory* (Englewood Cliffs, New Jersey: Prentice Hall).

Bass, B. M. (1981) *Stogdill's Handbook of Leadership: A Survey of Theory and Research* (New York: The Free Press).

—————— (1985) *Leadership and Performance Beyond Expectations* (New York: The Free Press).

—————— Waldman, D. A. and Avolio, B. J. (1987) 'Transformational leadership and the falling dominoes effect', *Group and Organization Studies*, 12, 1 (March) 73–87.

BDA (1989) *Profound Knowledge* (Salisbury: The British Deming Association).

Belbin, R. M. (1981) *Management Teams* (London: Heinemann).

Bem, D. J. (1965) 'An experimental analysis of self-persuasion', *Journal of Experimental Social Psychology*, 1, 199–218.

—————— (1967) 'Self perception: An alternative interpretation of cognitive dissonance phenomena', *Psychological Review*, 74, 183–200.

—————— and Allen, A. (1974) 'On predicting some of the people some of the time: the search for cross-situational consistencies in behaviour', *Psychological Review*, 81, 6, 506–20.

Bennis, W. (1969) *Organization Development: Its Nature, Origins, and Prospects* (Reading, Mass.: Addison-Wesley).

Bion, W.R. (1961) *Experiences in Groups and Other Papers* (London: Tavistock).

Blackler, F. (1986) 'Information technology and competitiveness: signposts from organizational psychology', paper presented at the British Psychological Society Conference, Occupational Psychology Section, University of Nottingham, UK, January.

—————— and Brown, C. A. (1980) *Whatever Happened to Shell's New Philosophy of Management?* (Teakfield: Saxon House).

—————— —————— (1985) 'Current British practices in the evaluation of the new technologies', ESRC/Lancaster Workshop, 24 May, University of Lancaster.

—————— —————— (1986) 'Alternative models to guide the design and introduction of new information technologies into work organizations', mimeograph, Department of Behaviour in Organizations, University of Lancaster, United Kingdom.

—————— and Shimmin, S. (1984) *Applying Psychology in Organizations* (London and New York: Methuen).

Blake, R. R. and Mouton, J. S. (1964) *The Managerial Grid: Key Orientations for Achieving Production Through People* (Houston: Gulf).

—————— —————— (1975) 'Group and Organizational Team Building: A Theoretical Model for Intervening' in C. L. Cooper (ed.) *Theories of Group Processes* (London: Wiley).

—————— —————— (1978) *The New Managerial Grid* (Houston: Texas: Gulf).

—————— —————— (1985) *The Managerial Grid III* (Houston, Texas: Gulf).

Blandy, A. (1984) 'New technology and flexible patterns of working time', *Employment Gazette*, 92, 10, 439–44.

Boddy, D. and Buchanan, D. (1984) 'Implications for development of new technology', *Management Education and Development*, 15, 2, 176–82.

Bowers, K. S. (1973) 'Situationism in Psychology: an analysis and a critique', *Psychological Review*, 80, 5, 307–36.

Brannen, P., E. Batstone, D. Fatchett, P. White (1976) *The Worker Directors: A Sociology of Participation* (London: Hutchinson).

Branthwaite, A. (1983) 'Situations and social actions: applications for marketing of recent theories in Social Psychology', *Journal of the Market Research Society*, 25, 1, 19–38.

Broedling, L. A. (1975) 'Relationship of internal – external control to work motivation and performance in an expectancy model', *Journal of Applied Psychology* 60, 65–70.

Brooks, E. (1980) *Organizational Change: The Managerial Dilemma* (London and Basingstoke: Macmillan).

Brown, J. A. C. (1954) *The Social Psychology of Industry* (Harmondsworth: Penguin Books).

Brown, W. (1960) *Exploration in Management* (Harmondsworth: Penguin Books).

Bryman, A. (1986) *Leadership and Organizations* (London: Routledge & Kegan Paul).

Bullock, Lord (Alan) (1976) *Report of the Committee of Enquiry on Industrial Democracy* (London: HMSO).

Burns, J. M. (1978) *Leadership* (New York: Harper and Row).

Burns, T. and Stalker, G. M. (1961) *The Management of Innovation* (London: Tavistock).

Burrell, G. and Morgan, G. (1979) *Sociological Paradigms and Organisational Analysis* (London: Heinemann).

Carnall, C. A. (1990) *Managing Change in Organizations* (Hemel Hempstead: Prentice-Hall).

Cartwright, D. (1971) 'Risk taking by individuals and groups: an assessment of research employing choice dilemmas', *Journal of Personality and Social Psychology*, 20, 36–378.

Cattell, R. B. (1946) *Description and Measurement of Personality* (New York: Harcourt).

Chell, E. (1976) 'A study of situational (cooperative/competitive) and personality ('high' and 'low' participation) factors on the role enactment of Human Relations problems', *Human Relations*, 29, 11, 1061–81.

———— (1977) *Participation in Joint Consultative Committees*, unpublished doctoral thesis, the University of Nottingham, UK.

———— (1980) *Worker Directors on the Board: Four Case Studies, Employee Relations*, vol. 2, whole No. 6 (Bradford: MCB Publications).

———— (1983) 'Political perspectives and worker participation at board level: the British experience', in C. Crouch and F. A. Heller (eds) *Organizational Democracy and Political Processes*, vol. 1 (Chichester: Wiley).

———— (1985a) *Participation and Organization – A Social Psychological Approach* (London: Macmillan).

———— (1985b) 'The entrepreneurial personality: a few ghosts laid to rest', *International Small Business Journal*, 3, 3, 43–54.

———— (1985c) 'Redundancy and unemployment: the role of the personnel manager', *Personnel Review*, 14, 2, 24–31.

———— and Cox, D. (1979) 'Worker directors and collective bargaining', *Industrial Relations Journal*, 10, 25–31.

———— Haworth, J. M. and Brearley, S. A. (1991) *The Entrepreneurial Personality: concepts, cases and categories* (London and New York: Routledge).

Chemers, M. M. and Skrzypeck, G. J. (1972) 'Experimental test, of the contingency model of leadership effectiveness', *Journal of Personality and Social Psychology*, 24, 171–7.

Chesney, M. A., Black, G. W., Chadwick, J. H. and Rosenman, R. H. (1981a) 'Psychological correlates of the coronary-prone behavior pattern', *Journal of Behavioral Medicine*, 4, 217–30.

———— Sevelius, G. W., Black, G. W., Ward, M. M., Swan, G. E. and Rosenman, R. H. (1981b) 'Work environment, Type A behavior, and coronary heart disease', *Journal of Occupational Medicine*, 23, 551–5.

Child, J. (1984) *Organization: A Guide to Problems and Practice* (London: Harper and Row).

———— (1985) 'Managerial strategies, new technology and the labour process', in David Knights *et al.* (eds) *Job Redesign – Critical Perspectives on the Labour Process* (Aldershot: Gower).

Chin, R. and Benne, K. (1976) 'General strategies for effecting changes in human systems', in Bennis, W. G., Benne, K. D., Chin, W. and K. E. Corey (eds) *The Planning of Change*, 3rd edn (New York: Holt, Rinehart and Winston).

Clegg, S. (1990) *Modern Organization: Organization Studies in the Postmodern World* (London: Sage).

Cooper, C. L. and Payne, R. (1980) (eds) *Current Concerns in Occupational Stress* (New York: Wiley).

Cox, C. J. and Cooper, C. L. (1984) 'Management and industrial relations' in A. Gale and A. J. Chapman (eds) *Psychology and Social Problems* (London: Wiley).

Dachler, H. P. (1988) 'Constraints on the emergence of new vistas in leadership and management research: an epistemological overview', in Hunt, J. G., Batiga, B.R., Dachler, H. P. and Schreisheim, C. A. (eds) *Emerging Leadership Vistas* (Lexington, Mass.: Lexington Books).

Dale, B. and Barlow, E. (1984) 'Facilitator viewpoints on specific aspects of Quality Circle programmes', *Personnel Review*, 13, 4, 22–9.

Davis, T. R. V. and Luthans, F. (1983) 'A social learning theory approach to organizational behaviour', in R. M. Steers and L. W. Porter (eds) *Motivation and Work Behaviour*, 3rd edn (New York: McGraw-Hill).

Delbecq, A. L., van de Ven, A. H. and Gustafson, D. H. (1975) *Group Techniques for Program Planning* (Glenview, Ill.: Scott, Foresman).

Deming, W. Edwards (1982) *Out of the Crisis* (Cambridge: Cambridge University Press).

Deutsch, M. and Gerard, H. B. (1955) 'A study of normative and informational social influence processes upon individual judgement', *Journal of Abnormal and Social Psychology*, 51, 629–36.

Dion, K. L., Baron, R. S. and Miller, N. (1970) 'Why do groups make riskier decisions than individuals?' in L. Berkowitz (ed.), *Advances in Experimental Social Psychology*, 5, pp. 306–77 (New York: Academic).

Drummond, H. (1991a) *Effective Decision-making* (London: Kogan Page).

———— (1991b) *Power Creating it Using it* (London: Kogan Page).

———— and Chell, E. (1991) 'Should organizations pay for quality?' *Personnel Review*, 21, 1, 46–54.

DTI (1990) *The Quality Gurus: What Can They Do for Your Company?* Nottingham: Services Ltd.

Duncan, W. J. (1981) *Organizational Behavior*, 2nd edn (Boston, Mass.: Houghton Mifflin).

238 *Bibliography*

Dyer, W. G. (1977) *Team Building: Issues and Alternatives* (Reading: Mass.: Addison-Wesley).
Dyer, W. G. (1984) *Strategies for Managing Change* (Reading, Mass.: Addison-Wesley).
Eiser, J. R. (1979) 'Interpersonal attributions', in H. Tajfel and C. Fraser (eds) *Introducing Social Psychology* (Harmondsworth: Penguin Books).
———— (1980) *Cognitive Social Psychology* (London: McGraw-Hill).
Ekehammer, B. (1974) 'Interactionism in personality from a historical perspective', *Psychological Bulletin*, 81, 1026–48.
Emerson, R. M. (1962) 'Power-dependence relations', *American Sociological Review*, 27, 31–41.
Endler, N. S. and Magnusson, D. (1976) 'Toward an interactional psychology of personality', *Psychological Bulletin*, 83, 956–74.
Epstein, S. and O'Brien, E. J. (1985) 'The person-situation debate in historical and current perspective', *Psychological Bulletin*, 98, 3, 513–537.
Erikson, E. H. (1963) *Childhood and Society*, 2nd edn (New York: Norton).
Etzioni, A. (1964) *Modern Organizations* (Englewood Ciffs, New Jersey: Prentice-Hall).
Evans, M. G. (1970) 'Leadership and motivation: a core concept', *Academy of Management Journal*, 13, 1, 91–102.
Farr, R. M. and Anderson, T. (1983) 'Beyond actor-observer differences in perspective: extensions and applications' in M. Hewstone (ed.) *Attribution Theory* (Oxford: Blackwell).
Fedor D. B. and Ferris, G. R. (1983) 'Integrating OB Mod with cognitive approaches to motivation', in R. M. Steers and L. W. Porter (eds) *Motivation and Work Behaviour*, 3rd edn (New York: McGraw-Hill).
Field, R. H. G. (1982) 'A test of the Vroom–Yetton normative model of leadership', *Journal of Applied Psychology*, 67, 523–32.
Fiedler, F. E. (1967) *A Theory of Leadership Effectiveness* (New York: McGraw-Hill).
———— (1977) 'What triggers the person–situation interaction in leadership?' in D. Magnusson and N.S. Endler (eds) *Personality at the Crossroads* (Hillsdale, NJ: Lawrence Erlbaum).
———— (1978) 'The Contingency Model and the Dynamics of the Leadership Process', in L. Berkowitz (ed.) *Advances in Experimental Social Psychology*, vol. 11 (New York: Academic).
———— and Chemers, M. M. (1984) *Improving Leadership Effectiveness: The Leader Match* revised edn. (New York: Wiley).
———— ———— and Mahar, L. (1976) *Improving Leadership Effectiveness: The Leader Match Concept* (New York: Wiley).
———— and Garcia, J. E. (1987) *New Approaches to Effective Leadership: Cognitive Resources and Organizational Performance* (New York: Wiley).
Fishbein, M. and Ajzen, I. (1975) *Belief, Attitude, Intention and Behaviour: An Introduction to Theory and Research* (Reading, Mass.: Addison-Wesley).
Fisher, C. (1980) 'On the dubious wisdom of expecting job satisfaction to correlate with performance', *Academy of Management Review*, 5, 607–12.
Fleishman, E. A. and Harris, E. F. (1962) 'Patterns of leadership behaviour related to employee grievances and turnover', *Personnel Psychology*, 15, 43–56.

———— Harris, E. F. and Burtt, H. E. (1955) *Leadership and Supervision in Industry* (Columbus: Ohio State University, Bureau of Educational Research).

Fowler, H. W. and Fowler, F. G. (eds) (1964) *The Concise Oxford Dictionary of Current English*, 5th edn (Oxford: Clarendon Press).

Fox, A. (1966) 'Managerial ideology and labour relations', *British Journal of Industrial Relations*, 4, 366–78.

———— (1974) *Beyond Contract: Work, Power and Trust Relations* (London: Faber & Faber).

Fraser, C. (1978) 'Small groups II: Processes and products', in H. Tajfel and C. Fraser (eds) *Introducing Social Psychology* (Harmondsworth: Penguin Books).

———— and Foster, D. (1984) 'Social groups, nonsense groups and group polarization' in H. Tajfel (ed.) *The Social Dimension*, vol. 2 (Cambridge: Cambridge University Press).

———— Gouge, C. and Billig, M. (1971) 'Risky shifts, cautious shifts and group polarization', *European Journal of Social Psychology*, 1, 7–30.

Frederiksen, N. (1972) 'Toward a taxonomy of situations', *American Psychologist* (Feb.) 114.

French, J. R. P. and Raven, B. (1959) 'The bases of social power' in D. Cartwright (ed.) *Studies in Social Power* (Ann Arbor: Michigan Institute of Social Research).

———— Rogers, W., Cobb, S. (1974) 'Adjustment as environment fit', in G. V. Coelko, D. A. Hamburg, and J. E. Adams (eds) *Coping and Adaptation* (New York: Basic).

French, W. L. and Bell, C. H. (1978) *Organization Development*, 2nd edn (Englewood Cliffs, NJ: Prentice-Hall).

Friedman, M. D. and Rosenman, R. H. (1974) *Type A Behavior and Your Heart* (New York: Knopf).

Georgopoulos, B. S., Mahoney, G. M. and Jones, N. W. Jr (1957) 'A path–goal approach to productivity', *Journal of Applied Psychology*, 41, 345–53.

Gergen, K. J. (1977) 'Stability, change and chance in understanding human development' in N. Datan and H. W. Reese (eds) *Life-span Development Psychology: Dialectical Perspectives on Experimental Research* (New York: Academic).

Goldstein, A. P. and Sorcher, M. (1974) *Changing Supervisor Behaviour* (New York: Pergamon).

Graen, G. B., Alvares, K., Orris, J. B. and Martella, J. A. (1972) 'Contingency model of leadership effectiveness: antecedent and evidential results', *Psychological Bulletin*, 74, 285–96.

———— Orris, J. B., and Alvares, K. M. (1971) 'Contingency model of leadership effectiveness: some experimental results', *Journal of Applied Psychology*, 55, 196–201.

Guest, D. E. (1984) 'Social psychology and organizational change' in M. Gruneberg and T. Wall (eds) *Social Psychology and Organizational Behaviour* (Chichester: Wiley).

Hacker, W. (1981) 'Perceptions of and reactions to work situations: some implications of an action control approach' in D. Magnusson (ed.) *Toward A Psychology of Situations: An Interactional Perspective* (Hillsdale, NJ: Lawrence Erlbaum).

Hackman, J. R. (1976) 'Group influences on individuals' in M. D. Dunnette (ed.) *Handbook of Industrial and Organizational Psychology* (Chicago: Rand McNally).

———— and Oldham, G. R. (1980) *Work Redesign* (Reading, Mass.: Addison-Wesley).

Hall, D. T. and Nougaim, K. E. (1968) 'An examination of Maslow's need hierarchy in an organizational setting', *Organizational Behaviour and Human Performance*, 3, 12–35.

Halpin, A. W. (1957) 'The observed leader behaviour and ideal leader behaviour of aircraft commanders and school superintendents', in R. M. Stogdill and A. E. Coons (eds) *Leader Behaviour: Its Description and Measurement* (Columbus: Ohio State University, Bureau of Business Research).

———— and Winer, B. J. (1957) 'A factorial study of the leader behaviour descriptions,' in R. M. Stogdill and A. E. Coons (eds) *Leader Behaviour: Its Description and Measurement* (Columbus: Ohio State University, Bureau of Business Research).

Hamner, W. C. (1979) 'Reinforcement theory and contingency management in organizational settings', in R. M. Steers and L. W. Porter *Motivation and Work Behavior* 2nd edn (Tokyo: McGraw-Hill).

———— Ross, G. and Staw, B. M. (1978) 'Motivation in organizations: The need for a new direction', in D. W. Organ (ed.) *Applied Psychology of Work Behavior: A Book of Readings* (Homewood, Ill.: Irvin).

Hampson, S. E. (1982) *The Construction of Personality* (London: Routledge & Kegan Paul).

———— (1984) 'Personality traits in the eye of the beholder or the personality of the perceived?' in M. Cook (ed.) *Psychology in Progress: Issues in Person Perception* (London: Methuen).

———— (1988) *The Construction of Personality* 2nd edn (London: Routledge).

———— Goldberg, L. R. and John, O. P. (1987) 'Category breadth and social desirability values for 573 personality terms', *European Journal of Personality*, 1, 241–58.

———— John, O. P. and Goldberg, L. R. (1986) 'Category breadth and hierarchical structure in personality: studies of asymmetries in judgements of trait implications', *Journal of Personality and Social Psychology*, 51, 39–54.

Harré, R. (1979) *Social Being* (Oxford: Blackwell).

Heider, F. (1958) *The Psychology of Interpersonal Relations* (New York: Wiley).

Heilmann, M. E., Hornstein, H. A., Cage, J. H. and Herschlag, J. K. (1984) 'Reactions to prescribed leader behaviour as a function of role pespective: the case of the Vroom-Yetton Model', *Journal of Applied Psychology*, 69, 50–60.

Heller, F. A. (1976) 'Decision processes: an analysis of power sharing at senior organizational levels', in R. Dubin (ed.) *Handbook of Work, Organization and Society* (Chicago, Ill.: Rand McNally).

Hemphill, J. K. and Coons, A. E. (1957) 'Development of the Leader-Behaviour Description Questionnaire', in Stogdill, R. M. and A. E. Coons (eds) *Leader Behaviour in Its Description and Measurement* (Columbus: Ohio State University, Bureau of Business Research).

Hersey, P. and Blanchard, K. (1982) *Management of Organizational Behaviour* 4th edn (Englewood Cliffs, NJ: Prentice-Hall).

Herzberg, F., Mausner, B. and Snyderman, B. (1959) *The Motivation to Work* (New York: Wiley).

Hewstone, M. (ed) (1983) *Attribution Theory – Social and Functional Extensions* (Oxford: Blackwell).

Hill, S. (1991) 'Why quality circles failed but total quality might succeed', *British Journal of Industrial Relations*, 29(4) 541–568.

Hogan, R., Desoto, C. B. and Solano, C. (1977) 'Traits, tests and personality research', *American Psychologist*, 32, 255–64.

Hosking, D. M. (1981) 'A critical evaluation of Fiedler's contingency hypothesis' in G. M. Stephenson and J. M. Davis (eds) *Progress in Applied Social Psychology* vol. 1 (New York: Wiley).

Hosking, D. M. and Morley, I. E. (1988) 'The skills of leadership' in J. G. H. Hunt, B. R. Baliga, H. P. Dachler and C. A. Schreisheim (eds) *Emerging Leadership Vistas* (Boston, Mass.: Heath/Lexington).

House, R. J. (1971) 'A path–goal theory of leadership effectiveness', *Administrative Science Quarterly*, 16, 321–8.

———— (1977) 'A 1976 theory of charismatic leadership', in J. G. Hunt and L. L. Larson (eds) *Leadership: The Cutting Edge* (Carbondale, Ill.: Southern Illinois University Press).

———— and Baetz, M. L. (1979) 'Leadership: some empirical generalizations and new research directions', in B. Staw (ed.) *Research in Organizational Behaviour* (Greenwich, Connecticut: JAI Press) vol. 1, 341–423.

Hutchins, D. (1985) *Quality Circles Handbook* (London: Pitman).

Ishikawa, K. (1985) *What is Total Quality Control? The Japanese Way*. (Englewood Cliffs, NJ: Prentice Hall).

Ivancevich, J. M. and Matteson, M. T. (1984) 'A type A–B person–work environment interaction model for examining occupational stress and consequences', *Human Relations*, 37, 7, 491–513.

———— ———— and Preston, C. (1982) 'Occupational stress, type A behavior and physical well being', *Academy of Management Journal*, 25, 2, 373–91.

Jago, A. G. (1978) 'A test of spuriousness in descriptive models of participative leader behaviour', *Journal of Applied Psychology*, 63, 3, 383–7.

———— (1981) 'An assessment of the deemed appropriateness of participative decision-making for high and low hierarchical levels', *Human Relations*, 34, 319–96.

———— and Vroom, V. H. (1980) 'An evaluation of two alternatives to the Vroom–Yetton normative model', *Academy of Management Journal*, 23, 347–55.

James, L. R. and Jones, A. P. (1979) *Perceived job characteristics and job satisfaction: An examination of reciprocal causation*, IBR Report No. 79–5 (Fort Worth, Texas: Texas Christian University, Institute of Behavioral Research).

———— and Sells, S. B. (1981) 'Psychological climate: theoretical perspectives and empirical research', in D. Magnusson (ed.) *Toward A Psychology of Situations: an Interactional Perspective* (Hillsdale, NJ: Lawrence Erlbaum).

Janis, I. L. (1971) 'Groupthink' *Psychology Today*, (November); reprinted in J. R. Hackman et al. (1977) *Perspectives on Behaviour in Organizations* (New York: McGraw-Hill).

———— (1972) *Victims of Groupthink* (Boston, Mass.:Houghton Mifflin).

Joe, V. (1971) 'Review of the internal–external control construct as a personality variable', *Psychological Reports*, 28, 619–40.

Jones, E. E. and Davis, K. E. (1965) 'From acts to dispositions', in L. Berkowitz (ed.) *Advances in Experimental Social Psychology* vol. 2 (New York: Academic Press).

———— and Nisbett, R. E. (1972) 'The actor and observer: divergent perceptions of the causes of behaviour', in Jones, E. E., Kanouse, D. E., Kelley, H. H., Nisbett R. E., Valins, S. and Weiner, B. *Attribution: Perceiving the Causes of Behaviour* (Morristown, NJ: General Learning Press).

Jones, J. E. and Pfeiffer, J. W. (1977) 'On the obsolescence of the term organizational development', *Group Organizational Studies*, 2, 3, 263–4.

Kahn, R. L., Wolfe, D. M., Quinn, R. P., Snoek, J. E. and Rosenthal, R. A. (1964) *Organizational Stress* (New York: Wiley).

Kanter, R. M. (1984) *The Change Masters* (London: Unwin).

Katz, D. and Kahn, R. L. (1966) *The Social Psychology of Organizations* (New York: Wiley).

Kelley, H. H. (1967) 'Attribution theory in social psychology', in D. Levine (ed.) *Nebraska Symposium on Motivation* (Lincoln, Nebr.: University of Nebraska Press).

————— (1972a) 'Attribution in social interaction', in Jones, E. E., Kanouse, D. E., Kelley, H. H., Nisbett R. E., Valins, S. and Weiner, B. *Attribution: Perceiving the Causes of Behavior* (Morristown, New Jersey: The General Learning Press).

————— (1972b) 'Causal schemata and the attribution process', in Jones, E. E., Kanouse, D. E., Kelley, H. H., Nisbett R. E., Valins, S. and Weiner, B. *Attribution: Perceiving the Causes of Behaviour* (Morristown, New Jersey: The General Learning Press).

Kenrick, D. T. and Funder, D. C. (1988) 'Profiting from controversy: lessons from the Person–Situation debate', *American Psychologist*, 43, 1 (January), 23–34.

Kerr, S. (1977) 'Substitutes for leadership: some implications for organizational design', *Organizational and Administrative Sciences*, 8, 135–146.

————— and Jermier, J. M. (1978) 'Substitutes for leadership: their meaning and measurement', *Organizational Behaviour and Human Performance*, 22, 375–403.

————— Schreisheim, C. A., Murphy, C. J. and Stogdill, R. M. (1974), 'Toward a contingency theory of leadership based upon the consideration and initiating structure literature', *Organizational Behaviour and Human Performance*, 12, 62–82.

————— and Slocum, J. W. (1981) 'Controlling the performance of people in organizations', in Paul C. Nystrom and William H. Starbuck (eds) *Handbook of Organizational Design* vol. 2 (New York: Oxford University Press).

Klein, L. (1976) *New Forms of Work Organization* (Cambridge: Cambridge University Press).

Klein, S. M. and Ritti, R. R. (1984) *Understanding Organizational Behaviour* 2nd edn (Belmont, Calif.: Wadsworth).

Knights, D., Willmott, H. and Collinson, D. (1985) (eds) *Job Redesign – Critical Perspectives on the Labour Process* (Aldershot: Gower).

Korman, A. K. (1966) '"Consideration", "Initiating structure", and organizational criteria – a review', *Personnel Psychology*, 21, 295–322.

Krahé, B. (1990) *Situation Cognition and Coherence in Personality An Individual Centred Approach* (Cambridge: Cambridge University Press).

Krantz, J. (1985) 'Group process under conditions of organizational decline', *Journal of Applied Behavioural Science*, 21, 2, 1–17.

Lakin, M. (1976) 'Experiential groups: the uses of interpersonal encounter, psychotherapy groups, and sensitivity training', in J. W. Thibaut et al. (eds) *Contemporary Topics in Social Psychology* (Morristown, New Jersey: General Learning Press).

Larson, L. L. and Rowland, K. M. (1974) 'Leadership style and cognitive complexity', *Academy of Management Journal*, 17, 37–45.

Lawler, E. E. III (1977) 'Reward Systems', in J. R. Hackman and J. L. Suttle (eds) *Improving Life at Work* (Santa Monica, Calif.: Goodyear).

———— and Mohrman, S. (1985) 'Quality circles after the Fad,' *Harvard Business Review*, 63, 65–71.

———— and Suttle, J. L. (1972) 'A causal correlation test of the need hierarchy concept', *Organizational Behavior and Human Performance*, 7, 265–87.

Lawrence, P. R. and Lorsch, J. W. (1967a) *Organization and Environment* (Cambridge, Mass.: Harvard University Press).

———— ———— (1967b) 'New management job: the integrator', *Harvard Business Review*, Nov./Dec., 142–151.

———— ———— (1969) *Developing Organizations – Diagnosis and Action* (Reading, Mass.: Addison-Wesley).

Legge, K. (1984) *Evaluating Planned Organizational Change* (London: Academic).

Levinson, D. J. (1978) *The Seasons of a Man's Life* (New York: Knopf).

———— (1980) 'Toward a conception of the adult life course', in N. Smelser and E. H. Erikson (eds) *Themes of Work and Love in Adulthood* (Cambridge, Mass.: Harvard University Press).

Lewin, K. (1947) 'Frontiers in group dynamics', *Human Relations*, 1, 5–42.

Lindblom, C. E. (1959) 'The science of "muddling through"', *Public Administration Review*, 19, 79–88.

Littler, C. R. (1982) *The Development of the Labour Process in Capitalist Societies* (London: Heinemann).

———— (1985) 'Taylorism, Fordism and Job Design', in D. Knights, H. Wilmott, D. Collinson (eds) *Job Redesign – Critical Perspectives on the Labour Process* (Aldershot: Gower).

Litwin, G. H. and Stringer, R. A., Jr. (1968) *Motivation and Organizational Climate* (Boston: Division of Research, Graduate School of Business Administration, Harvard University).

Locke, E. and Schweiger, D. M. (1979) 'Participation in decision-making: one more look', in B. M Staw and L. L. Cummings (eds) *Research in Organizational Behavior* vol. 1 (Greenwich, Connecticut: JAI Press).

Lorsch, J. W. and Lawrence, P. R. (eds) (1972) *Managing Group and Intergroup Relations* (Homewood, Ill.: Irwin).

Luthans, F. and Davis, T. R. V. (1979) 'Behavioural self-management: the missing link in managerial effectiveness', *Organizational Dynamics*, 8, 1, 42–60.

McArthur, L. A. (1972) 'The how and what of why: some determinants and consequences of causal attribution', *Journal of Personality and Social Psychology*, 22, 171–93.

McClelland, D. C. (1961) *The Achieving Society* (Princeton, NJ: Van Nostrand).

———— (1975) *Power: The Inner Experience* (New York: Irving).

McGregor, D. M. (1960) *The Human Side of Enterprise* (New York: McGraw-Hill).

Magnusson, D. (ed.) (1981) *Toward a Psychology of Situations – An Interactional Perspective* (Hillsdale, NJ: Lawrence Erlbaum).

Maier, N. R. F. (1963) *Problem-solving, Disussions and Conferences: Leadership Methods and Skills* (New York: McGraw-Hill).

———— (1970) *Problem-solving and Creativity in Individuals and Groups* (Belmont, California: Brooks Cole).

———— and Sashkin, M. (1971) 'Specific leadership behaviours that promote problem-solving', *Personnel Psychology*, 24, 35–44.

Mansfield, R. (1984) 'Formal and informal structure', in M. Gruneberg and T. Wall (eds) *Social Psychology and Organizational Behaviour* (Chichester: Wiley).

Mant, A. (1983) *Leaders We Deserve* (Oxford: Martin Robertson).

Margerison, C. and Glube, R. (1979) 'Leadership decision-making: an empirical test of the Vroom-Yetton model', *Journal of Management Studies*, 16, 45–55.

Marsh, P., Rosser, E. and Harré, R. (1978) *The Rules of Disorder* (London: Routledge & Kegan Paul).

Marshall, J. and Cooper C. L. (1979) *Executives under Pressure* (London: Macmillan).

Maslow, A. (1954) *Motivation and Personality* (New York: Harper).

Mattes, D. (1984) 'Attitudes to new office technology', *Employment Gazette*, 92, 10, 464–5.

Mayo, E. (1949) *Hawthorne and the Western Electricity Company: The Social Problems of an Industrial Civilisation* (London: Routledge).

Meadows, I. S. G. (1980a) 'Organic structure and innovation in small work groups', *Human Relations*, 33, 6, 369–382.

———— (1980b) 'Organic structure, satisfaction and personality', *Human Relations*, 33, 6, 383–392.

Mischel, W. (1968) *Personality and Assessment* (New York: Wiley).

———— (1973) 'Toward a cognitive social learning reconceptualisation of personality', *Psychological Review*, 80, 4, 252–83.

———— (1981) *Introduction to Personality* 3rd edn (New York: Holt, Rinehart & Winston).

———— (1984) 'Convergences and challenges in the search for consistency', *American Psychologist*, 39, 4, 351–64.

———— and Peake, P. K. (1982) 'Beyond déjà vu in the search for cross-situational consistency', *Psychological Review*, 89, 6, 730–55.

Mitchell, T. R., A. Biglan, G. R. Oncuen and F. E. Fiedler (1970) 'The Contingency Model: Criticism and Suggestions', *Academy of Management Journal* (September), 253–67.

Moscovici, S. and Lecuyer, R. (1972) 'Studies in group decision 1: social space, patterns of communication and group consensus', *European Journal of Social Psychology*, 2, 3, 221–44.

———— and Zavalloni, M. (1969) 'The group as a polarizer of attitudes', *Journal of Personality and Social Psychology*, 12, 125–35.

Mowday, R. T. (1979) 'Equity theory predictions of behaviour in organizations', in R. M. Steers and L. W. Porter (eds) *Motivation and Work* 2nd edn (Tokyo: McGraw-Hill).

Mower White C. J. (1982) *Consistency in Cognitive Social Behaviour* (London: Routledge & Kegan Paul).

Mulder, M. (1971) 'Power equalization through participation', *Administrative Science Quarterly*, 16, 31–38.

Murnighan, J. K. (1981) 'Group decision-making: what strategies should you use?', *Management Review*, (Feb.) 55–62.

Myers, D. G. and Lamm, H. (1976) 'The group polarization phenomenon', *Psychological Bulletin*, 83, 4, 602–27.

Nadler, D. A. and Lawler, E. E. III (1977) 'Motivation: a diagnostic approach' in J. R Hackman, E. E. Lawler and L. W. Porter (eds) *Perspectives on Behavior in Organizations* (New York: McGraw-Hill).

Neave, H. R. (1989) *Deming's 14 Points for Management* (Salisbury: The British Deming Association).

———— (1990) *A System of Profound Knowledge*. BDA Booklet No. 9 (Salisbury: British Deming Association).

Newton, T. J. and Keenan, A. (1983) 'Is work involvement an attribute of the person or the environment?', *Journal of Occupational Behaviour*, 4, 169–78.

Nicholson, N. (1984) 'A theory of work role transitions', *Administrative Science Quarterly*, 29, 172–191.

———— (1990) 'The transition cycle: causes, outcomes, processes and forms', in S. Fisher and C. L. Cooper (eds) *On the Move: The Psychology of Change and Transition* (Chichester: Wiley).

Opsahl, R. L. and Dunnette, M. D. (1966) 'The role of financial compensation in industrial motivation', *Psychological Bulletin*, 2, 94–118.

Paicheler, G. (1976) 'Norms and attitude change I: polarization and styles of behaviour', *European Journal of Social Psychology*, 6, 405–27.

———— (1977) 'Norms and attitude change II: the phenomenon of bipolarization', *European Journal of Social Psychology*, 7, 5–14.

———— (1979) 'Polarization of attitudes in homogeneous and heterogeneous groups', *European Journal of Social Psychology*, 9, 85–96.

Passmore, W. A. (1978) 'The comparative impacts of sociotechnical system, job-redesign, and survey feedback interventions', in W. A. Passmore and J. J. Sherwood (eds) *Sociotechnical Systems – A Sourcebook* (La Jolla, Calif.: University Associates).

Perrow, C. (1961) 'The Analysis of goals in complex organizations', *American Sociological Review*, 26, 854–65.

Pervin, L. A. (1968) 'Performance and satisfaction as a function of individual-environment fit', *Psychological Bulletin*, 69, 56–68.

———— (1990) 'A Brief history of modern personality theory', in L. A. Pervin (ed) *Handbook of Personality Theory and Research* (New York/London: The Guildford Press).

Peters, T. J. and Waterman, R. H., Jr. (1982) *In Search of Excellence* (New York: Harper & Row).

Pettigrew, A. M. (1973) *The Politics of Organizational Decision-making* (London: Tavistock).

———— (1976) 'Towards a political theory of organizational intervention', *Human Relations*, 28, 3, 191–208.

———— (1979) 'On studying organizational cultures', *Administrative Science Quarterly*, 24, 570–81.

———— Whipp, R. and Rosenfeld, R. (1986) *Competitiveness and the Management of Strategic Change: A Research Agenda* (Centre for Corporate Strategy and Change, University of Warwick, Coventry, UK).

Pfeffer, J. (1981) *Power in Organizations* (Boston: Pitman).

Porter, L. W. and Lawler, E. E. (1968) *Managerial Attitudes and Performance* (Homewood, Ill.: Irwin-Dorsey).

Powell, A. and Royce, J. R. (1978) 'Paths to being, lifestyle, and individuality', *Psychological Reports*, 42, 987–1005.

Rice, A. K. (1970) *Productivity and Social Organization – The Ahmedabad Experiment* (London: Tavistock).

Rice, R. W. and Chemers, M. M. (1975) 'Personality and situational determinants of leader behaviour', *Journal of Applied Psychology*, 60, 20–7.

Roethlisberger, F. J. and Dickson, W. J. (1939) *Management and the Worker* (Cambridge, Massachusetts: Harvard University Press).

Rosch, E. (1978) 'Principles of categorization', in E. Rosch and B. B. Lloyd (eds) *Cognition and Categorization* (Hillsdale, New Jersey: Erlbaum).

———— Mervis, C. B., Gray, W. D., Johnson, D. M. and Boyes-Bream, P. (1976) 'Basic objects in natural categories', *Cognitive Psychology*, i: 332–439.

Rose, M. (1975) *Industrial Behaviour: Theoretical Developments since Taylor* (London: Allen Lane).

Rosenbaum, R. M. (1972) *A Dimensional Analysis of the Perceived Causes of Success and Failure*, unpublished PhD dissertation, University of California, Los Angeles.

Rotter, J. B. (1966) 'Generalized expectancies for internal versus external control of reinforcement', *Psychological Monographs*, Whole No. 609, 80, 1.

———— Seeman, M. and Liverant S. (1962) 'Internal versus external control of reinforcement: a major variable in behaviour theory', in N. F. Washburne (ed.) *Decisions, Values and Groups* vol. 2 (London: Pergamon Press) pp. 473–516.

Royce, J. R. and Powell, A. (1983) *Theory of Personality and Individual Differences: Factors, Systems and Processes* (Englewood Cliffs, NJ: Prentice-Hall).

Rus, V. (1970) 'Influence Structure in Yugoslav Enterprise', *Industrial Relations*, 9, 148–60.

Sackmann, S. A. (1991) *Cultural Knowledge in Organizations Exploring the Collective Mind* (Newbury Park: Sage).

Sarason, I. G. and Sarason, B. R. (1981) 'The importance of cognition and moderator variables in stress', in D. Magnusson (ed.) *Toward a Psychology of Situations: An Interactional Perspective* (Hillsdale, NJ: Lawrence Erlbaum) 195–210.

Schanck, R. L. (1932) 'A study of a community and its groups and institutions as behaviour of individuals', *Psychological Monographs*, 43, No. 2 (Whole No. 195).

Schein, E. H. (1969) *Process Consultation: Its Role in Organization Development* (Reading Mass.: Addison-Wesley).

———— (1978) *Career Dynamics* (Reading, Mass.: Addison-Wesley).

———— (1980) *Organizational Psychology* 3rd edn (Englewood-Cliffs, NJ: Prentice-Hall).

Schmuck, R. A. and Miles, M. B. (eds) (1971) *Organization Development in Schools* (San Diego, Calif.: University Associates, Inc).

Schuler, R. S. (1976) 'Participation with supervision and subordinate authoritarianism: a path–goal theory reconciliation', *Administrative Science Quarterly*, 21, 320–5.

Seligman, M. E. P. (1975) *Helplessness* (San Francisco: Freeman).

Shaw, M. E. (1981) *Group Dynamics* 3rd edn (New York: McGraw-Hill).

Sheehy, G. (1976) *Passages: Predictable Crises of Adult Life* (New York: Dutton).

Silverman, D. (1970) *The Theory of Organizations* (London: Heinemann).

Sims, D. (1979) 'A framework for understanding the definition and formulation of problems in teams', *Human Relations*, 11, 909–21.

Smith, P. B. and Peterson, M. F. (1988) *Leadership, Organizations and Culture* (London: Sage).

Snow, B. R. and Glass, D. C. (1981) 'Differential reactivity of Type A and B individuals to congruent and incongruent environments', Paper presented at the Eastern Psychological Association, New York.

Stephenson, T. (1985) *Management – A Political Activity* (Basingstoke: Macmillan).

Stewart, R. (1982) *Choices for the Manager – A Guide to Managerial Work and Behaviour* (London: McGraw-Hill).

Stogdill, R. M. (1963) *Manual for the Leader Behaviour Description Questionnaire – Form XII* (Columbus: Ohio State University, Bureau of Business Research).

Stoner, J. A. F. (1961) *A Comparison of Individual and Groups Decisions Involving Risk*, unpublished Master's Thesis, School of Industrial Management, MIT.

Strauss, G. (1982) 'Worker participation in management: an international perspective', in B. M. Staw and L. L. Cummings (eds) *Research in Organizational Behavior* vol. 4 (Greenwich, Connecticut: JAI Press).

Tannenbaum, A. S. (1962) 'Control in organizations: individual adjustment and organizational performance', *Administrative Science Quarterly*, 7, 2, 236–57.

Taylor, F. W. (1947) *Scientific Management* (New York: Harper & Row).

Thomsett, R. (1980) *People and Project Management* (New York: Yourdon).

Tichy, N. M. and Devanna, M. A. (1986) *The Transformational Leader* (New York: Wiley).

———— and Ulrich, D. (1984). 'The leadership challenge – a call for the transformational leader', *Sloan Management Review*, Fall.

Trist, E. (1981) *The Evolution of Socio-technical Systems: a Conceptual Framework and an Action Research Program* (Toronto: Ontario Ministry of Labour, Ontario Quality of Working Life Centre).

———— and Bamforth, K. W. (1951) 'Some social and psychological consequences of the longwall method of coal-getting', *Human Relations*, 4, 1, 6–38.

Tsosvold, D. (1991) *Team Organization: An Enduring Competitive Advantage* (Chichester: Wiley).

Vecchio, R. P. (1977) 'An empirical examination of the validity of Fiedler's model of leadership effectiveness', *Organizational Behaviour and Human Performance*, 19, 180–206.

Vinokur, A. (1971) 'Review and theoretical analysis of the effects of group process upon individual and group decisions involving risk', *Psychological Bulletin*, 76, 231–50.

———— and Burnstein, E. (1974) 'Effects of partially shared persuasive arguments on group-induced shifts: a problem solving approach', *Journal of Personality and Social Psychology*, 29, 305–15.

Vroom, V. H. (1964) *Work and Motivation* (New York: Wiley).

———— (1984) 'Leadership and Decision-making', *Osaka University 50th Anniversary International Symposium on Democratization and Leadership in Industrial Organizations* (Osaka University: Japan).

———— and Yetton, P. W. (1973) *Leadership and Decision-Making* (Pittsburgh, Pa: University of Pittsburgh Press).

Wahba, M. A. and Bridwell, L. G. (1976) 'Maslow reconsidered: a review of research on the need hierarchy theory', *Organizational Behavior and Human Performance*, 15, 212–40.

Wall, T. and Lischeron, J. (1977) *Worker Participation: A Critique of the Literature and Some Fresh Evidence* (London: McGraw-Hill).

Walster, E., Bercheid, E. and Walster, G. W. (1976) 'New directions in equity research', in L. Berkowitz and E. Walster (eds) *Advances in Experimental Social Psychology*, vol. 9 (New York: Academic Press).

Walton, R. E. (1969) *Interpersonal Peacemaking: Confrontations and Third Party Consultation* (Reading, Mass.: Addison-Wesley).

Weber, M. (1947) *Economy and Society* (New York: Bedminster).

Weiner, B. (1974) *Achievement Motivation and Attribution Theory* (Morristown, NJ: General Learning Press).

————— Freize, I., Kukla, L., Reed, S. and Rosenbaum, R. M. (1971) *Perceiving the Causes of Success and Failure* (Morristown, NJ: General Learning Press).

————— Heckhausen, H., Meyer, W. and Cook, R. E. (1972) 'Casual ascription and achievement behavior: a conceptual analysis of effort and reanalysis of locus of control', *Journal of Personality and Social Psychology*, 21, 239–48.

————— and Sierad, J. (1973) 'Misattribution for failure and the enhancement of achievement strivings: a preliminary report', Unpublished manuscript.

Woodcock, M. (1979) *Team Development Manual* (Aldershot: Gower).

————— and Francis, D. (1981) *Organization Development Through Team Building* (Aldershot: Gower).

Wright, P. L. and Taylor D. S. (1984) *Improving Leadership Performance* (Englewood Cliffs, NJ: Prentice-Hall).

Yetton, P. (1984) 'Leadership and Supervision', in M. Gruneberg and T. Wall (eds) *Social Psychology and Organizational Behaviour* (Chichester: Wiley).

Zander, A. (1982) *Making Groups Effective* (San Francisco: Jossey-Bass).

Name Index

Subject Index